Also by Roger Caron
GO-BOY!

ROGER CARON

BINGO!

METHUEN

Toronto   New York   London   Sydney   Auckland

CANADIAN CATALOGUING IN PUBLICATION DATA

Caron, Roger, 1938–
  Bingo!

ISBN 0-458-99700-5

1. Prison riots — Ontario — Kingston.   2. Kingston Penitentiary (Ont.).   3. Caron, Roger, 1938–
I. Title.

HV9508.K56C37 1985   365'.641   C85-098999-X

Publisher's Note
Although the events described in *Bingo!* are true, some of the names have been changed in an effort to avoid further harassment of those involved.

DESIGN: Brant Cowie/Artplus

Printed and bound in Canada by John Deyell Company

1 2 3 4   85   89 88 87 86

*This book is affectionately dedicated to my sister
Sue, who epitomizes love and vigilance
and who has always been a pillar of strength.*

Special thanks to my editors at Methuen, Tanya Long and Kate Forster, for their smooth professionalism; and to Professor Frederick J. Desroches of the Department of Sociology, University of St. Jerome's College, Waterloo, for providing valuable research material.

CONTENTS

AUTHOR'S NOTE

IT WOULD HAVE been neat if my first book and I had both been released from the penitentiary on that same day back in 1977. However, *Go-Boy!* made it through the front gates first, though in a blaze of positive publicity that the parole board could not ignore. A carefully structured pre-release program aimed at integrating me slowly back into the outside world got under way early in 1979, allowing me to venture escorted outside the walls every few weeks for a few hours at a time. Then as my credibility grew I was trusted to go outside on my own, no longer under surveillance. This proverbial carrot was extended for six nerve-wracking months, until it was decided that I was ready for residency in a halfway house. In November 1978 I was released on conditional parole to Hull, Quebec, where I lived in one of two large houses under strict observation and curfew with two dozen other inmates on leave from federal institutions. In an effort to acquaint us with a normal job routine, we were put to work eight hours a day doing carpentry and upholstering in a large workshop operated by ex-cons and parole officers. I had so well prepared myself to blend into civilian life that in the first two months my unblemished behaviour caused paranoia in the committee that periodically reviewed my progress.

"You've got us worried," said the chairman. "We had predicted that your adjustment would be bumpy and spirited, but so far your transition has been too good to be true."

Dismayed, I blurted out: "You think that I might be lying low because I'm planning a caper?"

"That's exactly what we'd like to know," a bearded parole officer fired right back, "because according to your past records you're just not behaving normally."

"What do you want me to do?" I exclaimed. "Knock off a bank, break my curfew — something tangible for you gentlemen to sink your teeth into?"

"No, no," laughed the chairman, "it's just that we were prepared to help a lot more while you underwent a difficult period of adjustment."

So it was that my supervisors went on for several more months suspecting my quiet behaviour until finally they concluded that I was on the level, that all I was asking for was a little peace and tranquillity, and that I was prepared to tackle this new lease on life with the same single-mindedness that I had exhibited in my turbulent criminal career.

Unlike the other residents in the halfway house I was only too happy to avoid the bar scene and fast nightlife in favour of the simpler things. I was absolutely delighted just to have a carpet under my feet, to be able to use a telephone, raid the fridge, and play with the neighbourhood kids in the back yard. Sometimes I'd have as many as three boys on my back while riding a bicycle, and their families would sometimes invite me over for supper. I loved to visit nearby shopping plazas where I would hungrily absorb all the dizzying sights and sounds, particularly the mind-boggling array of colours, things that my senses had been deprived of for so many years. For the first time I was discovering that the best things in life were free.

Strangely enough, the things I had difficulty coming to grips with were little, ordinary situations. For instance, I found it terrifying to walk into a bank to make a deposit instead of a hasty withdrawal. As an ex–bank robber I just couldn't help looking admiringly at banks that had curtains covering all their windows and nice side exits, very much like an ordinary male leering at a pretty girl in a mini-skirt. I also had to come to grips with a new sensation — the lack of imminent danger and of the consequent gut-eating fear that had once been my constant companions. Realizing that I had become addicted to fear I cast around nervously for a legitimate substitute that would scare me without getting me into trouble with the law. I came up with the idea of joining a skydiving club in the Ottawa area. Twice a month I would drive forty-five miles into the countryside, don red coveralls, heavy boots, a helmet, and two parachutes, sit in the doorway of a small plane, climb above the clouds, and jump! Once in the dead of winter I appeased the fear factor in me for several months by crashing into a tall tree and hanging there for half an hour.

"Why do you do it?" people would ask.

"Because it scares me."

"Well, why don't you quit?"

"I will — when I'm not afraid anymore."

I pursued this thrilling sport for almost two years, and when I gave it up it was for flying school. I always landed the plane a little too steeply, thereby giving my instructor some anxious moments. I never did fully understand all the gadgets on the instrument panel, as I had almost no education.

It's been said that my life since my release from prison has been unfolding like a classic Cinderella story. I was extremely well received by the media, the public at large, and even by my traditional enemies, the police. When I won the Governor General's Award for *Go-Boy!*, Pierre Trudeau pronounced me a "great Canadian." A reception at the Governor General's mansion made me happy for my family and friends, but I dared not think of myself as a hotshot writer. Instead I saw the award as a coming-home party. The Canadian public was saying, "Roger, for twenty-four years, you did a lot of bad things to us, and we did a lot of things to you in the name of punishment, but now we're even."

Since my release from prison on ten years' parole I seem to have handled myself really well, but at a great cost in personal joy, since I have become my own jailer and very much a loner. I invite only my immediate family and a few friends into my home, where I live alone in a compulsively neat environment. It's a quiet middle-class neighbourhood, and I get along well with everybody on the street, especially the kids, but it's just a lot of "hello's." When asked to do media interviews or speaking engagements, I send "Go-Boy" because he's the more gregarious of the two of us and entertains delightfully.

The thing I missed the most while in prison was the exquisite pleasure of holding a woman in my arms. Upon my release I made up for lost time, and on each occasion I felt like falling to my knees and thanking god for having created such a wonderful partner. But all my solitary years in the prison system have created barriers that no one has been able to knock down, and I've stayed aloof from marriage. At the same time I astonish people with my easy-going nature because it clashes so dramatically with the individual in my books. However, my scarred body bears mute testimony that somewhere inside me there's still a volcano that needs watching; hence my consuming interest in physical activities like lifting heavy barbells four times a week to keep the lid on, a factor that has reduced my forty-seven years right down the middle.

Because of my parole I carry invisible chains wherever I travel, so I can't help imagining that I'm standing on a rug, and when I look over my shoulder I can see all these hands gripping that rug, ready to pull it out from under me the moment that I think I'm a big shot. For this reason I ride heavy shotgun on my emotions and my freedom, disciplining myself more severely than anyone else would. Anything so as not to go back to the slammer again.

The writing of my first book, *Go-Boy!*, was a voyage of self-discovery that spanned fifteen agonizing years during which I accumulated a grisly array of physical and mental scars. It was an odyssey that won me my freedom from prison, a spot on the bestseller list, a movie contract, and the Governor General's Award.

My second book, *Bingo!,* has been seven more long years in the making. It was written not from a prison cell, but rather from the privacy of my own home in a room that I referred to as my "torture chamber." I dreaded entering this room because of all the bloody phantoms I had to conjure up from my past. I wrote late into the night, every day. My typewriter seemed to take on mediumistic proportions. At times it was almost as if I was reaching into the flames of hell to grapple with my subjects. Afterwards I would fall exhausted on my bed and gasp for relief, but my mental exhaustion only acted as an open door for macabre nightmares to invade my sleep and wreak further havoc on me. There was never any question of giving up the task that I had undertaken with my two prison books, not only to inform the public on the evils of incarceration, but also to further purge my conscience so that it would rest and allow me to live a normal life.

Bingo! will be my last penitentiary-based book. I've now embarked on my first fictional effort, a thriller with a political plot that will astound the reader. For the first time in my long writing career I'm going to enjoy it!

Not the end,
                    rather the beginning.

ROGER CARON
Hull, Quebec
May 31, 1985

BINGO!

CHAPTER

1

WHEN THE HEAVY prison gates of Saint Vincent de Paul Penitentiary in Montreal swung open for my release in the summer of 1969, I knew that I'd have a lot of adjusting to do in the free world, having spent more years in the Big House than most retired guards. A few days earlier the warden had ordered one of his officials to drive me into the nearby metropolis to eat my first meal in a restaurant and to check me out in the rush-hour traffic. It was a new deal for long-term prisoners called "pre-release" that was supposed to acquaint us with the outside world.

Inside the steak house I felt that everybody was watching me and knew that I was an ex-con because of my prison suit. I ordered a T-bone steak. Because I was too shy to look up and around me, I didn't notice how the other customers were eating in the crowded place. However, I was quick to see that they gave me my steak on a battered old piece of board! I was so insulted at this mistreatment that I wanted to punch the waiter out.

"No, no, Roger!" shouted my escort as he grabbed both my wrists. "That's the way they do it now in mod places; they give you your steak on a carving board."

Well, that's crazy, I thought, as I sat back down all red in the face. What's this world coming to?

One hour after that fiasco my escort parked the prison station wagon near a busy intersection, then ordered me to get out and cross the street while he watched. Standing on the corner with all those aggressive vehicles roaring around me and the smell of gasoline fumes invading my nostrils made me very nervous. After many long minutes of waiting for the light to turn green I got really mad at my escort for sitting there like a dummy. Not wanting to wait any longer, I dashed frantically across the street amid squealing tires and blaring horns. "There!" I thought. "I'm still as fast as ever." Suddenly, in dismay, I noticed a lady holding her little girl by the hand and pressing a button that stopped all the traffic! I didn't know you could change traffic lights by just pressing a button. Instead of getting mad I just got sad; it made me remember all the things I'd rather forget.

I was thirty-one years old and had not yet come to terms with my nightmarish past. Under my right arm as I walked out of the prison was a bundle of tattered scribblers and notes, my primitive efforts at putting my prison experience down on paper. My memoirs were to be a frantic search to better understand why I had been so destructive with my life. Perhaps writing would prove to be more effective than stretching out on a psychiatric couch. Just about everything bad that could happen to an inmate in a Canadian prison had fallen upon me at one time or another. More than two thousand stitches were used to sew up the scars that criss-crossed my torso like a map of my past. But the real disfigurements were etched more deeply in my mind. Most of the punishment was inflicted upon me in the name of old-fashioned rehabilitation, strong-arm methods by uniformed goons trying in vain to make me see the error of my crime-littered ways. I needed only to close my eyes to conjure up vivid images of my formative years in the penal system, to see a boy of sixteen with no schooling naked and shackled to a concrete wall deep inside the bowels of the Ontario Reformatory, being whipped by a stuttering giant with sergeant's stripes while a prison doctor monitored my pulse. My silent screams engulfed me as I refused to beg for mercy through the black hood that covered my head. Instead of reforming me, the lash only fuelled my rebelliousness and drove me on to do crazy things.

Imagine putting a tame squirrel in a cage and poking at it with a sharp pencil for days on end. Afterwards if you poke your hand inside the door, see how many times it will bite the fingers that mistreated it. I wasn't a small animal, but I might as well have been. My inability to read and write made me a primitive being. It was understanding I needed, not legal torture; but back in those early days of penology, that's all there was.

Each time I got the strap the prison authorities informed me that it was for my own good. They told me the same story when they tried to break my spirit by lashing me tightly inside a strait jacket on a hospital bed and pouring an experimental anger gas down my throat to rid me of the devil they said was entrapped in my body. (I was seventeen years old!) The special gas gave me inhuman strength. It took six guards to hold me in position as I was reduced to a screaming primeval hulk. The guttural sounds coming out of my parched throat were so spine-chilling that the prison psychiatrist had to jam a towel into my mouth to mute them. Six times in two months I got the treatment, each time becoming more violent, until finally I ended up an amnesia victim. Days later when I came out of that mental wasteland thrashing and screaming I was told that the experiments on the prisoners had been discontinued. The next day I was caught sawing bars and was whipped again, then put to work in the quarry breaking rocks in the dead of winter. I managed the only successful escape ever made from the bull-gang; through deep snow I fled into the nearby woods bleeding and limping. Three days later I was arrested at a road-block. I had to be pried from the wreck of a stolen car and taken to a nearby hospital for some patchwork.

Not yet eighteen, I was dubbed by the Toronto newspapers as "Mad Dog Caron." Another headline read "Graduated from the Reformatory of the Big House with Honours." I was sentenced to Kingston Penitentiary. Because I was so young, the prison officials added a "Y" before the identification number on my clothes so that I could be more easily observed among the thousand hardened convicts I was now living with in a maze of cells, stacked tier on tier like a giant beehive. I was told that if I wanted to survive I'd have to become harder than nails overnight. Instead I chose to retreat deep inside myself. I went totally mute after a lifer nosediving over the top tier almost landed on top of me, spilling his brains onto my breakfast tray. My self-imposed silence lasted almost two years. During that time the prison shrink and warden tried desperately to make me talk by administering electroshock therapy. Once again I was strapped down to a hospital bed, but this time the white-jacketed orderlies glued electrodes to each side of my skull, placed a stick between my teeth, then pumped sodium pentothal into the artery of my left arm. When my backwards count got sufficiently groggy, electricity seared through my battered brain until I was flapping around like a fish out of water. Seven times I woke up in the recovery room with an enormous headache, and each time I remained mute.

This all took place in the early 1950s, when prison reform was still in the dark ages. My adult years during the 1960s were spent robbing banks and busting out of jails and accumulating more scars. It got so that neither the ''inside world'' nor the ''outside world'' wanted any part of me because I was too much of a disruptive influence. In fact I was the only prisoner ever turned down for admittance by a warden of a maximum security penitentiary. Standing there at the front gate of the New Brunswick institution with my hands and feet chained, I was shocked to hear the grizzled old warden tell my armed escorts that I was too heavy a risk to be allowed to rot in his prison! In the days to follow, the local papers headlined that story and the continuing efforts to get me admitted. That was the low point of my life — talk about feeling rejected!

My nature was strangely paradoxical in that I was always quiet and polite. I didn't smoke, consume alcohol, or take drugs. I was very much a loner. In prison I kept the lid on my frustrations by involving myself in sports to the extent that I won the middleweight title for boxing and weightlifting. I also spent a lot of time in the hole sleeping on a concrete floor, mainly because I had the disconcerting habit of escaping more often than any other prisoner. It was while in solitary confinement that I discovered the joy of reading books. I devoured as many as two volumes a day on every subject under the sun, and slowly I started seeing a light at the end of the tunnel. Because we were unable to converse openly in solitary, we had to find a new method of communicating. We did this by bailing the water out of our century-old toilets with our paper cups, doing so very quietly and cautiously so that we did not get caught. Then with the water gone we'd stick our heads in the commode and shout back and forth through the hollow pipes. Sometimes very late at night I'd tap three times on the concrete wall to let my next-door neighbour know that I wanted him to get on our phone system. When he did I'd ask, in a voice that must have sounded far away to him, ''What's happening?''

''Ain't nothing happening,'' croaked Jocko in a voice unaccustomed to talking, ''I've been down here two years.''

Sometimes our slow conversations would be interrupted by hordes of bloated sewer rats a foot long scampering madly through the pipes. At times like that one of us would shout: ''Hold the phone, here comes a wagon train!'' Mostly my time in the hole was spent curled up in a ball in the corner trying to escape by daydreaming. It was a vain effort, especially during the time when I was also recovering from a smashed nose and a near-fatal knife wound to the abdomen that left me with a foot-long scar. After that I realized I wasn't afraid of death, that in fact I welcomed it . . .

My kid brother Gaston, standing beside his old battered convertible in the prison parking lot, snapped me out of my reverie. He had come to take me home on this beautiful sunny June day, my family having agreed that he should be the one to do so. We had something in common on this particular day — we were both adjusting to our return to civilian life, mine from prison and his from the American army where he had served a stint in Viet Nam as a sergeant. With a flourish Gaston swung open the passenger door; bowing at the waist and grinning widely he ushered me into the front seat.

Tearing my gaze away from the prison gun towers I turned to my handsome brother and by way of greeting said, "You look like a screw in that monkey suit."

As he started the motor Gaston stared thoughtfully at my grey prison duds and brown shoes, bit back a retort, then with his white teeth gleaming through his tan said simply: "Not for long, buddy, because the first pit-stop we come to we're both getting out of our outfits."

Minutes later we were both in the washroom of a gas station climbing into faded jeans and white T-shirts. It was a wonderful casual feeling and I was starting to feel that I wasn't just dreaming about being free.

"Let's go home, brother," said Gaston, handing me a watch. "You're out for good this time."

In many respects I hadn't picked a very good time to be born. In the spring of 1938 Hitler was sabre-rattling throughout most parts of the world and everybody seemed scared. I was told later that this was the topic of conversation as I was being withdrawn against my will from my mother's womb in an old ramshackle house right next to the railroad tracks in Cornwall. In that kind of environment nobody had any patience for a little boy with a hyperactive nature who was always poking his nose into things, not when there were seven sisters and six brothers, many of whom would eventually march off to war. Mom and Dad were struggling on wartime rations. We were an impoverished family with deep religious beliefs that would eventually be shoved down my throat on a knuckle platter. Cluttering up the spooky old house we lived in were a collection of religious statues, crucifixes, and burning candles. My sleep was filled with nightmares about ghosts and devils. The big steam locomotive that roared past our house at all hours, shaking timbers and swaying the beds, didn't help the spooky situation any. Even strangers found the experience downright frightening.

My gregarious dad and my hardworking mom were both raised in very large families on small isolated farms. It was an upbringing that gave them very little schooling, just long hours labouring in the fields. Certainly neither of my parents knew anything about child psychology. To them my hyperactive nature embodied hordes of devils, and in those days there were only two ways to drum out evil spirits — beatings and prayers, both heaped upon me with devastating frequency. People would predict my future in the most ominous way, saying that I was going to end up on the gallows like a local bandit or in prison for the rest of my life. Others said that I was a bad seed. My mom was always throwing up her hands in despair and mentally thrashing herself for giving birth to such a wayward son. "What terrible sins did I commit that I should be cursed with such a bad boy!" she'd shout at me in French. That was heavy-duty stuff to swallow for a sensitive kid who had no real schooling and no other medium, such as television, to help develop another perspective on such things. So it was that I ended up accepting all the negative things people were saying about me as the gospel. I became convinced that I was fated to carry out all those evil prophecies. I'd say "If you think I'm bad now, you hadn't seen anything yet, just you wait and see . . ."

We were forever kneeling down around the old radio and reciting the rosary, at which times I would catch everybody sending knowing looks in my direction. My anti-social behaviour was further emphasized by the perfect conduct of my popular brothers and sisters. Well, they might be good at reaping brownie points, but I was real good at raising hell. That massive energy within me wouldn't let me do anything else. In a perverse way I came to believe that I was pleasing everybody by making their malevolent predictions about me come true. I don't think that I was mentally equipped to evaluate what the grownups were creating inside of me, since I spent most of my youth skipping classes. I was too hyper to sit still in school, and the nuns and brothers seemed happy not to report me missing. That was fine with me. It enabled me to go fishing and hunting, which made me feel happy and free.

The biggest influence on my formative years was my dad, with whom I had a love–hate relationship. He was a bullheaded individual with a barrel chest covered in grey hair, and whenever he wanted to make a point in his broken English he would pound that chest with a hamlike fist to get attention. He was full of inconsistencies and would never admit to being wrong about anything. He took a bigoted pride in being poor and uneducated, claiming that his religious fervour and inbred honesty were what counted. Anybody or anything that smelled of wealth was not to be trusted. "Capitalist" is what he called them. "Show me a millionaire and I'll show you a crook." He enjoyed making offhand comments like that as he puffed mightily on his pipe and made popping sounds with his heavy suspenders. Although he proclaimed his own honesty and integrity, his actions confused me. I witnessed many incidents of dishonesty and lawbreaking on his part. He would think nothing of catching fish out of season, especially if it was a prize specimen. He claimed that if he let the fish go some rich capitalist on a yacht would catch it, then mount it on a trophy board, while all he wanted to do was to bring the catch home to feed his family. When he worked as a carpenter at the paper mill in our home town he'd bring things back with him such as a metal saw or a keg of nails and a hammer. When I accused him of stealing (since he was always saying the same thing about me), he beat me for having the gall to criticize him. Then he took the time to point out that he did no wrong, that the company was filthy rich, and that he was poor and needed the materials to fix our leaky roof. In retrospect it's easy for me to see how my father's inconsistent ethics helped to create a criminal mind in me, one that later turned me into a bank robber who pitted his guns against the rich establishment. Perhaps my criminal career was an attempt on my part to win a grudging respect from the Robin Hood streak in my father.

In any case all attempts to stand tall in his eyes succeeded only in getting me more beatings and condemnations. By the time I was twelve years old I felt like a punching bag on whom everybody vented their frustrations. What bothered me was that no one would take the time to ask what caused me to break into a boxcar, or why I couldn't sit still in a crowded classroom, or why I had broken into that shed containing explosives and wakened the whole town with a spectacular display of fireworks. The severe beatings I got each time I did something awful did nothing to solve the root problems in my nature. Then again, no one figured that I had a personality problem; they simply assumed that I was born to raise hell.

When my father decided to become a bootlegger to make ends meet I was even more confused as to what was right or wrong. Bootlegging was a hazardous business that precipitated gangbuster raids on our house by squads of police searching roughly for illegal booze. From time to time the raids would be successful. My father would be arrested and have to pay heavy fines to the courts to stay out of jail. When this kind of pressure got too much for him he took to drinking heavily with his boozy customers and fighting furiously with my hardworking mother. Those ugly scenes left their mark on my mind. When I was fourteen I saw him pay protection money to a policeman to stay in business. He even gave a weekly portion of his take to our parish priest. In that way he figured he was getting the blessing of the church for selling booze.

The good memories that I cherish were of late winter evenings when my little sister Susie, my brother Gaston and I would slip from our brass beds in our longjohns, then curl ourselves snugly around the hot stove pipes in the attic above the kitchen to eavesdrop on my father entertaining a roomful of customers with spellbinding tales of his past. Among the crowd were many colourful characters, like the lumberjack who lost his legs and sang sad songs, a Charlie Chaplin lookalike who operated the barriers at the nearby railway crossing and who loved to play the spoons on his knee, and the old caretaker of the city dump who would play his harmonica at the drop of a hat. But usually my dad was the centre of attention, sitting in his rocking chair next to the red-hot stove, pausing in his story-telling only long enough to spit chewing tobacco on the burning coals. His stories, some of which bordered on the supernatural, never failed to send delightful shivers up and down our spines. In another tiny corner of the cluttered kitchen would be our mother, slim and prematurely grey, ironing huge mounds of laundry. Dad fancied himself as a bit of a healer and had a whole repertoire of dramatic cures for whatever ailment afflicted his friends and family. He claimed to have saved the life of one of my older sisters after the doctor had given her only hours to live. She was suffering from a deadly throat inflammation that was choking her to death. He wrapped a poultice made of herbs and coal oil around her neck until she vomited up what was trying to kill her.

My father died of cancer while I was serving time inside the French penitentiary. I had never felt such anguish in my entire life. That time around I had earned a bricklayer's diploma while in prison, thinking this accomplishment would please his critical nature, but now he was dead. Then the warden refused to allow me to attend my father's funeral, even under escort, although I was on short time. The volcano inside me erupted. With a wooden chair I smashed my cell furnishings to pieces, including the porcelain sink and toilet, which caused the water from the broken pipes to flood over the edge of the top tier like a miniature Niagara Falls. I then ripped my iron cot from the wall brackets and used it as a battering ram on my cell gate until the guards came running and sprayed me with tear gas. With tears running down my cheeks I grabbed a shard of glass from the broken mirror and slashed my right forearm from the wrist to the elbow. Watching the blood flow freely from the gaping wound, I fell to my knees in penance and waited for the screws to lug me off to the hole. . .

I noticed the countryside flashing past in a blaze of colour, and I stopped tracing the livid scar with my fingertips long enough to mutter, "Damn! Damn!"

"What's that all about?" Gaston shouted as the wind bristled around the open convertible.

Shaking my head and blinking the memory away, I smiled wistfully and said, "It's all about coming home, Gas."

With a laugh and a flash of teeth my brother tramped down on the accelerator and, as the car roared down the highway, he shouted in my ear: "Well, that's another hundred miles straight ahead."

I laid my head back against the leather upholstery and thought to myself, "This time you're home for good, Roger . . ."

2

WITHIN THREE DAYS of coming home I landed a job on a large construction project which consisted of rebuilding the front of the old textile mill at the edge of town. I also got myself a small furnished apartment, bought a second-hand convertible with money I had saved up, and found an attractive girlfriend who worked at the front counter of a dry-cleaning store. I worked incredibly hard, while minding my own business, relaxing only within my family circle and taking special joy in playing with my three little nephews. At first I was a bit uneasy with my good fortune, expecting every day to have it all rudely snatched away from me, because being on parole meant that I was vulnerable to many things. It was as though I was wearing invisible chains. I couldn't travel beyond a radius of twenty-five miles without written permission. Even an ordinary fist-fight could land me back in the slammer for four more years. But I was free, and that's all that counted.

A bricklayer's pay was excellent, and the competition very keen. But throughout it all there was a whiplike urgency that was conducive to accidents, especially while toiling in the hot sun on top of a maze of scaffolding one hundred feet high, rekindling the sense of danger that I had come to know so well. I was a quick learner and applied myself to each project with an energy that impressed my co-workers and overshadowed my criminal past. Off the job I maintained a healthy paranoia that kept me on my toes and on the alert for any trouble that might come my way. Because of my past record as a bank robber and my reputation for getting a tough job done, I received several offers to pick up a gun again. Being a tight-lipped loner who didn't drink further enhanced my image, and I was hard put to convince those who were seeking my services that I was clean and happy in my new vocation.

One individual who solicited my services was more insistent

than the others, and I almost had to get rough with him at a local dance where we were introduced by a mutual friend. Everything about him was super-smooth: his face, his clothes, the way he combed his sandy hair, even his approach to middle age. Lorne was a four-time loser with a syrupy voice that caressed and charmed his listeners like an old friend. The glib-talking con man said he had stumbled onto a dream heist that could put whoever had the guts to go after it on easy street for the rest of their lives. He was visiting Cornwall on shady business and urged me over and over again to come back to Toronto with him to see the bundles of green-backs firsthand. With an emphatic push I walked away from him.

Soon the picnics and the summer heat were gone, replaced by blustery winds and numbing cold that froze the mortar before we could set the bricks in place. From the top of the scaffolding we could see the wide expanse of the St. Lawrence river unfolding in the distance and ice building up around the edges. One by one the construction projects in my home town slowly ground to a halt as winter set in. I now found myself without a job, and I hadn't worked long enough to draw pogey like the veteran bricklayers did. Cornwall was also in the grip of a severe unemployment crisis, and with my criminal record, finding another kind of job was next to impossible. It was suggested that since I was unattached and had no one depending on me I should travel to one of the nearby cities and hire on as a tradesman. In the larger cities skyscrapers were sprouting like bad weeds, and most of the work was done indoors or under plastic domes. Bricklayers were a nomadic lot anyway, and I could always return home in the spring when construction workers would be in demand again. First of all I would have to get permission from my crusty parole officer, to whom I reported once a week.

I was still mulling over the idea early in November when the telephone rang in my apartment.

"Roger, old buddy!" shouted a familiar voice in my ear as the blare of loud music and tinkling glasses filled the background. "It's me, Lorne, calling from Toronto. Do you remember our discussion at the dance hall?"

"I recall," I replied non-committally.

"A mutual friend tells me you're out of work?"

"Yes."

"Well, I feel I owe you for putting you on the spot like I did, so now I'm going to put things straight by doing you a favour — something on the level. Are you interested?"

I was straining to detect any drunkenness in his voice, but he seemed to be straight. Still, I was suspicious. "What's your angle?" I asked point-blank.

"Angle!" he spluttered. "Man, I told you I was on the level. Hear me out, will you, or I'll hang up."

"What's up, then?" I replied, unsure of myself.

Lorne went on to explain that he was in the process of purchasing a catering company that serviced mostly construction sites in downtown Toronto. "I've made it a point to befriend the builders, and especially the foremen on each project. Even lined you up a job on a skyscraper. How's that sound to you, eh?"

"Shit," I muttered, still unsure of myself but feeling good at the same time, assuming that the reason for his generosity was that he had finally succeeded in locating someone else to do the heist for him. We talked for a while and I listened carefully as he spoke of the benefits of working on such a huge construction project. We finally agreed that I would travel to Toronto the following day (Thursday) and check into a hotel. Early on Friday morning Lorne would pick me up and drive me to the construction site for a personal introduction.

When I went to bed that night I found myself uptight. Something in the recesses of my mind was nagging at me and keeping me awake, warning me to be cautious of Lorne's eagerness to help me.

I travelled to Toronto by train because of the dubious mechanical condition of my car, which had been lured twice in one week onto the rocks by mini-skirted temptresses passing by me in the streets of Cornwall. Friday morning in Toronto dawned cold, with a bitter wind driving wet snow at us as we stepped out of my hotel and headed for Lorne's Buick Electra parked at the curb. The motor had been left running and I was grateful for the heat. Rubbing my hands together, I expressed my admiration for his white convertible. His reply left me strangely uneasy.

"You haven't seen anything yet," he said expansively as he lit his cigarette. "If all goes well I plan to buy something even more luxurious for my honeymoon." Turning to me with a wolfish grin he added, "I'm getting married, you know?"

"Lots of luck," I replied, as the big car pulled away from the curb and into the slippery downtown traffic. Little pinpricks were sliding up and down my spine as his words raced around in my head. My distrustful nature caused me to glance sharply at him in his tan raincoat and dark sunglasses. Finally, reminding myself of the depths of my paranoia, I rocked my head with a short hooking motion, as I was in the habit of doing when I thought I was being overly foolish. Startled by this gesture, Lorne gasped and blurted out, "Anything wrong?"

"No, nothing. Just getting my head screwed on right is all."

He was driving erratically through the congested traffic, so I thought it wise to explain that this was just a little thing I did to myself to drive home a point. Like sometimes when I found myself jaywalking through a red light and causing all those cars to pile up around me: on occasions like that I would clobber myself solidly, doing it right in front of all those drivers, who would cease blowing their horns and just gawk as I walked away shaking the cobwebs from my brain. I wouldn't be fooling around, either, because I was madder than hell at myself for nearly getting wiped out by something as common as a car. If ever I was run over and killed after surviving all those years in prison, I'd be so embarrassed that I'd come back to earth to haunt the roadhog right into his grave. That's one of the problems for a guy who has been locked away from the outside world for such a long time; he comes out craning his neck everywhere, forgetting all about these killer machines. And that's when one of them sneaks up on you and *wham!* it's game over.

Half an hour after leaving the hotel, Lorne entered a one-way street in the business section of the city. He expressed great relief at finding a parking spot next to the mouth of a dark alleyway. Directly across the narrow street was a boarded-off section of the sidewalk, and behind that was the skeleton of a huge skyscraper thrusting upwards. All around us was the hustle of construction activity, with heavy cranes lifting tons of material to the upper floors amid the usual sounds of jackhammers. On our side of the street was a variety of brick and concrete buildings three and four storeys high, all crammed tightly together. They housed mostly import-and-export businesses. Everywhere around us, people were hurrying along. Delivery vehicles snatched up the parking spaces as fast as they were vacated. The whole area smelled of money —

not crisp new greenery, but rather the kind that changes hands a dozen times a day.

"I guess this is it, huh?" I said to Lorne, pointing to a gate in the fence encircling the construction site.

With his eyes shaded by sunglasses, I couldn't read his anxious stare at first, but suddenly Lorne started talking very fast. "Roger, don't get mad when I say what I have to say, just hear me out, okay?" Taking a long nervous drag on his cigarette and shifting his weight to point over my shoulder down the alleyway, he continued. "At the very end of that laneway is a security door left ajar by a friend inside. The door leads to a room with a dozen people counting and bagging money. Now, that bread doesn't move until nine o'clock, when an armoured truck makes the pickup. That's thirty minutes from now. Jesus, Roger, all you got to do is go in there with a gun and take it all away from them. It would be easy for you and I'd wait for you out in the —"

I let fly with a right hook that bounced off the side of his head, sending his sunglasses flying against the windshield. Cursing wildly, he started to reach into the back seat for something when my fist connected a second time, pulverizing his left ear. With a cry of pain he fell back against the driver's door, moaning and groaning and holding his hands out for me not to hit him any more. Still barely in control of my rage at having been so easily duped, I slammed my head back in frustration against the doorpost, taking grim satisfaction at the sudden crack. I couldn't believe the creep had the gall to lay a colossal snow-job like that on me. Totally confounded, I glared at the bastard while he writhed in agony and sopped up the flow of blood with his scarf.

"You were out of work!" he cried out. "I did it for your own good, goddammit!"

"You're a fuckin' maniac if you believe that!" I shouted back to him. "Now you move this crate out to the highway, because you're driving me home!"

He continued reasoning with me for a while longer, explaining that the heist was a once-in-a-lifetime chance for the both of us. Finally, still mumbling to himself, he threw the big car into gear and moved out slowly into the heavy traffic. Half a dozen blocks further on we climbed up to the overhead expressway and, travelling high above the cluttered streets, we maintained the speed limit in icy silence.

About five minutes later, still travelling along the expressway, I became aware of a police cruiser on our tail, with just one uniformed bull behind the wheel.

"Lorne, is this car hot?" I said, swinging around to face him.

"No," he replied, still pissed off at me. "It's mine — bought and paid for."

"Well, how come we got a tail?" I answered, my voice suspicious.

"What?" His voice rose in alarm as he twisted his head to look at me.

"Sweet Jesus, Lorne, your face is covered with blood!" I groaned, realizing that the cop in the cruiser would also spot it. "Wipe it clean, dammit!" I punched him on the shoulder to shake him out of his stupor.

"Maybe he ain't following us," he croaked out, wiping vigorously at his face.

"Don't kid yourself," I replied. My heart sank lower. "He's on the mike right now, probably getting a make on your plates and asking for a backup. You're sure these wheels aren't hot?"

"No, Roger. I told you, no!"

"Okay. Just cool it and pull off at the next exit, then we'll see what his next move is." I wasn't too worried because I hadn't done anything wrong, but still I was in a bit of a sweat. I had a lengthy parole hanging over my head like an invisible axe. And there was something about Lorne's behaviour that conveyed a sense of danger to me. As we approached the turn-off a second cruiser joined the first, and they both started closing in on us. Sure enough, just seconds after we gained the exit there was the wail of sirens, and with a surge of power the cruisers nudged us firmly off to the side of the isolated road. At first, nobody pointed guns at us. Instead they asked for identification, taking particular note of my parole papers.

Suddenly an urgent call came over one of the police radios. When the cop returned to where we were standing beside the car, he informed Lorne that the B & E squad was interested in asking him some questions at headquarters.

Another policeman climbed out from the back seat of Lorne's convertible, pointing a gun at us. In his search he had discovered a black satchel. Inside it was a holstered .38-calibre revolver, a German luger, and two balaclavas.

3

I FOUND MYSELF a prisoner in a small window-less room in one of the most notorious police stations in Toronto. 54 Division was infamous for extracting involuntary confessions. The tiny room was stifling and thick with cigarette smoke. Both my wrists were tied securely with strips of cloth to the arms of a sturdy chair; my bare torso glistened with sweat so that the old prison scars criss-crossing my arms and chest stood out sharply under the powerful glare of the overhead light. Leaning against the wall a few feet away and glaring down at me was a big mustached detective in a baggy brown suit. His evil-eye performance was part of the psyching-out process before the heavies arrived from headquarters to interrogate me. It wasn't the first time I had been dragged into the back room of a police station. Only this time around I was about to be nailed to the cross on a bum beef. But with my kind of checkered past no cop was going to listen to my cry of innocence.

By ten o'clock that morning neither the cop in the baggy suit nor any of the others who came in to glare at me with hostility had uttered a single word. The overhead light was boring holes through my skull and causing perspiration to run into my eyes. I wanted to keep them squeezed shut, but at the same time I wanted to keep a close eye on those sadistic bastards. Directly on the other side of the thin door I could hear muffled voices, ringing telephones, and clacking typewriters. I thought to myself that the clerical staff and all the young shining knights in uniform bustling around out there would have to be deaf, dumb, and blind not to know what went on inside the tiny room. Just like the young screws inside prison, young cops learned all too soon to keep their mouths shut and not complain for fear of antagonizing the old bulls. They simply had to close their eyes to the strong-arm tactics, and swallow the humanity they learned in training, especially if they wanted to be accepted by the old goons.

In the underworld, Toronto was known as "Patch City" because the police excelled in cultivating stool pigeons to facilitate their police investigations. Taking such short-cuts saved the detectives a lot of brainpower and legwork. They'd hammer quick confessions out of suspects and clear their consciences by telling each other that criminals are animals and don't deserve better treatment. Most old-line cops made more deals than a pawnbroker any day, only the cops dealt in bodies, not commodities. It was common knowledge that if a cop in authority nailed a criminal on a minor beef he'd drop the charges if that individual could provide him with information on a bigger fish. At the very least the fink would be rewarded with minimal bail. It was a nightmarish scenario where patch upon patch is accomplished by offering the police bigger and better headlines which would lead to promotions.

In my case the Toronto lawmen were convinced that I would be an effective deterrent to the influx of French Canadians invading their fair city with machine guns to rob their banks. The Toronto police hated and feared the Montreal bandits, who were particularly tough and professional, much more deadly than their own home-grown bank robbers. Outright gunning down of Montreal bandits wasn't having much effect; the Toronto cops needed something more to scare them into staying on their side of the border, something like unheard-of prison sentences that turned a man into a living vegetable. Even before the heavies showed up it was decided that I would make an excellent example to scare off the invading hordes, especially if I was roughed up in the process. The rumour would circulate incredibly fast through the underworld that if you took your French guns to Toronto, you should be prepared to die on the streets or rot away in prison.

With the grace of baboons, two detectives barged into the room where I was still tied to the chair and slowly peeled off their dark overcoats and black fedoras. Seeming to ignore me, they made a big production of hanging their duds on hooks, aware that I was observing with mounting apprehension their every gesture, each of which was calculated to wear me down. They were a Mutt and Jeff team — one tall and hawkish, the other burly and barrel-chested. But there was nothing clownish about their nature and intentions. Both were feared and respected in criminal circles. The tall one with the crazy eyes was Sergeant Joseph Kane, a veteran cop who pulled no punches and allowed you no legal rights if you had a criminal record. His partner was Edwin Lupo, enormous by comparison, a great big shaggy creature with a shock of curly hair.

"We'll take it from here," said Kane to the detective guarding me. "Take our pieces with you and close the door when you go out."

"Yeah," muttered Lupo, rolling up his shirtsleeves after handing the cop his gun, "don't any of you pay any attention to the sounds you might hear coming from this room."

It was only then that the two gorillas turned around and faced me squarely. "Know who we are, boy?" growled Kane in a gravelly voice. Before I could reply Lupo swung around behind me and grabbed my hair, yanking my head backwards. "We're the guys who are going to make you wish you'd never seen the light of day!" "That's right," added Kane, "and we want you to do us a favour. When we ask you questions, refuse to answer, OK?"

"Yeah," breathed Lupo down my neck, "give us the pleasure of beating you to death!" With those words he delivered a vicious judo chop to my throat. I jerked my head forward as my eyes bulged and I gasped for breath. He immediately followed that with a punch to the face that drew blood from one side of my nose. One of them kneed me squarely in the groin. Then came more judo chops to the neck, followed by short punches to the solar plexus, all calculated to inflict the greatest pain while leaving the least trace. Every once in a while they would step back and watch me with leering faces as I gasped and wrenched and writhed in agony from their combined assault. Struggling helplessly against the restraints that bound me to the chair, I could only stare at them in silence and despair. I knew that I'd best dummy up and tell them nothing. There was no way they would believe that I knew nothing about the proposed robbery. I had stated my case upon my arrest and now it was up to me to hang tough and weather the storm. Certainly I wasn't about to sign a false confession that would seal my doom, even if my only alternative was to allow them to beat me to death. They kept insisting that the guns and disguises found in the satchel in the back of the car belonged to me. Sometimes I'd shake my head grimly by way of reply. Other times I'd just stare at them in sadness and shame. They shouted horrible obscenities at me. That bothered me even more than the physical beatings; they lowered all three of us to a sub-human level.

I later learned that whenever I passed out they would take the opportunity to pay a visit to Lorne in an adjacent room where two of their backhands had him babbling like a child. As a four-time loser, Lorne was desperate to make a deal for a lighter sentence. He spilled his guts in such a way as to place all the blame squarely on my shoulders. He especially wanted to wash his hands of the weapons, claiming that they belonged to me and accepting blame only for blueprinting the planned robbery. Kane and Lupo informed him that they would help him to squirm off the hook if he in turn would help to pin the rap on me. They pointed out to Lorne that I was a lucrative catch, with a Montreal reputation, and by laying me out to dry the word would get around about back-room justice.

"Hear tell you've done a lot of time, pisshead," Kane snorted at me in his hoarse voice. "We've been cops a long time too. That's how we learned how to treat you out-of-town hoods." He then kicked me in the belly so hard that he knocked my chair over and tore out the seat of his pants. "You fucking asshole!" he roared, pounding blindly away at me with his fist until Lupo pulled him off me. "You're going to mark him up!" was Lupo's rationale for halting the attack. They both took the time to smoke a cigarette and regain their wits as blood flowed from my nose and mouth and my head sagged onto my bare chest.

Then they were both back to chopping and punching away at me while slipping in some slaps, kicks, and chokes.

"You're going to sign a written confession stating that you own all that artillery," yelled Lupo, huffing and puffing from flailing away at me. "We'll type it up and you just sign on the dotted line that you and your partner conspired to commit a robbery, OK?"

Each time they said things like that I'd shake my head no, visualizing the penitentiary gates slamming shut behind me should I even open my mouth to complain that I was being taken for one hell of a ride. My stubborn silence never failed to get a rise out of Kane, who would then proceed to do strange things to my head and neck, like twisting it in directions I never dreamed it could go. Just before they took a break to go to lunch one of them hit me with something heavy on top of my head and the pressure almost blew my left eyeball right out of the socket. Lupo thought that was real funny.

Policemen came and went all that day while I sagged in the chair, my hands and feet always securely tied. Some of the cops would sit guard over me while the two goons made periodical visits next door to throw additional questions at Lorne. The uniformed cop who had been instrumental in our arrest reminded me of a boy who had shot his first bear. He kept coming in to stare with awe at his prize, proudly and yet sadly. I got the impression that he had been ordered to observe some of the beating, which might have been the old hard-line detectives' way of thumbing their noses at his academy training. The old-timers were trying to tell the young cops that they shouldn't waste a lot of leg- and paperwork following painstaking investigative methods, not when they could beat a confession out of a suspect in no time flat. If the guy was guilty and you sent him up the river with a prison sentence, great! If it turned out that the felon they were putting through hell was innocent, not to worry. They rationalized that this outcast from society had probably gotten away with many crimes in the past and was now receiving a belated punishment. That's how they cleared their conscience, and that's exactly what they told me.

"What happened to your partner's kisser?" Kane asked me many times. That was one part of the story that Lorne did not tell, for it would have established my innocence. By this time I didn't even bother shaking my head. I wanted to save what little dignity I had left. "Give us some answers, shithead!" I hated it when Lupo would grasp my head and shake it violently back and forth while breathing heavily into my face. I started to worry seriously when Kane threatened to hang my testicles in a desk drawer and kick the thing shut. That had happened before to friends of mine, and the results were gruesome, but fortunately Kane never carried out that threat on me.

I continued to say nothing, preferring to remain silent in the face of the attacks on my body and my mind, all calculated to break me down physically and mentally and to leave me feeling that I was all alone in the world. The prison officials had reduced me to that horribly lonely state of mind many times during my incarceration. Surely no one should have the power to make another human feel that way. Then again I kept telling myself that I had been an outlaw from society for such a long time, how could I expect any other kind of treatment? Nevertheless, the police cruelty only strengthened my resolve not to confess to a crime that I had had no intention of committing. I would die first.

I took some grim satisfaction from the fact that both detectives were nearing exhaustion from beating me up. It was warm in the tiny room and both were drenched with sweat. I heard them complaining to each other about what poor shape they were in, saying they should do something to get fit again, like climbing stairs instead of always taking elevators. I felt like telling them they should give up cigarettes too — the smoky atmosphere was choking me. Their failure to make me confess got them more and more riled up, but Lupo had a diabolical imagination. At one point he placed a thick Toronto telephone book on top of my head and beat on it furiously with a nightstick. The feeling was akin to being pounded over the melon with a two-hundred-pound bag of sand. I soon wished that I was dead. I could see how easy it would be to chuck the stubborn part of my nature and give in to the temptation to make a false confession. The struggle to maintain my resolve stemmed from the fact that they had taken everything from me in the past few hours, leaving me with nothing except the courage to fight back. Had I given in, I would have been left an empty shell, a broken human being, no good to anybody, least of all myself.

Whenever his arms got tired, Lupo would sit on the edge of a small table and place his big foot between my legs, making me flinch continually as I never knew when the blow would come. ''Talk, you fucking scumbag!'' Lupo would shout, grinding his shoe viciously down on my testicles. A scream would well up in my throat, only to be stifled immediately by a kick to the stomach. ''C'mon, you turkey,'' rasped Kane in that gravelly voice that I'll remember forever, ''sign this statement so we can go home to supper.''

In late afternoon they left me alone tied to the chair for almost an hour. When they returned they were bubbling over with victory. ''Your scumbag partner just spilled his guts in a new direction,'' said Kane as he rolled up his shirt-sleeves. ''Looks like we're going to be up to our necks in paperwork. The son of a bitch just cleared his conscience of more than a hundred break and enters clean across the province!''

In order to save his skin, Lorne was desperately attempting to arrange a package deal by making the detectives look good. To do that many B & E's in one year you had to be a really active cat burglar. He also ratted on the businessman to whom he fenced his stolen goods. Again the police would look good. Lorne was promised a five-year sentence for everything (only a few token break-and-enter charges would be laid against him) if he would help the police convict me of the conspiracy and weapons charges. He agreed to take the witness stand against me and to state that it was he and not me who decided not to do the heist because he hated any kind of gunplay.

Smug in their knowledge that they had me dead to rights, Kane triumphantly ticked off the circumstantial evidence piling up against me, pointing out that my co-accused's testimony would be enough by itself to convict me. I knew that what he was saying was true and that by clinging stubbornly to my innocence I was only pro-longing the torture, but I just couldn't live with the fact that I might expedite my return to the penitentiary.

Unable to keep my silence any longer I blurted out: "Why are you railroading me? I've committed no crime other than breaking my parole. You ought to know that rat-fink is selling you a bill of goods."

My outburst provoked a vicious attack. "A fucking masochist is what you are!" spewed Kane, livid with frustration. "I'll kill you right here before I allow you to spoil our confession record!"

"They all break sooner or later," Lupo yelled in my ear as he yanked my head back viciously, "and you ain't going into the bucket to brag about squeaking out of this one."

At one point, brandishing one of the balaclavas taken from Lorne and cackling like an old warlock, Kane tore out a handful of my hair. He held the mess up dramatically, then tossed the strands into the hood and declared in front of two harness bulls who had entered the room: "Guess what the lab is going to say when they compare what's left on your head to the strands found in the disguise?"

"You wouldn't!" I gasped, unable to contain my astonishment and despair.

"Try us!" retorted Lupo, kicking me on the shins. A moment later, as if summoned by a signal, a tall, bespectacled, middle-aged man in a white lab coat entered the room, snipped samples of my hair, placed them carefully into an envelope, and walked out of the room without uttering a word.

"This will prove to any jury that at least one of the disguises belonged to you, and since it was found in the black satchel with the guns, it goes without saying that the weapons must be yours too." After pointing all this out to me Kane then started bad-mouthing me once again. As for Lupo, he dug into his bag of tricks and came up with a new twist. Standing directly behind me he simultaneously slammed the palms of both hands violently against my ears, causing an explosion inside my skull that made me jerk spasmodically like an epileptic in seizure.

By this time I had shut my mind down, feeling grotesquely lonely and humiliated. Perhaps I should have admitted that I was defeated, signed the false confession, and then tried to fight back in court. But I just couldn't give in. I don't know why, except that it wasn't in me to give up even if defeat was facing me squarely between the eyes.

By five o'clock they had had it with me and were ready to give up. Not that it mattered much, because by then I was almost beyond hurting. Their expressions now were more respectful. No longer were they using degrading words against me. In voices that were strangely hushed, they took to pleading and reasoning with me, explaining that they were late for supper and that I shouldn't be so stubborn, that I should give them a signed confession for a reduced sentence; otherwise, they promised to have me put away for life. In great detail they went on to explain that the armed robbery squad in Toronto had the sympathy of a widely publicized high court judge who always did what they requested. "He gives out big time and has this special ability to sway juries and scare the shit out of defence lawyers," said Lupo, eliciting a sudden burst of cynical laughter from Kane that gave credence to his words. "He's an honorary member of our squad. If he doesn't bury you he'll at least put you on ice long enough that you'll be eligible for old-age pension when you get out."

I was now completely silent.

"It doesn't matter," said Kane in a weary voice, the sweat stains on his striped shirt spreading under his armpits. "We're going to settle for a brief verbal statement and it doesn't matter whether you said it or not. What does matter is that we're willing to swear in a court of law that you said you were guilty and that it was said voluntarily." Putting on his coat, Kane added, "Sorry it has to be this way, Roger, but you knew the name of the game when you came to Toronto. You knew what was in store for you if you got caught."

"You're guilty as hell," interjected Lupo, "and if we have to break your arms and legs and lie like the devil to get your type off the streets, then we'll do it with a clear conscience; otherwise all the jails would be empty.'' Patting me on the shoulder while I flinched, Lupo added, ''When word of this gets back to your underworld friends in Montreal, they'll steer clear of Toronto, maybe even learn to piss in their own backyards.''

''No hard feelings, Roger,'' said Kane as he walked out the door with my sunglasses on. ''We just did our job.''

Four policemen untied me from the chair. While they carried me to a cell inside the precinct, one of them said without a trace of mockery, ''Kane and Lupo like you.''

CHAPTER 4

TWO DAYS LATER, licking my wounds and urinating blood, I was removed before dawn from the steel-walled holding tank. Chained hand and foot, I was herded roughly aboard the meat wagon for the ride to the city courthouse. The weather had turned mean, and all the policemen were wearing greatcoats to protect themselves from the driving snow. It was not yet daylight, and inside the van everything was dark and miserable. Icy winter winds flowed freely through the barred window set high on the rear door of the vehicle. Shivering violently, I was hunched over on the hard bench as far as the chains would permit in order to ease the pressure on my stomach muscles. I was thankful that at least the vomiting spells had all but stopped. The black van plowed relentlessly through the empty streets, heedless of the moans of the prisoners within. My shadowy neighbours and I bounced crazily about like corks on a rough sea. With a final bump and a violent shake, the meat wagon swerved off the street through two ponderous steel gates and slid to a halt in the snow in the centre of an enclosed courtyard, seemingly anxious to disgorge its unwilling passengers.

Rays of sunlight were beginning to break through the overcast sky and snowflakes were falling silently as our keepers urged us out of the van toward the huge grey stone courthouse. We shuffled in.

We rode by elevator to an upper floor and emerged into a room bustling with police personnel. Here we were counted, mugged, and fingerprinted. From there we descended to the main floor and were nudged along a series of murky hallways by policemen gripping our wrist chains. We came to a halt before an imposing door with an eyehole. Directly inside were two holding pens for prisoners awaiting trial in one of the many upstairs courtrooms. Each cage was approximately thirty feet square, with hard benches secured to the three barred sides and a filthy toilet affixed to the one wall. Behind that wall was an identical cage containing a dozen or so female prisoners shivering in silent misery. The guards, bundled up inside their warm coats, refused to close the outside windows; they complained that the room stank too much. In the main bullpen there were about three dozen men from all walks of life, crammed so tightly together that there was absolutely no room to move around, let alone find a space on the bench to sit.

Inside the hallway door were the keepers of the gates, big disgruntled policemen in bulky black uniforms seated on hard-backed chairs with their shiny boots propped up on a scarred desk. They were short-tempered men, nearing retirement, who had grown calluses over their hearts from seeing too much for too long. They snarled at the prisoners when asked a polite question, and their black humour was enough to appall even a hardened ex-con. Each keeper was immune to the grief and drama going on inside that miniature zoo; if he weren't, he wouldn't be working there.

Free of my shackles and with the barred gate to the cage locked securely behind me, I stood looking through the smoky haze for a place to sit. I was just stepping around a bloodied hulk sprawled on the concrete floor when a gruff voice hailed me from a far corner: "Roger, ol' pal. Hope you brought some weed with you?" Turning toward the voice and squinting my eyes, I soon made out the form of an ape-like creature gesturing impatiently at me. As I got closer I recognized the mashed-in kisser of an ex-con who had done a lot of time with me when I was in Kingston Pen. Hugo was a sight to chill anybody's blood. He was as square and thick as he was tall, blue-bearded, and with saucer-like eyes that were as unemotional and pale-looking as a fish's. He was a hard-core, forty-year-old junkie, and was obviously fighting off a fit of nerves. There must have been a hundred cigarette butts scattered around his shoes.

"C'mon, pal, I'll make some room for you," said Hugo, and started shoving bodies around in his friendly but pugnacious way until I had a place to rest. Smacking a huge palm against his low forehead, he suddenly groaned in despair. Muttering to himself, he remembered and declared, "Aw, you don't smoke." Turning belligerently to the sleepy masses around him, he demanded, "Which one of you shits got a butt for me?" An elegant-looking dude seated straight across from us drunkenly held out a long cigar in a shaking hand. Hugo turned to the blond, willowy, middle-aged drag queen leaning against him and growled, "Quit using me for a goddamn pillow, knucklehead, and go and fetch me that cigar."

Ignoring his tough talk, I gingerly eased my weight back against the bars to relieve the pressure on my stomach and swollen groin. Barely able to summon up a whisper from my crushed vocal cords, I said, "I'll buy you smokes when Buster shows up — if he's still operating the courthouse canteen."

Hugo smiled amiably. "Yeah, he is, and would you believe that shitface still won't give me credit, after all these years as a regular customer?"

"I'll buy you a sandwich and coffee, too," I croaked, pulling my suede jacket tightly around me against the draft from the barred window.

"You're a pal, ol' buddy," replied Hugo, puffing greedily on the fat cigar. Suddenly pawing at the smoke billowing up between us, he inquired, "Where was the party?"

Closing my eyes against the memory, I said through swollen lips, "54 Division, in the company of Kane and Lupo."

"Shit, that figures. Hey, cut that out!" spluttered Hugo, slapping the queen's manicured fingers away from his biceps — a move that turned her look of propriety to a pout. Blowing cigar smoke into her painted eyes, he coolly went on to tell me about a recent experience of his own at another station — a con-wise way of indicating that he wasn't about to probe into my situation unless I volunteered more details. I wasn't about to. Soon I was lost in thought, struggling to cope with my injuries, steeling myself for survival now that I was back in the jungle. The beating had left my body and my mind at a disadvantage. That was probably why I was sitting next to Hugo, putting up with his bullshit until I got stronger and could fend for myself.

At eight o'clock that morning Buster showed up outside the bars hawking his goods, and the atmosphere inside the cage took on a new tempo. Everybody immediately stampeded in his direction, proffering coins in trembling hands. Those who didn't have any money offered rings and watches in exchange for coffee, donuts, and that all-consuming need, tobacco. A few of the men in the cage were obviously well heeled and quickly became the centre of attention, especially the well-dressed gent, who had never been busted before and thus did not know the ropes. Winos

beseeched him for coins, and mooches offered undying friend-
ship or veiled threats in an attempt to appease their growling bellies and their craving for nicotine. Even the girls in the neighbouring
pen got into the act. They shouted over, asking sweetly if anybody would stand them to coffee and cigarettes. If one of the men
refused them in a wise-guy manner, the iron maidens bad-mouthed
right back in language that would bring a nun to her knees.

By nine o'clock the tiny cellblock was transformed into bedlam
as the locked door leading to the hallway admitted a whole variety
of people "on business." This put our keepers in a terrible temper, because they had to get off their fat rumps to unlock doors
and answer telephones, all the while making room for additional
prisoners arriving from nearby jails. It wasn't long before the soul-
bargaining got under way. Misery flowed until you wanted to gouge
out your eyes and puncture your ears. Everybody on both sides of
the bars was looking for some kind of patch, and the auctioneering
reached a frenzy minutes before the courts convened in the rooms
upstairs. Gripping the bars from inside the cage, the bad guys
unburdened themselves to all who would listen, especially if there
was even a glimmer of hope that the good guy on the outside was
in a position to bend the judge's ear in their favour. Everybody
was trying to get points across with loud whispers and the occa-
sional shout and curse — priests in black suits, Salvation Army
personnel in their distinctive uniforms, impatient lawyers with
bulging briefcases, sad-looking social workers, arrogant detectives
wearing smug looks; it was a fantasia of characters bobbing and
weaving in the smoke-filled atmosphere, trying to be heard while
vigorously tugging at each other's sleeves through the bars.

"Check the action over there," whispered Hugo in my ear as
he pointed to a tall blondish beanpole decked out in a painter's hat
and coveralls. "That's Updike, a good second-storey man in one
of his working outfits. And man, will you dig the way he's got
them two coppers dancing up on their toes? What I'd like to know
is how come he's got them kissing his ass when they got him dead
to rights on a B & E?"

His words brought back thoughts about how that weasel Lorne
had sold me down the river to ease the pressure on him. Unlike
Lorne, this young guy was cool and sure of himself, blowing cigarette smoke upwards toward his peaked hat, smiling crookedly
as he spoke.

Still staring in disbelief, Hugo added, "Maybe the skinny-ass fox has got something on them coppers?"

"You mean like the hidden tape recorder that that nark used against your crowd?" I asked.

Groaning in mock despair and peeking out at me from behind his big paws, he blurted out, "Gimme a break on that!" (An undercover cop had infiltrated his gang of dope pushers, got everybody down on tape over a period of months, and then activated the raid that got them all busted.)

Hugo whispered hungrily, "Whatever line he's feeding them, I'd sure like to have some of it."

Grunting in agony, I suddenly bent double. My body was racked with muscle spasms and I felt warm blood running down my leg. When the haze cleared, Hugo's friend the queen was kneeling in front of me. Speaking for the first time that morning, she said in a concerned voice, "Can I help you?"

"No!" I grunted. "There isn't a fucking thing anybody can do." To soften my words I tried to smile, but succeeded only in gritting my teeth. Grabbing my heaving shoulders, Hugo slowly pulled me upright until I was resting against the bars. My eyes were still swimming in a red mist, but I was clear-headed enough to notice that no one else in the bullpen was paying me the least attention. I wasn't about to let them see me snivel for help, even if I bled to death.

"Get back here, Jezebel," said Hugo to his elegant friend in the leather pants. "Them pigs won't give him any satisfaction."

Closing my eyes and breathing deeply to clear the cobwebs, all I could hear was Hugo running off at the lip to Jezebel, laying track on her just as a guy would do to a hooker in a bar, and she was listening to his bullshit rapturously. Jezebel had the nervous habit of blowing upward on the long curls tumbling down over her sparkling eyes and clinging to people with her long, manicured fingers. Both she and Hugo had been in custody for seven months, each putting up with the weekly remand bit in the hope of manoeuvring themselves in front of the right judge for a jury trial. Jezebel was facing a manslaughter charge, having deliberately run over her lover with the new Corvette he had given her. As for Hugo, he was jacked up on possession of heroin for the purpose of trafficking.

It was a while before Updike finished his business with the two detectives. Looking jaunty, he started to pass our bench when Hugo called him over to offer a cigarette. As soon as he had Updike's undivided attention, Hugo lowered his voice conspiratorially and asked him, ''What was all that track you were laying down to the coppers?''

Blowing a lazy smoke ring, Updike answered with another question of his own. ''Did you know that somebody busted into Maple Leaf Gardens, beat the bug, and then swiped the Stanley Cup?''

''You mean —'' gasped Hugo, unable to finish the sentence.

''Well, it seems that the dicks are convinced that I know exactly where the trophy is stashed away,'' said Updike. Then, grinning like a thief who has just scored big, he made his way to the urinal.

''Goddamn!'' exclaimed Hugo in admiration. ''I told you, Roger, that skinny-assed fox was smart. Just like that he steals the most valuable trophy in hockey months in advance, for the specific purpose of having a patch for any rumble he might be nailed on. Jesus!''

Deals, everybody wheeling and dealing in bodies and merchandise. Steal something extremely valuable and you can count on trading it in for a clean bill of health. I had no doubt that Updike would have his break and enter charge dismissed on a technicality when he appeared in court. The following day all the local newspapers would be displaying large photographs of the Crown attorney sandwiched between the two detectives, clutching the Stanley Cup, all three grinning like Cheshire cats — claiming that an anonymous tip led them to the prize. It was good politicking, great for promotion, and at the very least it would get them box seats for the season's hockey matches.

It was nearly ten o'clock before the rear gate of the bullpen swung open with a crash to display the huge frame of a uniformed sergeant with a crew cut and a deeply lined face. All activity immediately came to a halt as he started ticking names off with a pencil on a clipboard.

''Carlan, David!''

''Updike, Craig!''

''Copeland, Raymond!''

''Brohaugh, Leon!''

''Barrett, Floyd!''

''Caron, Roger!''

The roll call went on as police officers herded us up a narrow flight of stairs. We emerged into a crowded courtroom filled with grim-faced people who were there to plead for others or to face wholesale justice themselves. Along one courtroom wall was a pen about the size of a jury box with a locked gate. They crammed us in there, more than two dozen of us forced to shove, smell, and curse each other. Standing in the front row gripping the railing, I had to fight back tears of pain and shame while deliberately closing my ears and eyes to the dickering going on around me. Defence lawyers, Crown attorneys, and the judge argued over the years a man should be sentenced to. I was strictly on my own in my struggle to prove my innocence; the odds were stacked against me so fantastically that it would have been easier to give up and settle for a lesser sentence. But I knew that if that came to pass, I would probably destroy myself.

Jezebel had to nudge me after the bailiff called out my name several times.

"On or about the seventh day of November in the year 1969 in the Municipality of Metropolitan Toronto in the County of York you did conspire with one Lorne Flannigan to commit an indictable offence, to wit: the crime of robbery, contrary to the Criminal Code."

"Not guilty!" I shouted in a hoarse voice, as I struggled fiercely to control my anger.

I was remanded in custody without bail until a preliminary hearing could be arranged. Pushed aside, I watched as the judicial sword went on slashing and thrusting remorselessly through the remaining prisoners in the dock. Slowly everybody was reduced to a mass of quivering jelly, including the parents, wives, and sweethearts. Even the spectators in the gallery were strangely hushed and humbled. As we expected, Updike walked out a free man.

By noon the courtrooms were all but empty. Those of us who had not been granted bail or a conditional discharge milled about restlessly in the bullpen downstairs, all of us waiting nervously for the meat wagons to arrive and cart us off to the county jails; being admitted and processed at any large jail is one of the most degrading experiences anyone can undergo.

The black vans were designed to hold no more than eight prisoners, but the policemen assigned to that duty usually doubled up prisoners to save extra trips. It made the three-mile journey to the

Don Jail something akin to travelling inside a revolving cement mixer, especially when the gum-chewing driver skillfully manoeuvred into every pothole along the route. The fat metal vulture lurched crazily from side to side as those of us in its belly shouted and pounded our chains in protest. Hugo, sitting near the front of the van, suddenly cut loose with bellows of rage after banging his melon once too often on the ceiling, and threatened to use his body weight to tip over the vehicle. By way of reply, the meat wagon screeched maniacally around a sharp corner so unexpectedly that all of us were sent tumbling into a heap. By the time we untangled our limbs, the tiny beam of light shining in through the barred window illuminated a fine sight to behold: graceful Jezebel gouging the eyes out of a bearded weirdo, a creep who had been tormenting her slowly and sadistically ever since leaving City Hall by silently twisting the handcuff chain that joined them. Resuming her seat on the hard bench, she coolly adjusted her golden curls and pouted about losing a prized fingernail. His mind too burned out on drugs to fully understand what had happened to him, the speed freak was left whimpering in agony as blood poured from his eyes.

The Don Jail was constructed like a miniature penitentiary, with high grey walls and gun towers guarding more than four hundred prisoners under sentence or awaiting trial. The news media and grand juries had been condemning the archaic dungeon for decades. The Don had been the scene of many grisly executions and gruesome suicides, men and women who preferred to take their own lives rather than spend another lonely night in one of the coffin-like cells with no plumbing or lighting. The majority of the staff were British, with a surprising number of Jamaicans and Orientals, immigrants who worked long hours for low wages and rarely got along with each other. The only time they became united was when they were able to pool their frustrations and beat up a recalcitrant inmate bound in chains.

"Awright, take that one to the infirmary," ordered the captain of the guards. The speed freak had tumbled out of the meat wagon onto the garage floor when the door was opened. Glaring at Jezebel — who was anchored to the other end of the chain — the captain demanded: "You know anything about that?"

With silent dignity Jezebel just shook her head.

"Take the bloody faggot to the hole!" said the captain to one of the guards. Hugo started to step forward, but Jezebel caught his eye and gave a slight shake of her head; he stopped whatever he was going to do and only watched as she was led away through the maze of tunnels and stone arches into the bowels of the jail. If she didn't complain too vociferously, the goons wouldn't kick her head in; at the most, she would spend a week or so languishing in an isolation cell in her birthday suit.

Soon I was sitting on a stool with a towel wrapped around my waist, mechanically answering the questions put to me by a guard in a white smock who transferred my answers to a data sheet used for all arrivals. When he arrived at the section asking that bodily scars be described, he threw down his pencil in mock dismay — I was covered with them. They were my visual reminders of past mistakes I didn't want to repeat.

We were fingerprinted, mugged, sprayed with DDT, and shoved through a bank of cold showers in a filthy dungeon-like atmosphere with guards constantly barking at our heels. We were finally issued with blue denims, laundry soap, and crushed chalk in lieu of toothpowder and paraded off through the damp tunnels to the cellblocks. Hugo talked a black sergeant into letting me bunk down on his range on the fourth floor of the new maximum security wing, where at least the cells had plumbing and there was a dim light to read by. After passing through numerous locked gates (the last two being electronically operated by a guard inside a bullet-proof modular) we entered a small block containing eighteen cells and three stainless-steel tables at which denim-clad inmates were playing cards. The entire area was enclosed by a curtain of iron bars stretching from floor to ceiling and from the front of the range to the rear for a distance of nearly two hundred feet. Beyond that imposing barrier was the outer wall of the cellblock with more window bars, which were enclosed in murky glass blocks that permitted only enough sunlight to seep inside for the prisoners to distinguish between day and night; certainly one couldn't tell if it was raining or snowing outside.

Living in a cell that consisted of three walls, 138 steel bars, a cast-iron sink and toilet and a narrow metal bunk was enough to make a guy wish fervently that he hadn't committed a crime–or at least that he hadn't got caught. Fixed to the wall of the cell was a set of rules. One in particular threw me for a loop: it said that it was strictly forbidden by penalty of the hole to communicate with the female prisoners on the top floor by way of the toilet.

The girls were in the habit of conversing with the guys on my range by means of the "telephone." Three sudden staccato bursts on the cold-water spring button above the sink was the signal that you were wanted on the phone by the person living above or below you. As we had done in solitary, a guy would bail the water out of the bottom of the toilets with a paper cup. This gave access to the air duct that stretched from the ground level to the roof; if you left just a few inches of water in the pipe, it acted as a conduit for the voices. Party lines could be formed with as many as four males and four females, all talking and joking at once, the voices sounding eerily hollow as they boomed through the pipes. Often you could hear the heavy breathing of some eavesdropper who didn't have a lady in his ceiling. You had to listen real close to catch the intruder as he filtered out the remaining water with his paper cup; this usually led to fierce denials and occasionally a fist fight when the doors swung open in the morning. You had to be tough to maintain a private line.

It was always in the evenings, shortly after the screws had locked us into our cells for the night, that the spring buttons started tapping out signals, letting us know that the gals were in their drums and ready to talk to whoever was directly below them. Sometimes the girl in your ceiling was cut loose or granted bail and a new arrival would take her place — always a pleasant thing to anticipate, that is unless she was three hundred pounds of brawn. Some of the guys were turn-offs, their language so foul that even the iron maidens were disgusted by them. A prisoner had to be really alert, because the screws were always sneaking around at odd hours trying their best to catch someone with his head inside the toilet. If you were talking on the phone very late at night, it was best to bundle a blanket over your head to keep your voice from being overheard outside your cell — which made it impossible to hear a guard tiptoeing up to your gate; consequently, we always had a six-man on point, standing at the bars with an open line ready to shout *"Six!"* into the toilet. This frantic warning was followed by a flurry of movement as toilets were flushed and bodies slid quickly under blankets, so that by the time the screws showed up on the range, all would be hushed.

Sometimes the girl you'd be talking to would suddenly go silent, either because there was imminent danger or because she was scooped by the matrons — especially if Terrible Hanna, the scourge of evil-doers, had floor duty that night. Hanna was three hundred pounds of raw beef, imported from England to maintain order and discipline. If one of the girls was shanghaied to the cooler for talking on the phone, a pall of gloom would fall over everyone, putting a damper on any exchange of words for the rest of the night. Apart from hearing their voices, we didn't have much opportunity to see the girls in person, unless we got a quick glimpse during our weekly court remands. If one of the girls a guy was communicating with was really daring, she could make herself visible briefly during our fresh-air walk in the cloister, a concrete yard enclosed by a forty-foot wall and three towering cellblocks five storeys high. The female prisoners got their fresh-air period on the roof, which was enclosed by a high, chain-link fence located a few feet from the roof edge. It was back far enough that it was impossible for the girls to look down into the yard, unless one of them was prepared to risk the wrath of Terrible Hanna by climbing up to the top of the barrier to wave and flash a thigh, a delightful treat for the male prisoners gawking far below.

Pacing back and forth in the cloister in regimented rows, under the intense scrutiny of uniformed guards above and below, was for the most part an ordeal because of the sounds assailing our senses from over the wall. Sounds of children playing and laughing and the clatter of the city streetcars hammered home to us our outcast status.

Awaiting trial on our range was a forty-five-year-old American millionaire who had been arrested at Toronto International Airport and charged with trying to trade off nine million dollars in stolen securities. (It was whispered that the shares belonged to "racket kingpins" who needed money to solve some tax problems in the United States.) His name was Emmanuel Greenberg, a huge man with thinning brown hair and features that were cruelly ravaged by acne scars. If he had any hangups concerning his appearance, he didn't let them show. Extremely articulate, Emmanuel always liked to be the centre of attention and sometimes went to appalling lengths to get there, mostly by forcing his strange sense of humour on people. For instance, where his right forefinger was supposed to be, there was now only a stub; he had lost the finger when he was a member of a youth gang in New York, as penalty for having impregnated the leader's kid sister. By utilizing the stub, he found he could shock prison officials — and especially the well-dressed ladies and gentlemen from various committees touring the cellblocks — by simply jamming the stub up one of his nostrils while conversing with them, swivelling it around vigorously and smiling blandly while appearing to be picking his brains.

Emmanuel not only had a stable of lawyers fighting his case in the courts (having been in custody almost a year) but he was also a keen student of law himself. His cell was stacked to the ceiling with expensive law books. It seemed that all the guys awaiting trials and appeals on cellblock 3-D were fast becoming jailhouse lawyers. They studied the thick volumes feverishly — some tricky words eluding their comprehension — forging ahead in search of the magic loophole that their lawyers might have missed. It really didn't matter that they were all reaching for something that likely wasn't there; what else was there for them to do? Besides, dreams and hopes have been formulated on a lot less. I became one of the most rabid searchers, compulsively burying myself in those pages from dawn to dusk in an anguished effort to retrieve my scalp from the law. At least it helped to alleviate the numbing fog that was threatening to engulf me.

Before I could make any startling discoveries, my court-appointed lawyer, Al Passman, showed up in a small room around the corner of the cellblock. "The Crown's office contacted me again yesterday and informed me straight out that if you'll plead guilty and save the courts a lot of time and expense, they'll deal time-wise with you."

"Never!" I raged, chopping the air with my hand. "Never!"

Waving off my protest with a long manicured finger, he went on as if this was all part of a ritual. "Don't blow your cool with me, I'm just outlining your options. If you don't latch on to this deal now they'll bury you with so much time you'll never see daylight again."

Pleading for understanding, I cried out, "Al, you know it's a frame-up, you told me before you believed me. What gives?"

Shaking his handsome head in disbelief, he said as patiently as he could, "Be reasonable, Roger. You haven't a prayer of winning an acquittal. Salvage what you can. Christ, I never saw a more airtight case."

"What you're really saying is that I'm a legal-aid case dumped on you by the court, and every day I tie you down is putting a crimp in your pocketbook. Right?"

"Wrong." Averting his eyes under the pretense of lighting a cigarette, he went on to say, "I just don't like going into a courtroom empty-handed and being made to look like a fool by blatantly accusing the police of torturing you. Don't you understand the magnitude of it all? It's your word against the police."

"It happened like I said, Al. What are they, gods?"

"They might as well be."

By this time I was trembling. "Al, you're all grossly underestimating me if you think I'm going to help Kane and Lupo put me back in the slammer."

"Case closed? Going all the way?"

Nodding my head, I stood up and walked out.

I had been in custody for four months awaiting a jury trial. When the day came, I found myself arguing vehemently with Al through a heavy wire mesh at the new federal court building in Toronto. Al was reiterating that, in his opinion, trying to get a not-guilty verdict was a futile effort, a waste of his time and the court's time. "You drag them through a lengthy trial and you're going to end up with a mountain of time."

"No way!" I insisted, gripping the screen.

Standing up abruptly and snapping his briefcase shut, Al just shook his head in dismay and said over his shoulder as he walked toward the elevator, "We've got twenty minutes before the trial gets under way. Let me talk to the Crown again."

My anger and frustration were swelling to the breaking point by the time he returned to the cubicle. He wore a smug look. Spreading the fingers of one hand wide, he whispered in a conspiratorial voice, "They don't like it, but they'll settle for five years if you cop a plea."

"No fuckin' way!"

"Either that or they'll bury you up there."

"Yeah," I hissed. "Well, you ain't going to be around to see the funeral, because I'm ditching you!"

My decision sent Al for a loop, and confounded courtroom seven. Escorted into the prisoner's dock by the bailiffs, I watched stubbornly as pandemonium broke out around me when the black-robed judge was informed that I had fired Al and was prepared to defend myself if they didn't delay the trial until I could obtain another lawyer.

The incensed judge cleared the courtroom of the prospective jury panel — sixty people from all walks of life — leaving behind spectators and a whole slew of policemen directly involved in my case. My lawyer, a beet-red judge, and a young-executive-type Crown attorney went into a frantic huddle. Finally, court was called to order. Standing up in the prisoner's box, I faced the judge, who was growing more livid by the second. Riveting his eyes on me, he pointed out grudgingly that it was my legal right to dismiss my court-appointed lawyer if I felt I was being misrepresented. "However," he added in an ominous tone, "I'll rule against you if you fail to present to this courtroom reasonable proof of your serious allegation." He then took the time to chastise me for choosing zero hour to make my move. "You are showing contempt for all the time and effort that the government and society has set at your disposal in order that you may get a fair and just trial."

Overwhelmed by the gravity of my decision and feeling very vulnerable, I mumbled incoherently about being steered into a package deal that made me feel that my lawyer was betraying me. But, like a fly trying to ward off a steam roller, my argument was to no avail. My request was rejected. Al nervously stated that he was willing to step aside. "No!" roared the judge. "Mr. Caron is not going to dictate this trial, and by the authority vested in me I order you to defend this man to the best of your ability."

My trial lasted two tension-filled days, with my lawyer fiercely attacking the police witnesses with new-found boldness and gusto. He was going out of his way to show me that I was wrong about him. When people are lying, they find it increasingly difficult to cover their tracks; under intense cross-examination, Al decimated those who dared to perjure themselves on the witness stand, dredging up their lies for the jury to digest. Finally, my so-called co-accused slunk into the courtroom hemmed in between Kane and Lupo. Soon Lorne was dancing to the tune that the Crown had set for him. Slick and cocky on the stand, he appeared to be devoid of shame. He lied time after time, damning me with each word as he tried to clear himself of all blame. But his slick demeanor was so offensive that it soon became obvious that the jury members were turning against him. As if his life depended on my conviction, he embellished everything he had written earlier in his statement. His effusiveness was his undoing; through cross-examination, Al was able to trip him up in numerous lies and inconsistencies, until finally the veneer started to peel away. As we began to make headway, my lawyer paid more and more attention to my whispered suggestions.

The inconsistencies in the testimony of the witnesses were too much for the jury to swallow. After deliberating for almost three hours, the jury foreman returned with a verdict of not guilty on the weapons charge. A current of excitement rippled through the courtroom. On the main count of conspiracy, it was announced that the twelve jury members were divided and unable to reach a unanimous verdict. Trembling like a leaf in the prisoner's box, I watched with conflicting emotions as the judge ordered the jury to try again for a conclusive verdict, even if they had to deliberate all night.

After a few more hours it was obvious that the jury members were hopelessly deadlocked, and they told the judge so, leaving him no other option than to officially declare a hung jury. Because of the rare verdict, the first trial was voided, which meant that I would have to go through a second trial on the conspiracy charge. Even so, I was overjoyed at the outcome. Al was flushed with victory, pumping my hand enthusiastically and looking at me with renewed respect. As for me, it was a struggle to keep a straight face because of the devastating effect the verdict had had on detectives Kane and Lupo, both of whom were staring daggers at me.

Later, in the basement of the new courthouse building, Al was bubbling over with confidence. He tried to allay my worries on the one remaining charge. "They threw everything they had at us, and the next time around it will be a cinch, because we'll know exactly what their cards are."

I told him that I wanted to believe that what he said was true, but my paranoia was warning me that Kane and Lupo would stop at nothing to secure my conviction — including dredging up new false evidence that would nail me on the conspiracy.

"You could rack your brains until the next trial," Al replied, "but it will only be a waste of energy, because whatever evidence they had they were compelled by law to tender during the original trial."

Just then the door to the visiting cage swung open to reveal three policemen. "Let's go, Caron, the wagon's waiting."

Flashing a V-sign to me through the wire mesh, Al smiled and explained that he was going to Florida for a week of sunshine. "Sit tight and don't worry about a thing. Remember the odds are now in our favour!"

Biting back a sarcastic reply, I stood glumly as my hands and feet were wrapped in chains for the bumpy ride back to the Don Jail.

I did worry and brood — and with good reason. While my lawyer was eyeballing bikinis south of the border, Kane and Lupo — with the help of the Crown attorney's office — were busy plotting my downfall. Somehow they were able to manoeuvre me in front of one of the toughest judges in the country. It was said that when Judge Walter Martin was finished with you, you could consider yourself martinized and hung out to dry with a cruelly long sentence. The judge with the bushy eyebrows was a courtroom dictator in every sense of the word and was feared by defenders and defendants for his biting cynicism and manipulation of the jury. His bullying tactics often got him in hot water with the Supreme Court judges whose job it was to untangle the legal nightmares he created through unorthodox decisions made in the name of the law he represented. Lawyers shuddered when informed that they were defending a client in front of that old devil, knowing that the chances of an acquittal were diminished by half and that the sentence upon conviction would be at least double that of any other judge. The old man was as self-righteous as they come, almost to the point that he considered himself godlike with the power invested in him to protect the public. To Judge Martin, anyone with a past criminal record was guilty of any new accusation, especially if the police whispered so.

It was early summer when my second trial got under way, and on the very first day Judge Martin lived up to his reputation for eccentric courtroom behaviour by falling asleep several times while the trial was under way. To make matters worse, he sometimes snored, the sounds drifting alarmingly across the courtroom floor and into the gallery of spectators. He was also able to catnap while appearing to be awake. He would accomplish this by resting his head in the palm of his left hand while grasping a pen in his right hand; high on the podium, he masked his eyes behind the thick-rimmed glasses so that it was difficult to determine whether he was awake or not — unless of course he was snoring. The third time that happened in my trial, Al was cross-examining my "accomplice" on the stand. It was difficult for him to maintain his line of questioning because of the snores, especially with everybody snickering and trying to conceal their incredulity. That's when the ancient court clerk would come into the picture. Tall and thin like an overripe undertaker, he would slowly and creakily get to his feet and awkwardly climb up to the judge's side. As in a well-rehearsed ritual he would solemnly and noisily pour water into a glass from a pitcher, while thumping the padded swivel chair with his hip until Judge Martin snorted and came to life, scribbling furiously on the scratch pad without raising his head.

Some ten minutes later the judge interrupted Al during crucial cross-examination of Lorne's testimony. "Mr. Passman!" he shouted. "You are leading the witness and I must warn you to permit him to choose his own words."

"But Your Honour," spluttered Al in indignation, "it's on record that the witness had earlier in his testimony volunteered that information."

"Mr. Passman, are you questioning my ability to follow this trial?" retorted the judge, barely concealing his disdain.

"No, Your Honour," replied Al, mortified. How could he explain to the judge that His Honour had obviously been sleeping when Lorne had admitted that he did tell the police upon his arrest that the guns were his? For Al to accuse Judge Martin of having been sleeping was akin to a servant telling the Pope that he had ring-around-the-collar. Since it was my hide that was at stake, I had no such trepidation and was about to make a scene when Mr. Clayburgh, the prosecutor, rose wearily to his feet and declared, "With greatest respect, Your Honour, I do concur with the defence."

Judge Martin, turning crimson with embarrassment, muttered, "Well then, I stand corrected."

Kane and Lupo were successful in having additional bogus evidence introduced against me, including a trumped-up diagram of the planned robbery site. When Judge Martin asked why this new evidence hadn't been introduced at the first trial, Lupo took the stand and swore that he had forgotten it in an inside pocket of his old suit on the day of my arrest, and that it was only located by accident a few days before this second trial started! The judge accepted this explanation, especially after it was pointed out that the drawing was found in the black satchel with the guns and disguises — a bag that the two detectives swore I had voluntarily told them belonged to me. All kinds of little odds and ends were accepted by Judge Martin as new evidence, though Al protested vehemently.

My lawyer just didn't have the balls to accuse Kane and Lupo of torturing me and making up the verbal statement in which I was supposed to have admitted that I owned the black satchel. This was the summer of 1970, and the backroom tactics of the police in Toronto hadn't yet been publicly exposed. But two years later, after a Royal Commission did glaringly uncover police brutality, then and only then did defence lawyers have the courage to dangle their battered clients before juries.

After deliberating for more than nine hours on my case, the jury rendered a verdict of guilty. The only expressions of emotion were the snapping of my lawyer's pencil and the intake of my breath. As far as I was concerned Judge Martin was the deciding factor — the thirteenth member of the jury.

Standing stone-faced in the prisoner's dock, I had to accept the further indignity of the judge's long-winded verbal attack on my character and past behaviour that left my knuckles visibly white. Then came the coup-de-grace: he sentenced me to *twenty-nine years* in the slammer! The scream that welled up in my throat did not explode from my lips until I was back in the holding cells. Then it echoed throughout the basement of the courthouse. As I beat the steel walls and myself with bloody fists, I damned the detectives all to hell and vilified the judge with curses. I was now serving one of the longest sentences in the entire province; certainly it was the most severe meted out by a judge anywhere for a crime of a similar nature. The irony and anguish of being warehoused for something that I was innocent of was almost enough to drive me crazy.

What to do now? I was broke, desperate, and striving for a

miracle in the appeal courts. At the very least I would need the help of a very prestigious lawyer. Victorious appeals, even with the best lawyer, were as few and far between as Halley's Comet. It was in the depths of my despair that I ran across an article in the local paper concerning a bona fide legal genius by the name of Desmond Morton. He was a professor of law at the University of Toronto, revered by his students for his brilliant mind. A frail and sickly little Irishman who drank too much for his own good, he was nevertheless a fierce fighter for justice. Outspoken and rebellious, he was always championing the underdog, whom he would defend with pugnacious tenacity. Although he seldom left the classroom to venture into the courts, I took the chance that he just might accept the challenge of defending me.

Immediately upon receipt of my request he dispatched two of his young students, a married couple, to interview me in jail. Gunter and Nadia shared a profound passion for justice. Together they pumped me for the facts in the case and took down the information on a note pad. The two of them left the tiny visiting room convinced of my innocence. "We can't promise you anything right now, at least not until the professor has had a chance to study the facts, but if he does champion your plight you'll have a heavy-weight in your corner!"

I returned to my cell cherishing a small glimmer of hope, impressed by the profound reverence the two young law students had for their mentor. The very next day Gunter was back in the visiting room, trembling with repressed excitement.

"Good news!" he blurted out, "Professor Morton has agreed to fight your appeal. What's more, he's convinced after reading the notes that he's going to win for you!"

When I staggered back to my cellblock, all my neighbours rejoiced with me at my good fortune. Not only was Professor Morton going to undertake my defence free of charge, but he was also going to involve his entire classroom! Kane, Lupo, and Judge Martin had made damn sure that I got more years than I could sanely handle, but at the same time fate balanced the scale by providing me with a small army of legal defenders.

The appeal courts were ponderously slow, and I was informed that I must be patient, that my turn at bat might take up to a year. Meanwhile, I was still an officially convicted felon serving a lengthy sentence for a crime I hadn't committed. I was also considered a high security risk because of my past escapes. One hot summer afternoon I overheard the governor of the city jail say to the guards, "Let the hard-nose begin serving his time in Kingston Penitentiary, where he can go on dreaming of winning his freedom in the appeal courts. He's not staying here another day!"

CHAPTER

5

THE GOVERNOR'S CRUEL WORDS and derisive laughter were still with me the following day when a dozen of us prisoners were chained together and herded aboard an eastbound passenger train. Sharing the coach with us were a dozen hard-hearted sheriff's deputies watching our every move. They couldn't have cared less if we were guilty or not. What mattered to them was our safe delivery to Kingston Penitentiary, midway between Toronto and Montreal. Seated in the rear half of the coach were civilians whispering and gawking at us until most of us blushed with shame. I wasn't interested in gabbing to anybody. I sat there peering through the window, watching the images blur past. Although it was only mid-morning the sky was dark; a summer storm was rumbling. In the passenger car most of the prisoners were puffing greedily on tailor-made cigarettes purchased from the vendor, knowing only too well that the cigarettes would be confiscated upon entry into the hellhole that awaited our arrival. Our names would also be taken away from us in exchange for a number, as would our civilian clothing. The guys on the chain who had never done time before would have to learn to roll their own tobacco and to save their butts for recycling. Our grey denim would be issued with pockets, but the knowing cons always kept their hands in the clear. You never knew when you might need them to fend off an attack. Prison was a hostile environment that could destroy you in the blink of an eye. This time I for one wasn't going in blindly. I had long ago learned how to survive in that unmerciful, unforgiving place.

About a hundred miles west of Kingston the train came to a grinding halt at a small railroad station to pick up an unwilling passenger in the custody of three policemen. He was a stir-crazy old burglar by the name of Step-Ladder, who more than anyone else represented just about everything that was insane and futile in the prison world. Just by looking at him you could tell that he was a strange bird. He was tall and stooped, with long ape-like arms that dangled to his knees. Although emaciated, he had the biggest bones I ever saw in a man, and when he snapped his gnarled fingers the sound was like a pistol shot. Black, unkempt hair half covered his cavernous eye sockets, from which glared crazy little eyes.

"Shitheads!" spewed Step-Ladder to the police hustling him aboard. "Bunch of cowfuckers!" He was quick to let his keepers know that he absolutely dreaded being touched by human hands. Nor did he take lightly to being shackled to the chain. His cobra-like hissing caused the deputies to handle him with more than a little trepidation. Rubbing his massive wrist where the chains had dug in, he kept muttering to himself ill-naturedly as he jerked about in the seat next to me.

"Go easy, man," I said softly as I shifted my weight to ease the pressure that Step-Ladder was exerting on the leg-irons, "You're cutting into my leg."

My voice coming so close to his ear caused him to recoil to the far edge of the seat, where he continued to wriggle and eyeball me with suspicion, so paranoid that he didn't even recognize me as an old cellmate. Of course, that might have been because a heavy bandage covered most of the right side of my face, concealing the grim results of a beating at the hands of the goon squad for refusing an order a few days earlier. Just as a glimmer of recognition crossed his scarecrow features the train gave a sudden lurch and slowly pulled away from the tiny station. This movement gave Step-Ladder a further target; he began bad-mouthing the engineer with a barrage of hayseed remarks. By this time the heavens had finally opened up and down came a wall of rain battering the train window, followed by thunder and lightning. We were all left breathing heavily in the ensuing silence.

Continuing to angle my mug toward the window, I gave a sudden tug on the chain in irritation, which caused Step-Ladder to quiver like a fugitive from a bughouse. I was uptight myself at the thought of returning to that hellhole that had robbed me of my youth. As was my habit when I was hurting a lot, I cast around looking to see if I had the corner on grief, but no way, not with Step-Ladder in the same boat as I was. Staring hard at my neighbour, I couldn't help thinking that things could be worse — I could be him! The poor guy was convinced that he was adrift in a sea of devils, all of whom wanted to nail him to the cross.

Whenever Step-Ladder felt threatened, he'd try to climb to dizzying heights, maybe to get himself closer to the pearly gates. That's how he got his nickname — from climbing up the ladder to the crow's-nest platform in the cellblock whenever he felt hassled. These were tiny observation posts affixed to the far wall in each wing of the central dome. The height enabled the guards to observe all activity in the cells and any infraction of the rules. The warden's crew always had a devil of a time coaxing Step-Ladder down and usually had to resort to powerful jets of water or tear gas. On one occasion Step-Ladder almost climbed the prison wall by utilizing stout weeds growing straight out through the century-old barrier. He reached the top in broad daylight, whereupon a guard's bullet creased him across the buttocks, causing him to fall to the ground and break both wrists.

During his most recent trip to the outside world the old con had been fleeing late one evening from a bungled burglary when a shot rang out. With a hoot and a holler Step-Ladder clambered straight up the side of a granite church and didn't stop until he was able to cling to the belfry like a modern hunchback. He remained in that position for almost twenty-four hours, raving and ranting at his enemies far below. He was finally enticed down by his brother, who held aloft a bottle of booze to tempt him. The crazy old goat had a powerful affinity for alcohol which was always getting him into tight scrapes.

The weather turned really sour as we got closer and closer to Penitentiary City. So did the cloud of cigarette smoke in the passenger car. Peering through the window, I flinched each time lightning flashed. The thunder that followed seemed to herald our coming as if to say that we were in for a hard time. You could feel the uneasiness grow as the chains scraped more loudly against the floor. Finally Kingston loomed up in the distance, distorted and eerie through the solid sheets of rain, and the guys were puffing like crazy on their remaining TMs.

Three long black limousines were drawn up to the wooden platform of the old train station, waiting to receive us, a dozen convicted felons, for the five-mile drive to the penitentiary. We were all lined up under an overhanging roof and chained together in pairs by the sheriffs, who were now wearing yellow ponchos. We were feeling even more miserable than before because the rain had soaked us as we got off the train. We must have looked like something the cat dragged in, decked out in motley civilian clothing and dripping wet.

"Light up your last butts, lads," grunted the chief honcho, "and from now on I want you all to keep your hands in sight."

The trip to the prison was completed in stony silence, so that by the time we pulled up before the grey fortress Step-Ladder was twitching a mile a minute and just raring to go. Watching our every move as we clambered from the vehicles and shuffled toward the massive gates were the tower guards bunched up inside their raincoats. Some of us were returning to the big house for the second or third time, and it was bitter to find ourselves once more confronting the concrete obscenity that clung grimly to the shoreline of Lake Ontario. Two sides of the penitentiary were hemmed in by the water that was as deep and cold as a hangman's heart. On this grey day the wind was blustery. A large boat moored to one side of the prison wall tossed to and fro and crashed noisily from time to time against the concrete wharf. When the weather calmed down, a crew of prisoners would be detailed to unload its cargo of coal for the institutional powerhouse whose sleek chimney rose high into the sky. Kingston Penitentiary had first opened its gates way back in 1835, and had long ago been condemned to the wrecker's hammer by investigative committees, but it somehow survived and continued in its role as a human warehouse of death and horror. In through its gates had marched some of Canada's most infamous outlaws, a mind-boggling array of volatile characters all struggling for survival within six square acres of despair. In the summer months the cavernous cellblocks were sweatboxes; come winter they were as cold as a morgue, year-round howling winds whistling through the tiers like avenging phantoms.

"You! Third from the front, eyes forward."

"Straighten out that goddamn line."

"Hey you! Dummy up back there."

Once the front gates had closed behind us and we were in the custody of the prison officials, we all steeled ourselves for the finger-jabbing and verbal abuse that went hand-in-hand with shaking rough time. Most of the time the screws were so uptight and ill-tempered that they would spoil for some sign of rebellion so as to have an excuse to unleash their frustration. Just make one wrong move and they were sure to bum-rush you into the digger, where unfeeling goon squads would use your melon for a pounding block. Afterwards the screws could go home feeling that at least they could pull rank over the felons in their charge, especially if a particular prisoner's reputation made them feel inferior. Most of the cons were upfront enough to admit that they had not played by society's rules and regulations. They were prepared to pay their pound of weary flesh. But the screws took it on themselves to extract a lot more than the courts demanded, transforming some of the inmates into avenging monsters. Serving time inside the walls of Kingston Penitentiary seemed so pointless, so futile, that it was no wonder those of us wearing numbers engaged in so many bizarre acts of disorder and violence. Our only possession was our private thoughts, and even these were chipped away at day by day.

By now my ankles were raw and bleeding from the wear and tear of the steel shackles, so it was great to have the shackles and handcuffs removed; but with the relief came a sense of doom because it meant that we were almost inside the belly of the beast. In fact right where I was standing inside the North Gate a guard had been shot to death years earlier by a would-be escapee. A hail of bullets from one of the gun towers caused the fleeing vehicle to crash into a telephone pole. The lifer who had struggled so desperately to regain his lost freedom was later hung by the neck until dead. With this memory in mind I reluctantly allowed myself to be prodded through the final gate and on down a long winding driveway toward a massive cluster of cellblocks and industrial shops. As we got further away from the front wall the few flowers and blades of grass faded behind us. In their place were acres of grey concrete and gravel.

"I warned you lads to keep your hands clear of your pockets," growled the keeper herding us along. "Let the gun towers see what your hands are doing."

The rain was still falling lightly. We hunched down deep inside the collars of our suit coats with just our eyes poking out and darting all around. Everything was still painfully familiar to me. I had spent so many of my formative years inside this vegetable factory. The air was thick with the bad vibes of so damn many individuals struggling for survival. Whether you were a con or a screw, you had to be constantly alert and on point, never permitting yourself to relax fully. Although there was no official executioner in the prison, killings and suicides were as common as breathing. You could even bet on some individuals' early demise. There was so much open anger and hostility that it wasn't at all unusual for someone with an unpredictable temper to kill his best buddy over an imagined slight. We all gave up the rights of law-abiding human beings when we stepped through those front gates. Very quickly the prisoners developed their own brand of justice, labelling and condemning one another in a kind of barnyard pecking order. You just had to step out of order once and a calloused fist would come crashing out of nowhere to put you back in line. Or you might even end up with a homemade shiv between your shoulder blades. This jungle-like behaviour was especially heightened during times of unrest or pill popping. Whenever illicit drugs were smuggled into the prison, a dealer could buy an enemy's death warrant for as little as a dozen goofballs.

The guards were anxious to get us out of our civvies and into prison denim, relishing the thought that they had the power to exchange our names for numbers, so they hustled us along a little faster as we approached the reception centre. Some of our keepers had a way about them that made the cons feel that the simple act of breathing was a privilege, that just permitting us to stay alive was a dubious act of kindness on their part. When they called us by numbers, they stood taller. If they had had their way we wouldn't have been allowed to utter a single syllable, since each time we spoke we were forcing them to acknowledge us as human beings. It was the way they bad-mouthed us while we paraded by in single file that indicated to me that they pictured inmates as unfeeling zombies. It was no wonder that the joint was preparing to blow its collective top. And sitting right on top of the human volcano were the screws.

Finally we passed between the hospital and kitchen complexes and arrived at the main gate to the east cell block where the R & D centre was located. Blinking our eyes in the gloom and running our fingers through our wet hair, we followed instructions and seated ourselves along two wooden benches facing a short counter. We were all keeping very quiet. The only activity came from the uniformed staff and the prison barber talking about a baseball game. The keeper in charge was a silver-haired, crew-cut veteran with a sharp tongue and a perverse sense of humour. Giving his full attention to Step-Ladder, the officer sneered, ''Couldn't hack it out there, Coolidge? What's the matter, the garbage cans starting to freeze over?''

Glaring ominously through long strands of unkempt hair, Step-Ladder muttered, ''Shithead.''

''And a good day to you, too!'' interjected the R & D officer with good humour from the other side of the counter, cooling the situation by ordering us all to strip down to our birthday suits. They all knew Step-Ladder, but nobody seemed to notice that the old con was more paranoid than usual. When the discharge officer came to my name he inquired suspiciously, ''Is that you, Caron, under all those bandages? Looks to me like you had a run-in with the prison dump truck,'' then laughed cruelly at his own joke.

''Shithead!'' repeated a voice from nowhere.

Suddenly getting all red in the face and big in the chest, the keeper with the crew cut interjected violently by pounding his fist down on the counter and yelling at Step-Ladder, ''Anymore of that shit from you and you're going straight to the digger!'' Step-Ladder turned his back, displaying two white cheeks as he stooped to gather up his clothes and plunk them down on the counter.

Accepting the bundle of rags, the discharge officer told the rest of us to undress too. Shortly afterwards, we each got on an old-fashioned scale for weighing, like cattle going to slaughter. Among our group was a sharp-looking black guy with an enormous afro. The sight of all that hair seemed to agitate the keeper, who kept making snide remarks as he gleefully anticipated the black dude's turn in the barber's chair. The guy, whose name was Alexander, had been toking one joint after another ever since we were chained aboard the train at Toronto. The deputies had noticed the smell and had passed this information on to the penitentiary officials. In fact anybody would have to have been blind not to notice his spaced-out look.

''You!'' shouted the crew-cut keeper to Alexander, ''bend over and let's see you touch your toes, see if we can't locate the source of all that smoke.''

The black man just stared back with owlish eyes, seeming not to comprehend the order. The keeper repeated his command, emphasizing it with a hard slap of his hand on the counter. Jarred out of his reverie, the black man gave out a yelp and with arms flailing fell over backwards right on top of Step-Ladder! With a howl of protest, Coolidge flung the naked body from his own, and in doing so, revealed that the afro was a mammoth wig. That wig was now gripped in Step-Ladder's hammy fist. With a shriek that surpassed the first, Coolidge was on his feet and running!

Pandemonium reigned supreme as reefer after reefer tumbled from the wig and guards and naked cons scrambled to scoop them up. At this point the barrier leading out to the prison compound swung open, and two guards burst in to investigate the noise. With a horrified look on his face, Step-Ladder ran for the opening and made it through. He bounded across the yard like a huge flapping albatross, shrieking like a banshee, brushing away imaginary demons, oblivious to anything standing in his way, searching desperately for something lofty to climb.

"Come back here, you son of a bitch!" shouted the crew-cut keeper. He blew his whistle and took up pursuit.

More shouts of "Halt! Halt!" and one pompous "You're going to get it, boy!" reverberated across the yard as Step-Ladder made a beeline for the towering prison smokestack. Turning a deaf ear to more warnings from the nearby gun towers, Coolige slid to a halt at the base of the chimney, and with the guard pack howling at his heels, Step-Ladder gave a mighty leap upwards and grasped the first metal rung of a ladder embedded in the concrete. Suddenly a guard on the wall fired a warning shot. As it echoed within the compound Step-Ladder continued his bare-assed scramble up the side of the smokestack! Like a human crab he went ranting and raving all the way to the top until he was able to grab hold of the lightning rod. It was there that he decided to roost, convinced that he was safe amid the black smoke belching from the chimney. Far below him was a miniature penitentiary and uniformed guards who now looked like ants. Beyond the walls loomed the city and the vast expanse of a cold and forbidding Lake Ontario. The awesome view caused the frightened prisoner to jerk up and down on the ladder in excitement.

Although his narrow perch was dangerous and precarious, Step-Ladder now beat his chest like King Kong, and from time to time shouted down challenges, urged on by hordes of prisoners at the shop and cell windows. His little red beady eyes seemed to blaze out of a face that was getting blacker by the minute from all the smoke. Alerted by the out-of-the-ordinary activity within the prison, people on nearby boats stopped to observe the goings-on with the aid of binoculars. Fearing that Step-Ladder's defiant behaviour might trigger off an even greater disturbance among the prison population, the warden gave orders to lock everybody up until the crisis was over. This didn't sit too well with the prisoners, who expressed their discontent by beating on the cell bars with their steel cups and hammering their iron bunks on the floor.

Meanwhile the prison staff tried all kinds of things to flush Step-Ladder down from his perilous perch. They sent huge quantities of dense smoke up the chimney, a dirty trick that only succeeded in turning the poor guy completely black. Next on the scene was the institutional shrink, whose sweet talk also failed to dislodge him. Finally the crusty old warden took hold of the bullhorn and mustered up all kinds of dire threats, including the evil spirits he knew were bedevilling Step-Ladder. All this was to no avail. Not being terribly articulate, Coolidge responded to it all by urinating on the upturned faces, a steady downpour that was greeted with howls of rage as the warden and his men leaped to safety. It was then decided that Step-Ladder be allowed to cool off before new tactics were attempted. Babbling incoherently, the naked prisoner clung grimly to the top of the chimney, determined not to come down . . .

Being put under lock and key immediately upon arrival at the penitentiary was a downer for us new fish, because the first thing we wanted to do upon admittance was to renew old acquaintances in order to alleviate some of the crushing loneliness we all felt. Then, too, we were all bogged down with messages from those still awaiting trial in the Toronto bucket, bits and pieces of scandal and rumours about partners and contacts — little things to break the stagnation that comes from being cut off from the outside world. Stepping through that front gate with a brand new bit left each of us with the feeling that the whole world had just given us the thumbs down and nobody cared a damn about us. That's why old buddies made sure that they were on hand to greet you with warm handshakes. There was also the traditional sharing of meagre canteen rations to provide us with some of the necessities to start off a sentence. Sometimes, too, there were hostile reception committees for a newcomer, especially if he was a notorious rat or a skinner. The grapevine always knew in advance where each and every chain was coming in from and who was on it.

Sitting on the edge of my iron cot I tried to control the violent trembling of my hands as the guys hollered back and forth in the cellblocks with the latest reports on Step-Ladder's activities. I was bunking down on the top tier of B-block and couldn't see the chimney because the new kitchen blocked my view, but others could see some of the action and they made sure that the grapevine hummed with wild rumours. There was a lot of rattling of bars with steel cups, much as apes do in a zoo when frustrated by their keepers or the insensitive public. Some of the prisoners flipped their lids because of all the noise and excitement and smashed their cells to pieces, creating additional chaos within the institution as their broken toilets sent water cascading over the tier. Some were led away quietly to the digger in handcuffs to cool off while others went berserk in an orgy of self-destruction, their frenzy so intense that they mutilated their own bodies in protest against their confinement. The latter wouldn't come out of their devastated drums in quiet fashion but waited for the goon squad to drive them out with tear gas and attack dogs, clubbing the struggling prisoners all the way to the digger. Strangely enough, it feels great to blow your cork once in a while, especially in an institution that violently discourages any unruly behaviour. The sudden euphoria that comes from going haywire can be intoxicating and cause you to lose your common sense. Only later does remorse come into the picture, but by then you're languishing in the cooler on bread and water. Sitting in a barren cell gives a guy plenty of time to think, to contemplate whether he regrets committing the crime or just getting busted.

Step-Ladder was still perched on the smokestack when jug-up time rolled around and we paraded down tier by tier to pick up our supper trays. Idly stabbing away at the boiled fish with a blunt fork, I realized with a shudder that I might very well end up having to serve the full thirty years of my sentence. If that was the case I had an obligation to myself to find a chink in the prison's armour. In the event that my appeal failed, I could always try to escape. Then again, with KP a powder keg ready to explode, anything could happen to prolong my stay. With an overflowing population, tight restrictions, and day-to-day upheavals, all it took was a character like Step-Ladder to spark things off. The staff really believed their positions to be impregnable, despite frequent crises. Nevertheless, their underlying fear was displayed through their attitudes. Although pugnacious and taunting, the guards could be seen to sweat profusely, and they always patrolled in pairs and avoided blind spots.

In many respects Kingston Penitentiary was like a small city. It had a name, a mayor (the warden), a city council (classification board), a police force (goon squad), and a jail (solitary confinement). There were also things that approximated a hospital, a movie theatre, a recreational hall, churches, and industries—everything to sustain life, but no warmth and no love. The heart of the institution was housed inside the dome, which rose to a cathedral-like cupola, below which was a circular catwalk with gun ports. Inside the dome were eight cellblocks branching off from the centre like the spokes of a wheel: a beehive of more than six hundred cells stacked next to and on top of one another like building blocks. Here one could see no floors above ground level; instead there were tiers four stories high, two deep, back to back. Everything led to the dome, which contained a maze of metal stairways and circular galleries, illuminated during the day by hazy sunshine and at night by a dozen spotlights. Inside the dome fresh air was at a premium. The atmosphere was stifling, making it difficult to breathe. The cells were so narrow that by stretching out your arms you could easily touch both walls at once. The only pieces of furniture were an iron bunk fastened to the wall by a short chain, a table affixed to the opposite wall, a folding chair, and a century-old toilet and metal sink with two kinds of water, "running" and "cold." The only opening in the cell was a barred gate less than thirty inches wide set in concrete a foot thick. The drums were damp and cold, and the sewer system was infested with bloated rats, some as big around as groundhogs, with large yellow teeth. Sometimes late at night when pressed by hunger the rats would crawl forth from the lidless toilets and chew viciously at the toes of a sleeping convict. The rest of us would be awakened by horrified screams that sent us all searching for something to cover our toilets with. The hospital was just as primitive. Dr. Frankenstein would have felt right at home within its huge concrete walls and cave-like cells where bats flew around at night. Other structures were not connected to the dome with its eight tentacles but were spread throughout the four walls. There were smaller cellblocks and industrial shops, in all a mind-boggling array of concrete buildings designed to destroy hope in the convicted felons.

When Kingston Penitentiary first opened its gates to prisoners in 1835, it was in the separate village of Portsmouth. Its inmates were seldom treated as people. The lash was administered for infractions as minor as talking, and the cost of feeding a convict was only five and seven-tenths pence, not enough to purchase a package of gum by today's standards. A classic example of the prisoner's non-status as a human being is the recorded fact that male members of the public were charged a shilling and three pence, women and children seven and a half pence, to see what amounted to a custodial circus at the edge of town. Positioned at peepholes cut into the walls of the sweatshops, the townspeople were able to observe the prisoners labouring in forced silence, giving them the solid feeling that their tax money was being put to good use. For one hundred and fifty dollars a year the guards worked twelve-hour shifts, seven days a week, all of which encouraged graft and cruelty, the results of which continue to permeate Kingston Penitentiary today.

The town of Kingston is known cynically as Penitentiary City because within a radius of sixteen miles there loom thirteen penal institutions, including the federal penitentiary for women. That means big business: millions of dollars are spent annually to keep these human warehouses functioning. If they were all closed down, the city of Kingston would become a ghost town. That is also true of other penitentiary cities spread out across the country, so it's no wonder that the prisoners are skeptical when they hear politicians talking about curbing the national growth of prisons.

The big yard was where the real action was, a thieves' bazaar and a den of iniquity, the hub being the baseball field where the home team, the Saints, filled the bleachers every Sunday. Some of the players were powerful home-run hitters, and frequently the guard in the wall tower had to duck to avoid being hit. Whenever our home team played against outside players there was a great deal of cheering and heckling, and heavy bets were exchanged with the prison bookies. Other activities on the yard included weightlifting, handball, horseshoes, and floating crap games. Whenever prison brews were being consumed you could always count on a fair amount of blood being spilled. If there was a score to be settled it was usually carried out behind the baseball bleachers out of sight of the gun towers. Unlike in the movies where actors knock off foes with the greatest of ease, in real life the human skull proves awesomely hard to crack. Countless times I've seen a prisoner still standing, albeit in a puddle of blood, numbly feeling the top of his melon where a bulky baseball bat has been splintered in two in an effort to kill him. I've also seen inmates struck several times over the head with mighty blows from a solid iron bar who are still standing and cursing. Only in the movies do men die without a struggle from a single stab wound. I've seen cons still standing their bloody ground after being stabbed through and through a dozen times. And I have never seen a guard manage to knock out a prisoner with a nightstick or a blackjack, no matter how many blows he delivers. The human body is mighty durable, and so is the will to survive. There may be lots of blood, but there's lots of angry fighting back too!

The situation when I entered Kingston Penitentiary in the summer of 1970 was electrifying, mostly because all of the legitimate activities that usually took place in the yard had come to a standstill. In their place was a lot of restlessness and brooding. Eyes darted furtively and tempers flared. With no sports or social activities to channel all the nervous energy, the atmosphere became almost unbearable. Both camps did a lot of sabre rattling to get their point across. Contact with the outside world through self-improvement programs was also curtailed in order to increase the pressure of mass discipline. ''Security reasons'' were given as a blanket excuse to turn the screws even tighter. Actually the warden was bowing to pressure from the old hard-line guards, who wanted zombies for prisoners. Often a screw would mistake a prisoner's hangdog look as a sign of brute obedience. He would push the anguished convict just a little bit further, then with a look of astonishment would suffer the grisly consequences. Perhaps that's what happened late one night in one of the large dormitories behind the main cellhouse when a burly guard with many years of service was slaughtered.

Like the killing of a policeman, the murder of a prison guard was the ultimate act of desperation, the result of a mind-boggling violent emotion that defies description. The killer would have to be pushed beyond endurance, because if and when he was apprehended for the crime, the police or guards would extract their own measure of punishment for days, weeks, even months, making the gallows seem like a merciful ending. But prison walls rarely disclose their secrets. The code of silence was so strictly enforced that any individual who infringed on it was doomed to a macabre death at the hands of his fellow cons.

Often as I lay awake late at night inside the confines of my cell, an eerie chill would penetrate my space and I would feel a dreadful presence brushing against me. Other times I would quake in horror as a mutilated spectre moved past my gate and shuffled drunkenly away into the darkness. At such times I would punch myself on the side of the head and tell myself that I was hallucinating, that the ghastly shapes prowling along the tiers were created by the winds and spotlights. But I *have* seen them. One night a creature appeared to me on several occasions. It was a young man, terribly mutilated around the head and face, stumbling mournfully past my gate in search of god knows what. I believe he was a suicide who had plunged from the top tier and who even in death was destined to serve out the remainder of his sentence.

Who, then, I often asked myself, in this caged world of numbered men waiting in vain for a spark of hope, butchered the senior guard in the dormitory? Daylight revealed an appalling sight amid the dormitory latrines and shower stalls: a uniformed senior guard lying in a pool of blood on the marble floor. He had been stabbed seventeen times in an orgy of rage. The walls of the lavatory were splattered with blood and gore, yet none of the sleeping prisoners a few feet away reported having seen or heard anything. Is the answer hushed up by the convicts' code of silence or by the phantoms that move freely through the night?

The only real flesh and blood permitted to move legally through the night was the handful of screws working the graveyard shift. Grim-faced, they prowled with flashlights and attack dogs through the cellblocks, yards, and workshops, twitching nervously at the sudden sounds made by the wind and by the sewer rats raiding the garbage cans. In the keepers' hall more guards sat around a table playing poker with guns and clubs at hand, mumbling softly amid a thick cloud of cigar smoke. Among these keepers of men are those who almost seem to beg for trouble in order to break the gruelling monotony of staying alert while the institution sleeps. Every hour on the hour two screws take their turns making the rounds of the maze of tiers. One guard mans the locked gate and the spinning wheel while his partner moves stealthily along the tiers illuminating the way with his torch until the long rows of cells are exhausted. Reaching the end he punches a time clock and backtracks to the exit. If along the way he wants a little action, he'll pause at the cell of a convict he dislikes and concentrate the powerful beam of light into the eyes of that particular sleeping con until he disturbs him.

"Keep your face uncovered, Blake," growls the screw to the prisoner. "You know the rules, boy!"

"Shove that flashlight up your ass!" is the usual reply as the prisoner hauls his blanket over his head.

The guard reacts with a wolfish grin. Now he has the scent of blood. He calls for the other screws to rush the cell with clubs and tear gas. The gate swings open and blackjacks arc through the air and land with sickening authority. A cry of rage and pain shatters the stillness, and moments later the helpless prey is dragged bodily out of the drum. The violence awakens the sleeping giant and soon hundreds of angry voices roar their disapproval and steel cups pound the cell bars. The guards freeze briefly in their tracks wondering if perhaps they've gone too far this time. But inertia soon sets in, and as quickly as the pandemonium started up, it subsides. A few more cries and rattling of the bars, then silence again cloaks the tiers as the numbered men slip back into their own little worlds. The screws who have paused momentarily to shudder and listen now resume pummelling and dragging their prisoner toward the cooler.

Although it is a pulsing, throbbing world of gloom, the Pen is nevertheless the home of men who can still weep, who will give up a treasured possession to bring relief to a friend. You see examples of giving every day in the yard, where emotions can run the entire gamut. Philosophical opinions bounce back and forth across the yard like ping pong balls, and they did so especially when all sports activities were shut down tight, leaving only walking and the spoken word as exercise. Some of the prisoners indulged in mad walks under the guntowers inside a territorial boundary no more than two feet wide and a hundred feet long. Like lone wolves they would be extremely hostile to anyone who infringed on their space as they walked back and forth trying to get their priorities straight. Still others used their walks to daydream, racking their brains while replaying old scenarios, exhausting their bodies and minds so they could fall asleep when they got back to their cells, for only in slumber was there any escape. The best pacers were the cons who had been incarcerated a long time, flowing back and forth across the yard like a chorus line, never missing a step and never invading the next guy's space. Always they'd be puffing away furiously on joint tobacco while swapping stories about bygone capers, exaggerating their exploits like anglers telling fish tales. The screws patrolling the yard in pairs would be itching to listen in on what was being said in certain groups, but whenever they ambled too close the prisoners would switch to a bastardized pig latin, their own special language that the screws couldn't understand. The guards on top of the walls would also try to tune in by reading lips through powerful binoculars, but the cons would foil this attempt too, by making very little lip movement.

Everywhere in the joint there were spies snooping around in search of information that would buy them favours with the prison administration. A guy had to be careful who he confided in and not let himself be overheard, else he'd end up in the digger or the segregation block. Whenever there was heat in the joint and both sides were uptight, there were bound to be overreactions from either camp. Certainly the conditions in 1970 bred both hostility and mistrust, and Warden Arthur Jarvis overreacted as much as anyone else. No sooner would he receive a clandestine note from one of his stool pigeons stating that certain inmates were plotting to disrupt the orderly flow of the institution than he'd immediately assume those inmates were guilty and send out the goon squad to lock them up. The segregation unit was situated inside the East Cellblock, and as punishment it was rated only one step above the hole. By the fall of 1970, it would be overflowing with suspected troublemakers, very few of whom were actually guilty of the vague accusations made against them. Many devious individuals used the warden's paranoia to get rid of enemies by fabricating plots and then sending in accusations in the form of anonymous kites. Such a kangaroo tribunal left a lot of prisoners bitterly vengeful.

So it wasn't surprising that some of the prisoners were willing to go to extraordinary lengths to avoid shaking time under these conditions. Some of the guys took their lives in the most horrifying ways in order to escape the daily pressures, slitting their throats in the dead of night and cursing bitterly as their blood soaked into the decaying mattress. Still others mutilated their bodies with glass shards in a silent plea to be heard and understood. One inmate was placed naked in an observation cell after he attempted suicide. Still he found a way to kill himself. He died horribly by fire after he wrapped his body in toilet paper and set it alight. Probably the most painful death was that of an old-timer who swallowed a whole can of Drano, an acid used to clean out drainpipes. It took him twenty-four hours to die.

Kingston Penitentiary was one of the few federal institutions that still insisted on keeping the prisoners dead-locked in cages for as long as eighteen hours a day for no better reason than punishment. Other jails wisely decided that such oppression was contrary to their responsibility of rehabilitating an inmate. So instead of warehousing a man and creating a vegetable, they would leave the doors open for longer periods so that the inmate could involve himself in self-improvement programs or get rid of tension by participating in sports. In the old days the prisoners had no recourse but to accept the daily drudgery and bullying tactics, as they had no legal rights and were mostly uneducated. The jailers could get away with the "lock them up and throw away the key" attitude. Not so in today's world. Even the most unsophisticated individual realizes that such primitive treatment only creates avenging ex-cons and as a result the average person on the street suffers. Unfortunately it is not the hard-line guards with their frustration and thirst for power who suffer the backlash for having created evildoers. When the felon has completed his sentence and the gates of hell swing open, his natural instinct is to put as much distance between himself and his uniformed tormentors as possible. Blindly thirsting for revenge while licking his wounds, the ex-con heads for the nearest city and strikes out blindly at the taxpayers whom he's convinced have condoned his harsh treatment. My impression is that prison guards consider themselves second-class citizens. Certainly the screws are cliquish, almost to the point of shutting out the outside world. I believe that deep down they don't much like the public at large. A certain percentage of them seems to take a perverse pride in the creation of their Frankenstein monsters, ex-offenders about to wreak havoc on society.

6

STEP-LADDER CONTINUED his silent protest as the institution held its collective breath throughout the long foggy night. The only sign of activity was the spotlights from the towers illuminating the tiny naked figure way up at the top of the chimney where billows of smoke poured forth non-stop in a further effort to dislodge the defiant prisoner. By early morning the damp chill and smoke had finally taken their toll and, encouraged by some additional sweet talk from the prison shrink, Step-Ladder slowly started to ease himself down the metal rungs toward the waiting guns. He was nearing the base of the chimney when an overzealous keeper grabbed him by the ankle. Immediately there was an explosive reaction. Emitting spine-tingling howls of rage that rooted his keepers to the spot, Step-Ladder bounded away in the early morning fog with hordes of uniformed guards pursuing him. He zipped around the powerhouse bare-assed, shrieking like a banshee, and slid to a halt in front of the entrance to the massive building containing all the workshops. Directly above the portal was an empty gun cage used during work hours to survey the shops and the yard perimeter. Since it was only six o'clock in the morning the cage was deserted, its gate was agape, and the metal sliding ladder was down.

Step-Ladder took one look over his shoulder at the hue and cry and leaped up the metal rungs, looking like a singed refugee from a burning oil rig. Upon reaching the gun platform he used the horizontal bars encircling the cage to help him clamber up the remaining distance to the slanted roof of the shop building, which had a glass dome in the middle. Like a live spark dancing crazily in a shed filled with high explosives, Step-Ladder continued to disrupt the good order of the institution. Ranting and raving and zipping dangerously up and down the four slanted roofs that were still wet from the previous night's rainfall, Coolidge finally roosted at the peak near the dome and shook his fist in all directions. Again the situation was stalemated since no guard would volunteer to clamber up after the elusive fugitive.

By 8:00 a.m. it had started to rain, and once again the prison population was dead-locked until the crisis could be resolved. One of the rumours circulating inside the dome was that the officials had given Step-Ladder until nine o'clock to come down peacefully or they'd have him shot off the roof. The prison psychiatrist, now convinced that he was being deceived, swore to the warden that Coolidge was faking being nuts to get attention and preferred treatment!

Among the uniformed crowd on the ground far below was the stiff-necked chief keeper, whom everybody addressed as Mr. Bristow. A rigid stickler for the strict enforcement of rules and regulations, his sharp tongue cut a daily swath through both cons and screws. His ill nature was as consistent as his grim fairness if he found that you were in the right, but if you were wrong . . . look out! A bulky man with a handlebar mustache, Mr. Bristow was never without his black cane, which he used effectively to intimidate everybody he came into contact with, especially when he was pointing out the quickest direction to the hole to some rebellious con. The chief keeper was within a few months of retirement, having been a guard for nearly forty years, and on this day he seemed strangely subdued as he tried to coax Step-Ladder down from his perch with a bullhorn. They had known each other for many years, and several battles for the possession of home brew had been won and lost between the two of them. Step-Ladder had laid the moniker Old Brew Nose on the keeper because of his uncanny ability to sniff out hidden potato and tomato brews which he would then pour down a toilet before they could reach maturity. Mr. Bristow hated home brews with a passion because, he claimed, they were always at the root of prison unrest.

But those battles had been a long time ago. Right now all the chief keeper wanted was for Step-Ladder to come down so the joint could get back to normal. One of the inmates, a fellow named Barrie Mackenzie, was thinking along the same lines. Mackenzie's loyalty to the inmate code and his natural leadership often got him in trouble with the prison brass. He was an extremely muscular, clean-cut-looking country boy who worked in the kitchen and loved to drink home brew and kid around with his many friends.

Although Barrie was only twenty-seven years old, he had already spent the majority of those years behind bars, his last beef being for assault and jailbreak. He was the institutional weightlifting champion and tough as nails. Although he always appeared friendly and in good humour, you just did not trifle with him. I guess you could label him a "con's con," as he always adhered rigidly to the prisoners' code, and in struggling for prisoners' rights he wasn't afraid to stick his neck out to help a friend.

"I'll go up there and drag Step-Ladder down," Barrie was saying to Mr. Bristow through his cell bars, "on the condition that you take the poor bugger to the hospital and not the digger."

"You summon me up here from the yard to dictate terms to me," spluttered the chief keeper, "when we got a bare-assed crazy son of a bitch out there turning this place into a laughing zoo!"

Bristow wasn't about to give in lightly. He went through his verbal routine, spluttering to a stop only when Barrie pointed out that it was also his ass that was on the line if he climbed up there.

"Awright," growled the chief keeper. "You get him down from there and I'll see that he goes to the psychiatric ward for a few weeks' observation, just long enough to dry out."

"Yeah," muttered Barrie through his cell bars, "just long enough to give him shock treatments, which will turn the guy into a living vegetable for sure."

"Ha!" snorted the keeper in a voice dripping with sarcasm. "He likes them! Anyhow, it's either that or we'll shoot him off the roof."

With these ominous words ringing in his ears, Barrie stepped out of his cell and was escorted to the yard by heavily armed screws. The grapevine was quick to carry word of what Barrie was about to attempt, and immediately the cellblocks got deathly quiet.

At first Barrie tried coaxing Step-Ladder down with the bull-horn, pointing out that the prison population was solidly behind him and that nobody wanted to see him blasted from his lofty perch. Eyes blazing and hair billowing in the wind, Step-Ladder turned a deaf ear to any talk directed at him, warily observing the uni-formed crowd far below, always ready to scoot off if anything threatening came his way. It was decided that Barrie might as well climb up and give it a try from there.

"Hey, man! Where in hell are you going?" Barrie shouted as

he gingerly poked his head above the overhanging roof about ten feet from where Step-Ladder had slithered in alarm.

"Go to hell!" screamed Coolidge as he fired first one small tar pail, then another, at Barrie's unprotected head. Barrie ducked the onslaught while scrambling up onto the wet roof on all fours, grimly trying to dig his nails into the one-inch metal ribs to stop his backward slide. Barely holding his position and with his breathing coming in laboured gasps he muttered, "Why me?"

"Mackenzie!" bellowed the chief keeper from the ground. "What do you think you're doing?"

"Help!" croaked Barrie in terror as his fingers slowly lost their grip on the slanted roof.

"Mackenzie," shouted the keeper again as Barrie's legs started sliding out over the edge, "you ask Coolidge to give you a hand."

"Step-Ladder, old buddy, help me, will ya?"

Nimble as a cat burglar, Coolidge skipped along the slanted roof until his big bare foot was poised only inches above Barrie's hands, ready to stomp down with glee.

"Coolidge!" bellowed the chief keeper. "You do that and I'll give the order to have you shot off the roof!"

Groaning in despair, Barrie rolled his eyes in disgust and in a strangely calm voice asked Step-Ladder: "Well, for pete's sake, what are you going to do?"

Suddenly looking bewildered, Step-Ladder paused and asked "How come you know my name, huh?"

Barrie's legs flailed as he tried to tighten his hold. He exploded in disgust, "Jesus Christ!"

"It ain't that, you stupid bastard, it's Pete," then in a whimper, "but nobody ever calls me that."

"I did and I will, because you're my friend. Now c'mon, Step-Ladder, gimme a hand, will ya?"

With a fierce look Coolidge growled, "Gimme a smoke if I do?"

"Sure, Pete," gasped Barrie with a grimace as spasms shook his muscular body and his grip weakened. "First you pull me up."

Far below, the crowd of horrified prison staff gave a unified sigh of relief as the drama came to a peaceful end. Pawing the light mist of rain from his craggy features, Mr. Bristow stared incredulously up at the two of them talking and drawing smoke from soggy butts and barked out: "You two all through playing Peter Pan?"

Thus went my first twenty-four hours in the Big House this time around. But all too soon the daily routine of shaking rough time set in with crushing monotony. The custodial circus started off each morning with the nerve-wracking wake-up bell inside the dome reverberating throughout the eight wings. The sound pierced every nook and cranny inside the cellblocks, including the deepest recesses of our minds. By the end of each prison day the bell would have rung 128 times. Sitting in splendour on a solid metal pedestal in the centre of the dome floor, the brass bell had ruled authoritatively over its numbered subjects for well over a century. To the guards it was a symbol of authoritarian rule, and our keepers did everything but bow and pay homage to it as they rallied around it for security. To the convicts it was an abomination, a symbol to be hated with a passion. Over the years there were all kinds of attacks against the bell, all doomed to failure. One colossal-sized convict flipped out and like an enraged bull charged head-first across the dome floor into the bell and split his skull wide open. Even before they got around to lugging the guy off to the hospital, the screws were busy wiping the gore off their cherished bell with their handkerchiefs.

Wake-up was at 6:30 a.m., the bell causing our eyes to pop painfully open, our bare feet to plop automatically onto the cold concrete floor, and our kissers to point up to the cell gate for the morning count. Some of the guys were able to continue sleeping in that stooped position while seeming awake.

By 7:00, we would have washed, brushed our teeth with ground chalk, swept the floors of our cells, and fastened our narrow cots to the wall. All of us would be hungry as we gripped the bars of our cell doors waiting for the inmate tapper to pop the handles up. Our last meal would have been at four o'clock the day before. The screw at the head of the tier would spin two spoked wheels that permitted two travelling bars two hundred feet in length to move back and forth simultaneously to place the cell doors in the "unlock" position. This would be followed by the tap-tap-tapping sound of the inmate tappers running along the tiers as nimbly as mountain goats and with the dexterity of magicians popping up the protruding handles at full speed. Some of the trusties had been doing exactly that every day for years and took great personal pride in their speed.

The penitentiary always looked its gloomiest early in the morning when long lines of convicts paraded zombie-like down to breakfast. Placed strategically along the maze of metal staircases were uniformed sentinels like buzzards watching their prey. As the men passed along a blank wall steel cups and trays would be shoved out to them through food slots. Once they were back inside their cells most of the men seemed indifferent to what was served to them. They just pushed the grub through the hole in their faces until their bellies said "enough."

At 8:00, the maze of tiers was again tapped open to the sound of the bell, one peal for each range, until all the prisoners had vacated their cages for labour in the sweatshops. It would take a full thirty minutes for the long lines of silent prisoners all to crisscross the prison compound and reach their work locations. It was near the guard shack in the middle of the yard that Mr. Bristow was most visible, jabbing away with his cane, bad-mouthing the passing inmates like some old disgruntled traffic cop.

"Button up that coat!"

"You — straighten up that goddamn line!"

"Where's your hat? Go back and fetch it."

"What are you trying to hide, boy?"

"This is your last warning . . . "

To the great delight of the cons looking on, the rank-and-file guards would receive the same tirade from the chief keeper if their shirts were unbuttoned or their ties askew.

At 11:00, the first work gangs would parade from their respective industrial shops for the noon-hour jug-up inside the dome. By noon all the prisoners would be dead-locked inside their drums and the head count confirmed, allowing most of the guards to wander off to the officers' mess for lunch. We would spend the next hour sleeping, reading, or listening to the radio headsets.

Some limited activity would take place during the noon hour. Some of the cons would go to the joint hospital for various reasons and others were interviewed by an assortment of social workers. The warden would also dish out discipline during this hour in his infamous "kangaroo court" just inside the entrance leading to the hole. It was a small office with a big desk flanked by Canadian and British flags and lots of burly guards ready to pounce on any rebellious prisoner reacting violently to the sentence handed down to him by the warden.

"How do you plead, lad?"

"Not guilty, sir!"

"Well, I think you're guilty . . . ten days in the hole."

At 1:00 p.m., the cells would be tapped out and the inmates would dump their trays near the kitchen and parade off to work.

At 4:00, the shop whistle would blow for supper, and again the sequence would repeat itself until all the prisoners were dead-locked.

Baseball, hockey, and football games were hot betting items while we were locked away in our cells for the evening, but since our government canteen credits added up to only nickels and dimes, the winnings were totalled in pennies. Many of the guys simply drifted off into an early uneasy sleep in a desperate bid to escape doing time, but because all of us were hungry between meals a guy first of all had to fill his stomach with tap water in order to trick his belly into thinking that it was going to bed full. On the other hand a lot of the fellows felt that sleep left them too vulnerable, permitting all kinds of crazy things to invade their dreams, so instead of dozing they just closed their eyes and stayed real quiet for hours on end. There were others who spent most of their cell time labouring lovingly over crafts and hobby pieces of all shapes and sizes. There were always the solitaire players and those who played chess with their neighbours by numbers. But the most popular pastime was reading and listening to the various radio stations on the headset.

If a guy slept on one of the top tiers he could stand at his cell bars and observe the antics of his neighbours by staring into the cellblock windows, which acted as reflectors. It was like studying the inhabitants of a giant beehive that had been sectioned. There was little Angelo, who night after night displayed monumental patience in erecting a miniature Eiffel Tower with nothing more than glue and hundreds of toothpicks spirited out of the officers' mess. He would stop only when the lights went out, and then his closest cellmates would hear him crying himself to sleep. There were oddballs like the Arab, who would masturbate using a hollowed-out cucumber filled with warm water. He burst into sorrowful wails one night after the cucumber ruptured from over-use. The Owl wasn't quite as exotic. Night after night he fished in the toilet bowl for large sewer rats, then he would fry bits and pieces of them on the bedsprings and eat them.

At midnight the bell would sound and the lights would suddenly go out. There would follow the flushing of toilets, a few coughs and muted whispers, and then the screws would show up with their flashlights for a final head count.

As the winter of 1970–71 approached, the few so-called privileges we prisoners had left were taken away. Contact with the outside world that had once been encouraged to help develop a social consciousness was abruptly curtailed for "security reasons." Even the responsibility of conducting our own social affairs at the simplest level through officially sanctioned elected committees was abolished for fear of political activity. The obsession with tighter security turned out in the long run to be the downfall of the law and order our jailers were trying so desperately to achieve. In fairness, the warden and most of his administrators were in favour of rehabilitation programs to alleviate the tensions and create a healthy outlook for everybody concerned, but always they had to cave in to the devious pressures exerted by the rank-and-file guards. Many of those guards were frustrated and didn't even bother to disguise their hostility toward and contempt for any form of penal progress. The guards claimed that any proposed programs were futile, dangerous, and unrealistic. Like stubborn mules with burrs under their saddles, they bucked violently each time the brass showed any interest in proposals from civilians to defuse the powder-keg conditions inside the walls, even when the proposals were for the betterment of everyone concerned. The guards never failed to get even with any individual who dared to change the course of action they'd taken, including the warden and his immediate superiors. Revenge would take the form of a polite cold-shoulder, snarly looks, taking an inordinately long time to unlock barriers to let them through, and all kinds of similar unfriendly gestures. In the hostile environment of a maximum security penitentiary, even a warden liked to feel that if he was backed into a corner he could count on a quick rescue by his subordinates. Knowing that he couldn't, that he was on his own, was enough to break the resolution of any man. The biggest weapon in the guards' arsenal was their powerful union, which numbered about ten thousand. Pressure would be brought to bear on the warden in much the same manner that organized labour outside the prison walls dealt with their employers when dissatisfied with working conditions. On occasions when the screws did strike and the warden was left with no one to guard his institution, the army would be called in on a temporary basis to maintain security. That happened quite often, and usually after a few days a horrified warden would come down on the side of the guards' union. Bitterly the prisoners would smash their cell furnishings and beat vainly on their iron bars to protest the unfairness of it all. At times like that they became mere pawns.

Not only were the cons and the brass subjected to pressure from the hard-line guards to knuckle under to their caveman attitudes; so were the social workers, chaplains, volunteers, and civilian instructors, and even the odd guard with a kind heart. Anybody not wearing a number who showed any sympathy and concern for a prisoner would be branded a "con lover" and given a hard time — deliberately left waiting behind locked barriers, insulted, given the silent treatment, their cars sabotaged in the parking lot. The idea was to make life so miserable for anyone who did not join forces with the hard-line guards that they would quit their positions and never come back. The worst treatment was reserved for any guard who wanted his job to be fulfilling, who wanted to be not just a turnkey but someone whose fairness could help turn the tide of recidivism. Those who displayed such a spark of humanity were rewarded by their fellow guards with beatings at the local Legion Hall, slashed tires, rocks thrown through their living-room windows, and threatening phone calls.

But none of this had much to do with Step-Ladder's penchant for rubbing Mr. Bristow the wrong way. Newly released from the bug ward after nine weeks of shock therapy, the man was as spinny as a shithouse flea. Put to work as a range cleaner inside the dome through the direct influence of the chief keeper, Step-Ladder almost immediately showed his appreciation by concocting, along with two other hard-drinking cronies, several gallons of potato brew. Making the booze was no big deal in itself. What was difficult was finding a place to stash the foul-looking mixture, at least long enough for the blend to ferment, say a day or two. Over a period of a hundred years the guards got to know every single nook and cranny where a home brew could be secreted. Thus, although he was a canny brewmaster, Step-Ladder was hard put to find a spot where the brew detail wouldn't sniff out his liquid treasure. He concluded that the best bet was to be bold. In the dome next to the barrier leading into A-block was the keeper's desk where most of the screws hung out under the maze of staircases. Hanging on the wall was an old-fashioned fire extinguisher containing several gallons of water. Step-Ladder thought that if he managed to switch the contents for the brew he was making, no one would dream of searching that area. Only a sudden fire would uncover the plot. So, on the pretext of polishing up the red canister, Step-Ladder lugged the extinguisher into the mop room, unscrewed the metal top and poured out the water, then carefully stuffed his plastic brew bag into the dark cavity. Minutes later the thing was securely back in its bracket on the wall behind the keeper's desk. For the next forty-eight hours, in anticipation of a mindless drunk, the three old pirates kept a paternal vigil over their prize as it quietly gurgled and fermented just a few feet above the heads of their uniformed keepers.

Old Brew Nose came onto the scene just before breakfast parade. He was sitting behind the battered desk handing out work assignments to his subordinates when suddenly he went rigid and his nostrils flared in alarm. Whirling around in his swivel chair, he stared in utter amazement as droplets of hazy liquid dripped slowly from the tip of the fire extinguisher nozzle. Upon closer inspection his sensitive snout confirmed his suspicions, and he up and roared like a demented lion.

"Them sons of bitches are at it again!"

Dismayed to see his keeper so disgruntled, a young screw leaped to his feet and stuttered, "I'll dump it for you, sir."

"Not this time, lads," grinned the old chief. "I've got a better idea."

Being careful not to disturb the gurgling contents, Mr. Bristow undid the shoelace that sealed the plastic bag. Then he emptied a bottle of powerful laxative into the mixture, stirred it well, and capped it off. Beaming up at the shiny extinguisher, the chief keeper tapped his cane excitedly against the palm of his left hand and muttered malevolently, "There's more than one way to flush a jailbird!"

Not long afterwards, Step-Ladder and his two accomplices, concluding that the brew had completed its organic cycle, pounced on the canister when the screws deliberately vacated the area for a few minutes. Stretched out in the mop room, the three prisoners greedily guzzled down the soup-like brew until their throats were seared and they were pleasantly drunk. When the noon-hour bell reverberated throughout the dome signalling dinner and lockup, the terrible trio were astonished to find their individual cell gates padlocked! That's when Old Brew Nose showed up to herd them downstairs onto the main floor of the dome and order them to sit quietly on a wooden bench right next to the desk.

With bated breath both sides waited as the wall clock ticked ever so slowly. Little by little the three cons started to squirm uneasily on the bench. Soon came painful grimaces as all three started eyeing the single toilet inside a tiny cubbyhole across the cement floor. All of a sudden there was a mad scramble as they bolted simultaneously from the bench seeking relief, each shoving and tearing at the others in an effort to reach the commode first.

"C'mon man, I'm first!"

"Oh, oh, oh, hurry, let me at it!"

"Hey, man, I can't breathe!"

"Jesus, how about me, you assholes!"

"Oh my god, I think I'm going to miss the boat!"

Meanwhile a dozen uniformed guards were gathered around the keeper's desk splitting their sides, laughing so uproariously that the prisoners in the nearby cells started banging their steel mugs against the bars in protest. The end result was a sight to be seen: three palefaced brewmasters mincing around the cellblock days later in a subdued manner.

That was the black humour. Still to come were the real horrors of doing time, scenes that no human being should ever have to witness, at least not this side of purgatory.

CHAPTER 7

JANUARY 1971 found me stuck in the mailbag department, a notorious sweatshop. It seemed that all the institutional misfits landed in there sooner or later. The warden must have felt it was better to have the rebels all under one roof where they could be under constant observation. But the interior of the shop was so noisy and murky that the shotgun guard inside the barred cage was hard put to see half of what was going on. That's why they had three uniformed instructors constantly prowling the floor through huge mounds of mailbags in various stages of repair seeking out trouble before it erupted into something major. There were rows and rows of heavy-duty sewing machines whose humming sound filled the rafters with what sounded like an enormous heartbeat. Here and there the pounding of clamping machines added a discordant note to break the monotony. Because of the harsh sounds a conversation with your neighbour was almost impossible, unless you shouted directly into his ear.

The mailbag room was a hotspot because so much wheeling and dealing and plotting went on during the rap sessions. Everybody was vying for the latest scoop coming in off the joint grapevine. Some guys even fabricated information just to give the impression that they had the inside track. One of the rumours that was being whispered about was the possibility of a forcible takeover of the prison by a mysterious group who wanted to bargain for more humane conditions and less pressure from certain goons in uniform. As for the names of those involved in the attack unit, the guesses were way off base. High-profile cons frequently had their names tossed around. That was a dangerous thing for them because of the state of mind the warden and his administrators were in—nervous and paranoid. If any of those names dropped in their laps they'd act upon it and lock the person up. That's why one day I got riled up when two tough shooters came over to my workbench where I was driving home rivets and asked me point-blank, ''Rog, ol' buddy, can you clue us in on when the joint is going down?'' Turned out they had heard that I was going to be one of the leaders in the plot to bingo. They wouldn't believe me when I said I didn't know what they were talking about. They thought I didn't trust them. Nor was I able to track down the source to put an end to such a dangerous rumour. There were a lot of prisoners who for a variety of reasons would give anything to know when the place was going to blow up. I think they wanted to make sure that they were not on the spot when an eruption occurred.

The second most talked-about subject was the new multi-million-dollar super maximum security penitentiary near the village of Millhaven. We had seen pictures of it in the local papers. The ''Haven,'' as it came to be known, was rumoured to be designed to replace old Kingston Pen. Hidden from the road and the shores of Lake Ontario, it was eighteen miles from the city of Kingston. It was white in colour and sprawled on cleared land within dense bush. The new penitentiary was constructed in the form of an octo-pus, low to the ground with the suckers on the tentacles forming a network of escape-proof cells. The maze of marble hallways was so long that electric carts were used to get around from cellblock to cellblock. Just one guard securely locked inside what became known as the ''space ship'' could do the normal duties of a dozen screws. Instead of turning cumbersome keys, the guard would manipulate a maze of buttons on a console littered with blinking lights. He could punch open a single door or a hundred doors in seconds. He could also pour out a hail of gunfire or a cloud of tear gas. There were about a dozen of these space ships spread through-out the penitentiary and cellblocks, not counting the gun cages in the shops and the gun towers outside the barbed-wire perimeter where powerful telescopic military rifles were pointed at every-thing that moved in the exercise yard. The entire complex was encircled by two chainlink fences topped with rolls of razor wire. Killer dogs, huge and ferocious, prowled between the fences look-ing for something to sink their fangs into. Even the dog handlers were frightened of them. In the beginning more screws got chewed up than cons. The dogs even killed each other off inside the kennel. The guards had enthusiastically transformed these dogs into drool-ing killers in order to impose their will on the inmates in this new super maximum security institution.

Everything connected to the imminent opening of the Millhaven complex was shrouded in mystery and was threatening the peace of mind of almost every convict inside Kingston Penitentiary. It was official that the first few hundred inmates to be transferred to the "Haven" would come out of old KP, as would the guards. In the Haven these screws would be in a position to screw the lid down even tighter than before. That's why some of the prisoners wanted to make a last-ditch stand while they were still in KP. Any thoughts of rebelling inside the new electronic fortress would be futile.

The rumour that angered us the most about the Haven concerned the extensive bugging system that could monitor every sound, even your breathing while you slept at night. It was said that any conversation you had anywhere inside the prison could be picked up even from the towers, recorded, and used later against you in the warden's kangaroo court. The grapevine talked about two-way monitors inside the cells that could zoom in close enough to distinguish the colour of your eyes. The fear was that we would have absolutely no privacy, not even to go to the toilet, and that even in the visiting room your most tender exchanges would be recorded through bullet-proof glass. We all heard about tough new parole statutes that would make it infinitely more difficult to win your freedom. Release on full parole would be impossible while incarcerated in the Haven, because of the stigma attached to being a resident of a super maximum security penitentiary. In there a convicted felon could consider himself doing dead time and would have no incentive to better himself.

What made the rumours surrounding Millhaven even more confusing was the attitude of secrecy on the part of Warden Arthur Jarvis and his staff. Undoubtedly our keepers took a grim satisfaction in seeing us squirm. Aware of the falsity of some of the rumours and the paranoia they were generating, the screws nevertheless fanned the flames of anxiety, using the threat of being transferred to that unholy place as an invisible club to keep us in line.

But the prisoners were not the only ones sweating and squirming under the daily pressure of staying afloat in this man-made hell. Warden Jarvis had his own share of problems to deal with. He was struggling bitterly to cut through red tape with letters to the Commissioner of Penitentiaries and the Regional Director, desperately trying to convince them of his immediate needs. For instance, the position of deputy warden was vacant. In the report of the Parliamentary Investigation Committee into Disturbances at KP, the warden was quoted as saying in his letter, ''This means that the assistant deputy warden is flooded with paper work and has no time for inmates. Naturally he is not interested in taking on greater responsibilities for the same pay.'' Complaining about the loss of mature and experienced staff who had recently been transferred to Millhaven, he noted that they had as replacements people without experience trying to fill a slot which at that time they were not capable of filling. Expressing his acute anxiety about overcrowding and the type of prisoners he was receiving, he went on to say,

> God knows what will happen if one of us breaks down under pressure. I don't. After all we have 700 of the most difficult inmates in the country to deal with and in my opinion the number will not deplete to less than 350, even if Millhaven is operating at full capacity. We have dozens of disgruntled inmates who have been returned from medium or minimum security institutions, who claim they don't know why they were returned, or in some cases, because they were under suspicion or simply because they just can't get along in medium security. Some examples of this are inmates being returned directly to maximum security from minimum, etc. for escape or mediocre disciplinary problems.

The warden's second letter continued,

> I cannot afford to let more experienced staff transfer to Millhaven until something is done about reducing our count substantially. There is a very high degree of tension at Kingston Penitentiary at this time. In fact it appears to be almost at the point of explosion. We are doing all in our power to lessen the tension and to control the inmate population. There are, however, too many factors outside our jurisdiction which affect the situation over which we have no control. The most important problem is that the inmates are not getting the attention that they require and this is for several reasons, as follows:
> a) Divisional heads, etc. are too busy with paper work and have no time to communicate with the inmates, i.e. position descriptions, variance reports, Union matters, including grievances.
> b) We have been short three Classification Officers since August

1970 and it seems no one can fill these positions. As a result of this and the extra load being created by Bill C-150 as well as the number of paroles and violators of parole, along with 1,200 newcomers and about 300 returnees from other institutions each year, inmate problems are not being attended to.

c) Our psychiatric facilities are too small. Many of the people who should be confined there for treatment are released to the population before they are ready because someone else in poorer mental condition needs the cell. These are a constant source of trouble and are being used by the psychopaths to stir up trouble.

d) This exceeds by far the number of the type of desperate inmates that we should have in a maximum security institution. Moreover, our Segregation and Disassociation cells are practically full. I don't know where we can house inmates if a disturbance erupts.

e) There has been, and continues to be, widespread anxiety among the inmate population because of the contemplated transfer of inmates to Millhaven Institution. I feel sure that there are many inmates who would like to see Kingston Penitentiary in shambles before the transfer is completed.

f) Last Saturday it was necessary to cancel our Alcoholics Anonymous Anniversary Meeting because we had tips that there would be trouble. The names of the inmates we received certainly were likely candidates to attempt violent action. There also seems to be some relation to the inmates involved in the several violent acts which have occurred recently at this institution, namely assaults on my officers and the taking of hostages.

g) Unless some immediate action is taken with reference to the above, I expect many serious incidents to occur in the very near future.

All of us in the prison population were aware of the administrative problems the warden was having and his frustrating impotence when it came to making the rebellious guards toe the line. Unlike the old days, a prison warden just didn't have any clout, was in fact reduced to pushing papers. Certainly he didn't have the power to fire a screw. As a result of all this red tape nobody wanted to stick his neck out and maybe lose a promotion. Instead there was a lot of undermining going on among the staff to make an associate look stupid. The inmate leaders used this throat-cutting to their own advantage to pit one prison official against another to get what they wanted. With so many guards running around in circles to cover their asses and save their skins, no one had the time or inclination to worry about anything else. It was no wonder that the convicts had so much contempt for their keepers and rattled their bars in anger.

That kind of environment makes a guy do things he wouldn't ordinarily do on the street; it keeps him uptight and on edge. As always upon entering a prison with a brand new bit, I found myself very touchy and explosive as I re-adapted to survival in the prison jungle and got myself once again in top physical condition. The pain of my defeat in court was still fresh and almost overwhelmed my good sense; I tended to think with my guts instead of my brains. It was as if the sudden transition of having to get used to shaking time all over again brought with it temporary madness. A guy had to make awesome emotional decisions in split seconds, which left the question of right or wrong for later scrutiny. The will to survive was uppermost in all of our minds. I had sworn to myself a long time ago that I'd never let anybody get the drop on me again. I reaffirmed that thought each time I saw the horrible scar next to my heart, recalling how I had to stem the flow of my life's blood while gripping my guts that squeezed through the knife wound. It's memories like these which twist a man in prison, which can make him sick and crazy and vulnerable to the system.

My anger at being in on a bum rap made me strike out with my fists time and time again whenever some goon started sabre rattling around me. I just wasn't up to arguing with anyone who displayed a mean streak toward me. That angry, primitive part of my nature seemed alien to me. On the surface I was always extremely polite and amiable and not the least bit pushy. However, those qualities can be detrimental to one's survival inside the walls because there are so many loud-mouths who take them as a sign of weakness and try to test your resolve by seeing how far they can push you. That's what happened to me one day in the mailbag department during a break. A group of us cons were busy washing up at a large white basin at the rear of the shop when a big beefy newcomer named Chard came up behind me and spun me around. Jabbing a gnarled finger into my bare chest, he growled, "That's my towel you're wearing!" Yanking it roughly from my neck, he added threateningly, "Don't let it happen again."

My right fist exploded against his jaw, then my left. As his knees started to sag I followed through with another haymaker to the side of his head. He was hitting the floor as I walked away. It happened so quickly that only a few guys saw the play, and everybody else assumed that the new guy had suffered some kind of seizure. In fact one of the instructors rolled the unconscious man onto his back and put a pencil between his teeth so he wouldn't swallow his tongue! When they were able to bring him around, they lugged him out on a stretcher to the joint hospital. I learned later that the guy used to be a heavyweight boxer and had a reputation for being a bully. He was trying to make a name for himself at my expense. After that he shied away from me and kept shaking his head in amazement that a middleweight could knock him out cold. I had practised hundreds of hours on that particular technique. Besides, he was wrong — the towel was mine.

Every day there was more and more talk of hostage taking by various gangs, for various reasons, until the air became thick with feverish whispers, everybody greedily gulping down snatches of conversation and rumours until they were overflowing with conflicting stories. The institutional runners who moved freely delivering goods to the various industrial shops also brought with them an abundance of grapevine gossip and proudly picked out individuals or small groups to lay their tracks on. It was flattering to be singled out to receive such secret information because it meant that you were considered a solid con and trustworthy. Even more important, it was testimony to the fact that you were considered an important cog in the prison machinery. Most of the prison population was kept in the dark about precisely what was going on and had to settle for insignificant and wildly inaccurate morsels of information. Some of these cons were in fact responsible for the wild stories that were circulating. They made them up as they went along just so they could appear knowledgeable.

Sometimes hostage plans were formulated so quickly that they never had the chance to become rumour. One such incident occurred in the winter of 1971, instigated by two amateurs whose kamikaze act was doomed to failure. The two prisoners, an Indian and a black, suddenly decided while guzzling home brew that living in Cuba was preferable to shaking rough time in KP. So, arming themselves with two wicked-looking knives, they pounced on their two shop intructors on the floor of the carpentry department right under the nose of a shotgun guard in a barred cage. When the screw manning the locked gate responded to the cries of alarm, he too was taken hostage, and all three were dragged into the glass-enclosed office in the centre of the workshop. With razor-sharp blades pressed to their throats, the three victims were tied securely to office chairs with quarter-inch rope. The two angry rebels then poured gallons of solvent down the stairwell leading to the main floor of the carpentry shop and threatened to set fire to the fluid if any rescue attempt came from that direction. A bungled rescue attempt was made and the stairs were indeed set ablaze. The warden had to order the raging flames to be doused with fire hoses. A second rescue attempt was made. This time the goon squad was greeted with a barrage of furniture, including a stack of toilet seats. The would-be rescuers retreated only after the young black man pressed a sharp blade to the throat of the uniformed guard and shouted, "Come any closer and he gets it!"

The prisoners' bid for political asylum in Cuba failed after twenty-four hours of tense negotiations with the warden and his staff, who rejected the demands as "impractical." The deciding factor was the two prisoners' sudden sobriety, which took all the fight out of them and brought them back down to earth. They became such good buddies with their three hostages that in the final hours they freed them so they could all play cards. This was a mistake. Their "friendly" victims suddenly overpowered them long enough for a rescue squad to jump into the melee. The fiasco made headlines clear across Canada, and the two disgruntled mutineers languishing in the hole could only daydream of smoking cigars in Cuba.

Meanwhile, alone in the darkness of my cell, I continued tossing about in my nightmares and crying out in rage at the judge who had so cruelly banished me to this cold, empty place to vegetate. Once I dreamed that the screws were planting me in the prison garden and chanting,

"What kind of vegetable do you want to be?"

"A goddamn turnip!" I gasped in despair.

"He wants to be a fucking turnip!" they roared with glee, dancing mockingly around me. "We'll water the bastard once a week!"

I woke from that one in a cold sweat and pinned my bunk to the wall so that I could get down on the concrete floor to grind out hundreds of push-ups and shadow box until I was physically exhausted. Afterwards I sat trembling at my tiny table scribbling down furiously the torrent of words that was gushing out of me until finally I slumped over in relief. I had so much to say, so much to confess and discover about myself, but first I had to teach myself how to write coherently if I wanted to share my experiences with the outside world. And I had to do it while alone in a world of swinging fists and cold contempt for human life. Also I wasn't so thick-headed that the damning things I had done didn't scrape away at my conscience like a wooden ladle in the hands of a famished man. I was a human being with a heart and soul and a conscience that was battered and soggy with regret. But I was almost drained of repentance as I was paying the price for a crime I didn't commit. Certainly I wasn't about to be a target for anyone any more.

One Sunday afternoon in February, I was out in the yard pacing back and forth in the snow when my old friends Hugo and Jezebel interrupted my thoughts.

"The lug you clobbered in the shop is out to do you in," the drag queen informed me, her blond curls looking indecently out of place under her grey prison cap.

"Yeah," echoed Hugo, blowing steam in the cold air, "he's stoned on goofballs and mouthing off that he's going to shank you before the whistle blows for jug-up."

I stopped dead. "Where is he?"

"Looking for you," replied Hugo, with concern. He withdrew a short iron bar from a coat-sleeve that was far too short for his ape-like arms.

Mechanically I slid the heavy bar inside my winter coat. Pacing once again with my two buddies, I whispered softly, "Is he serious?"

"Dead serious," said Jezebel, clutching sympathetically at my coat-sleeve.

"You don't know that for sure, knucklehead!" snorted Hugo.

"Dead serious," repeated Jezebel stubbornly.

Shrugging his massive shoulders, Hugo advised, "I think you better beat him to the draw, Roger."

That was the nature of things inside the walls—kill or be killed. On the surface I was unnaturally calm, but deep down where it counted I could feel my guts churning. Such an encounter was the last thing I wanted. Damn him for threatening my existence; it was tough enough surviving as it was. Damn him all to hell! I would have to defend myself to survive, but I always did well when my back was to the wall. I'd been there so many times.

"Ain't hardly anybody in the yard," I muttered, shifting the iron bar around in my waistband.

Shivering violently from the icy cold, Jezebel replied through chattering teeth, "Everybody is inside in the TV room watching the hockey game."

As we stopped in the snow to give Hugo a chance to light up a cigarette, I said to him quietly, "I'd hate to get busted on this; see what you can do, OK?"

"Don't worry, Rog, we'll do our best to run interference for you, maybe get a few more guys to block the screws."

The three of us continued across the snowy yard to the auditorium entrance where we told the screw manning the barrier that we were cold and wanted to see the last half of the Montreal game. Half of the prison population was locked up in their cells, having had their recreation period that morning. The warden wisely utilized the two television rooms like a doctor handing out placebos, pacifying the sports fanatics among the prison population — anything to get us through another day in the big house.

I figured I'd look for this Chard guy in the TV rooms first, which were away from the gym floor and not far from the prison library. That's where most of the scores were settled — away from the lighted auditorium where everybody played cards and chess and where there was a gun cage. There was no gun cage in the TV rooms. Because there was no weaponry in that area the screws beefed up their patrols, but not very enthusiastically. They were scared shitless of the dark room, so they tended to linger around the entrance. Hugo and Jezebel had managed to gather around them half a dozen tough characters to run interference for me. The cons were all bored stiff and itching to see some blood flow. They didn't care much who won, as long as it was a good fight. I had just squeezed past two screws at the entrance to the larger of the two rooms and was trying to pick out Chard's big shaggy head from the other silhouettes in the smoky atmosphere when Jezebel tapped me on the shoulder.

"He's in the shower room in his birthday suit!" she blurted out. "He won't have his shank with him, right?"

A moment later I slowly swung the big green door leading into the shower room open and was greeted by billows of steam. I must have looked bizarre standing there in my winter coat with my right hand hidden. Straight ahead of me was a low wall with two banks of shower nozzles under which naked bodies were lathering up, all indistinguishable in the heavy vapour. Along the other walls were men either undressing or drying off, none of whom was my target. So intense was my concentration as my eyes roamed the area that the shouts and buzz of conversation reached my ears in a strangely disjointed manner. I had just spotted Chard on the other side of the wall spouting water like an African buffalo at a water hole when a hand gripped my shoulder and a thick syrupy voice whispered in my ear.

"Don't do it, Roger. Put it off, please."

Trembling violently and fighting back the explosion that was gathering in me I spun around and, glaring at the chunky figure standing slightly behind me, muttered, "Stay out of this, Billy; it's no skin off your ass."

Pompously he replied, "But my friend, I'm not trying to prevent this rumble for purely selfish reasons, it's for the good of the whole inmate population."

When I looked back at Chard, I was further ticked off to see that the big lug had quit spouting water long enough to stare at me with a shocked expression; the element of surprise had now evaporated because of Billy Knight's untimely appearance.

"C'mon pal, let's go out into the gym like two reasonable men so I can explain the situation better."

At that moment Billy Knight was only the prison barber, but in a few days he would become known as the man who tried to reshape the dark history of Kingston Penitentiary. A politician by nature, Billy was always bubbling over with revolutionary plots and ideas to better the conditions of his fellow prisoners. He had started out in group foster homes, then thieved his way up the ladder on mediocre beefs, picking up short-term sentences along the way. He felt that the penal system was moulding him like an assembly-line product. He was bitter to the point of self-destruction and vocal about his dissatisfaction. In fact he was so mouthy that the guards eventually sloughed off his attitude as eccentric and harmless. However, the sparks of rebellion that were burning in his mind were about to ignite with a roar that would be heard all around the world. At a later date he would grow himself a beard, and damned if he didn't look like Charles Manson. His attitude and mannerisms did mirror that infamous fellow outcast. Billy wasn't much taller or heavier than Manson, and he had the same visionary eyes and bony features. His hair was the same colour, only it was slicked straight back. At the age of 28 he was ready to set the world of penology on its ear, if not through grandiloquent speechmaking then through brute force.

He led me into the washroom adjacent to the recreation office, pleading emotionally for me to hear him out.

"My friend," said Billy, "we have all got a bellyful of bitterness eating away at us for one reason or another, and I know you're disgusted right now, but be of good cheer and remember principle has a thick, thick skin."

"What's that got to do with me squaring things with Chard?" I swiped his hand angrily away from my coat-sleeve. His speechifying act was starting to rub me the wrong way and I thought I'd give him a little jab of rebuttal. "The grapevine says you want to take over the joint just so you can get your mug on the front page."

"Groundless suspicion," he spluttered, dropping most of the tobacco from the cigarette he had been rolling. "A lot of pea-brain jealousy is all."

"Anyhow," I repeated as I tried to calm myself, "what's all this got to do with my beef?"

Grabbing at my sleeve again, he pulled me closer and whispered in my ear, "We've got all our gear planted in the shower room in one of the vents, stuff we're going to need to take over the joint, and if you pipe that big ape the pigs will tear the place apart."

That was something I could understand, and I said so, but right after that he had the nerve to ask me to join his group. "We can use your fists because this is going to be one helluva bingo, but this time nobody is going to get killed. Speed and surprise are going to be our weapons!"

"Shit!" I remarked in disgust as I walked away. The guy was nuts if he thought he could take over the joint with just an arsenal of knuckles. I was thinking that the prison scene was changing too fast for me, things were being conducted differently than they were in the old days when I first started doing time. One thing shouldn't change — a guy should never meddle in his neighbour's beefs. Still in possession of the iron bar, I went prowling for Chard on the assumption that he was no longer in the shower room.

"Hey, Roger, hang on there!" says this big bruiser coming out of the TV room toward me. It was Honky, an old friend, bringing me the news that he had overheard Chard asking the keeper to lock him up because somebody was gunning for him. "Jezebel asked me to run interference for you, so he must be running from you."

I asked in surprise, "Are you sure he's asked to be dead-locked?"

"Sure, sure, ask Do-Die, he heard him talking to the man too. The guy froze and asked to be locked up in protection."

I didn't know whether to be relieved or sad. Rumbling was one thing, but being responsible for another con's broken spirit was something that weighed heavily on me.

The next morning I received a kite from Chard through one of the runners saying that he hadn't been gunning for me at all. A con named Eastwood had set the whole thing up to get rid of him. There was bad blood between the two of them, a conflict that had flared up while they were shaking time in another penitentiary. It was Chard's guess that Eastwood had capitalized on our earlier beef to manoeuvre me into zapping him. With Chard out of the way Eastwood could breathe easier; his paranoid mind told him that Chard was gunning for him. To someone in the outside world this explanation of the chain of events must sound like a comedy of errors, but to anybody shaking time it was all perfectly logical, in a crazy way.

Believing what Chard said to be true, I was now obliged to settle accounts with Eastwood for trying to set me up. That same day I caught up with the manipulator in the jug-up line. Quick as a wink I spun him around just a few feet from two screws and smashed my fist into his face. The powerful blow sent him and his supper tray sprawling across the concrete floor with a terrible racket. In the ensuing confusion I was able to lose myself in the excited crowd, grimacing in pain as I had almost busted my hand.

In the prison environment there is a lot of poetic justice. Eastwood (who ended up with two shiners) got so anxious that he demanded to be locked up in the protection block, a few cells down from Chard, because, as he told the warden, he feared for his life. Nobody felt sorry for the guy, certainly not Chard. He was now totally gripped by paranoia and refused to sign himself out of dead-lock, thinking that I was only trying to trick him so I could lead-pipe him. I felt terrible that a fellow con was vegetating because he was afflicted with the stir bug and that it was indirectly my fault.

Although I was not interested in getting involved in Billy Knight's scheme, I did have some plans of my own, and Step-Ladder came to figure heavily in them. Apart from being a "range cleaner," Step-Ladder also had the assignment known as "water boy," an extra duty that gave him additional canteen. Because KP was so old, none of the cells had hot water taps and we sure as hell couldn't shave with cold water, at least not with the cheap blades they issued us once a week. So it was up to a handful of cons rushing up and down the tiers with water pails to keep us supplied after lock-up. If you were jailwise, you'd create your own method of boiling water with an illegal little gadget called a "dunker." Half-a-dozen old razor blades were banded together in such a way that a positive and negative flow of electricity could charge between the two stacks. A piece of rubber acting as a buffer between both forces ensured that your hot-wiring did not create a short circuit that could knock you on your ass or plunge the whole cellblock into darkness. If you were careful to splice into your cell wiring just right, then you could boil a can of water in less than ten minutes. If you did blow the lights out with your dunker, not only would the screws get mad, but your neighbours would also get pissed off at the inconvenience. Mostly the dunkers were used to make contraband coffee out of chicory beans.

"Hey, Coolidge, pull up, will you?" I whispered to Step-Ladder from my bunk one day as he lumbered laboriously past my cell door gripping the heavy pail of boiling water in both hands. Stopping in the shadow of my doorway all hunched up with the billows of steam giving his gaunt features an ominous look, he stood there numbly with the spout resting on the metal cross-piece. "Hey, old buddy, don't you recognize me?" I asked as I switched on my cell light and held out my water pail to be filled. Jerking back his head so that the unkempt mass of black hair was clear off his face, he peered hard at me through the cell bars, and with a look of surprise lighting up his haggard kisser he exclaimed "Cowfucker!"

(When I had first come into the joint as a kid many years before I worked on the sports gang with Step-Ladder and sort of got into the habit of looking after his welfare. Whenever he was lucid he'd joke and shadow-box with me. Each time I managed to tweak his hawk-like nose, he'd get madder than hell and rap his big knuckles on top of my skull. When he wanted my attention he would snap his fingers with a sound like a pistol shot. One winter day I found him alone in the dark stone shed struggling with invisible webs that he said were trying to choke him to death.)

I was glad to see that he still remembered me, because I had a big favour to ask of him related to his work as a cleaner. I didn't believe in putting all my hopes in one basket, so all the time I was in the joint awaiting the outcome of my appeal, I had not been idle. In the event that my legal route fizzled, I had been wracking my brain for a second way out — one that would lead me over the wall. With my enormously long sentence and lengthy record of jailbreaks, it was natural that the warden had his men keep me under close scrutiny. Hardly a day went past without my person or cell being searched. The uniformed staff were forever looking for sawed bars or some other proof that I was trying to bust out. Up to this point all the manoeuvres had been done in my head. Finding a chink in the prison's armour was becoming an obsession with me; I could think of nothing else. At night in my cell and during the day in the workshop my eyes were constantly probing the four walls, searching for that elusive crack that would enable me to crawl out to freedom if my appeal failed. I knew the beast well, having spent most of my adult years inside its belly, and I also knew that it had learned to close any remaining gaps in its defences, having had more than a hundred years to do so. Nevertheless it was eerie how the old bastion would surrender its architectural secrets to me if I exerted enough mental energy on the various structures strewn across the six acres.

One possible escape route that intrigued me was up through the top of the dome's glass cupola, which from my workshop window looked like a round flying saucer with countless tiny windows. I spent weeks and months staring up at that towering structure. I thought if I could find a way to get up there from my cell, I could crawl out through one of those tiny windows, slide down the slanted roof, and hop over to the roof of the chapel. Then, clinging to the stone chimney, I could throw a pronged hook over the railing of the gun tower fifteen feet away, fasten it tightly around the base, and cross over hand-over-hand. It was a centre-wall tower and was used only during the day. Guards in the corner towers could see me crossing the empty space, but I could solve that problem by choosing a foggy night, which was no problem since we lived right next to a large body of water which created a smoky mist. I knew for sure that nobody had ever attempted a jackrabbit parole by going through the top of the dome; maybe no one ever would because no matter how hard I looked I just couldn't see any way of reaching the top without being seen by the screws. In fact there seemed to be no way for even a legitimate work crew to get up there from the outside or the inside. Yet away up at the top was a tiny metal circular catwalk just below the small windows. I couldn't imagine any ladder being long enough to reach it, so I concluded there had to be a hidden trap door somewhere inside the main cellhouse. Ironically it turned out to be no more than ten feet from my cell. I slept on the top tier of B-Block in number two cell, and right in front of me was an old gun cage that was no longer in use; inside was a tiny trap door leading up to the attic. I became convinced that somehow through that trap door there was a roundabout way that led to the top of the dome. The only way I'd know for sure was to get inside that locked cage, pick the heavy lock on the ceiling trap door, then explore the attic above for a hidden passageway. That's where Step-Ladder came into the picture. He had a photographic memory that enabled him to observe an object like a key, then minutes later draw on paper the exact dimensions. He had used this same gimmick before to have keys made in the machine shop to hide his home-made brews. I asked him to make me one for the gun cage. "Sure, OK," he agreed. "I'll get my friend Do-Die to help me." He was enthusiastic about the idea of doing something out of the ordinary and asked me no questions.

"Well, he's your buddy, and I trust him." In fact I had my doubts. At one time Do-Die was a classy can-man who could crack any pete on the market, until booze and technology slowed him down; afterwards he became a skid-row bum with a thousand stories. His final safecracking caper turned out to be a fiasco: he used so much nitro that when the safe door blew off its hinges it went straight through a brick wall. Moments later the short, stocky prowler with the enormous belly was fleeing down an alleyway ducking police bullets. Gasping for breath he turned to his partner and shouted, "It's do or die!" Thus the nickname, plus a bullet in the leg that gave him a permanent limp and a disability excuse. But despite my misgivings, I told Step-Ladder, "I guess it's okay if you get Do-Die to run interference for you." As I spoke, I was watching Step-Ladder pawing at something in front of his face. "What's the matter? Is the steam getting in your eyes? I've got enough water; you can move the pail away."

"Naw, it ain't that," he grunted in confusion. "It's the cobwebs, cowfuckers are getting so thick that some days I can hardly move around."

Setting my water can down on the table I gripped the bars and, leaning close to his gaunt face, said, "You gotta quit thinking like that or else the man will use that weakness against you! C'mon, Step-Ladder, you're too shifty to fall into that kind of trap."

Shaking his shaggy head from side to side, he looked up at me like a little boy and in a painful voice added, "You ask Do-Die, he almost got tangled in my webs, he'll tell you I ain't crazy, because he's seen them."

Exasperated, I blurted out, "If you keep letting that old pirate bend your ear with all that funny farm talk you'll go bananas for sure! Use your head and do your own thinking."

"It's not easy, you know," mumbled Step-Ladder, slowly rolling a cigarette between thick fingers.

"Sure, I know where you're coming from, but that out-to-lunch friend of yours is going to do a number on your head each time you guys booze together. Just don't be telling him about spider webs or anything along those lines. He'll twist the facts and throw it back at you all full of knots."

Lighting up his butt, he reiterated in a faraway voice, "It's easy for you to say. You've got smarts, Roger, but not me. It always takes me so long to come up with the right answers."

While the two of us were talking, some guys further down the range were hollering for Step-Ladder to show up with his water pail. They wanted to feed their caffeine habit or get their shave over and done with so they could get some shut-eye.

"C'mon Step-Ladder, I got a date with a babe soon as I get these whiskers off."

"Yeah, and she's got three legs," cried out a wiseacre, "and the third extremity is what you're aiming for!"

That and other wisecracks started echoing along the tier, making Coolidge self-conscious. After mumbling something incoherently he picked up his pail and shuffled off. Just then my next-door neighbour January Jones piped up, his words directed at a guard making the rounds far below, "Hey screw, open a window, will ya? I breathe once in awhile, you know."

"Right on, January," I blurted out, laughing, as I gripped my cell bars. "You sure know how to influence people."

"Is that a challenge I hear?" retorted the old jug-man as he energetically rummaged around under his bunk.

"You got the message, old buddy," I teased, as I too dug into my personal effects for my chess board. "Get your jaws on the board because this time I'm going for the guzzler!"

Our little banter was almost a nightly occurrence as we two chess fanatics rattled our pieces at each other, both lusting for a quick checkmate that we could tease the other with. Sandy-haired and freckled, January was a keen athlete who hated to lose, though he was in his early fifties. When he beat the pants off the younger players in the institutional handball championships, he razzed them mercilessly about the age difference. His biggest loss came when the judge handed him a double sawbuck for bank robbery, a bitter pill that he never swallowed very well.

Because there was a wall and bars separating us, we had to play each other using numbers carved into the squares on our boards, which we had made in the carpenter shop. That meant there was a lot of hollering back and forth. Sometimes half a dozen teams would be playing at one time in the cellblock, with other guys following the best games on their own numbered boards while wagering. All in all it was a damn good way to kill time.

Even after the silence bell sounded January and I were able to continue the game by simply passing a string to each other's drum and writing our moves down on a tiny piece of paper. On this particular night the first thing my neighbour wrote down was a message of warning: "Do-Die and Step-Ladder—you've got to be kidding?" Obviously he had overheard my talk with Coolidge. I replied simply, "You're right, but I've got no choice, smile."

8

I WAS TRULY IMPRESSED. With just a small hobby-craft knife and a piece of wood, Do-Die and Step-Ladder actually came up with a working model of the key that unlocked the barrier leading into the gun cage. It took them one week of patience and painstaking work to copy and carve those teeth that would turn the tumblers in the massive lock, and they did it without causing any suspicion, which was no small accomplishment for those two misfits. Now both of them had me cornered in the hallway leading into the gym. Smirking and beaming with pride, they asked me point-blank when the three of us were going to bust out!

Astonished, I said to them as patiently as I could without ruffling their feathers that going up through the trap door was just exploratory, that I was simply following a hunch that might lead to a dead end. "You guys have got to cool it, OK? Even if something does pan out, I don't think you should be dreaming about making a jackrabbit parole. It's tough out there in the streets, and it's a hell of a lot shakier when you're running and hiding."

"Aw, Roger, no problem," piped up Do-Die in that shifty way of his. "You'll have us as partners."

"Yeah," added Step-Ladder, chewing on a raw carrot pilfered from the back of the kitchen, "I'll be your getaway driver and Do-Die can go into the banks with you."

Shuddering at the thought, I changed the subject and told them I had no intention of escaping until I got the results of my appeal, which could come any day.

"Well, I sure believe you've found a way out," said Do-Die in a stubborn voice. "You wouldn't have asked us to stick our necks out if you hadn't."

"Well, one thing for sure," I added as I glanced around to make sure that no one could overhear us, "the trap door must lead up into the attic above A- and B-blocks, and once a guy is up there he could always punch a hole through the roof. That would be a bit noisy, but effective."

"See, Step-Ladder, what did I tell you, eh?" gloated Do-Die as he did a little excited jig.

Interrupting his dance, I continued sombrely, "There's a catch — a real fucking monkey."

"What's that?" Do-Die wanted to know.

Smiling slightly to take away the sting, I stared down hard at his huge belly and stated flatly, "There's no way that you're going to fit through the trap door."

Throwing his two cents' worth in, Step-Ladder exclaimed: "The cowfucker will go on a diet and drink no more brews!"

"Yeah, right," chimed in Do-Die in a shaky voice. "Just gimme a couple of weeks and I'll be so skinny I'll slide through the key-hole." To illustrate his point he sucked in his gut and his pants fell down.

I was convinced that they were just blowing in the wind, that when it came down to a crunch they'd quickly change their minds. Meanwhile, I'd let them go on dreaming. Besides, my appeal was sure to be a success, but just in case . . .

I sent the wooden key to the metal shop and had a solid replica made which I planned to try out on the weekend. Saturday afternoon the screw spun the wheel and the cells on my tier were tapped out. Then, while my neighbour January Jones occupied the guard, I slid the key in the gun-cage lock and was elated when I felt the tumblers turn over easily. With that question answered, I quickly re-locked the gate and followed the crowd down the maze of stairways and out to the big yard. The following afternoon, on Sunday when the cell gates swung open, I slid into an empty cell further down the tier, pulled the door shut and hid under the bunk. An hour later the gate again swung open and I could hear Step-Ladder saying: "It's going to take at least an hour to clean it up, boss."

"In that case I'll leave it open until the lads troop in from recreation," replied the guard as he walked away.

"All clear," whispered Step-Ladder as I stared out from under the bunk at his big feet and mop pail. "Do-Die is mopping the dome floor and he says he will keep the screws down there busy with some of his stories."

Groaning from the pain of being cramped up and from the thought of having to rely on my round little cohort, I dragged myself to my feet. Looking around at the cell that was littered with wreckage, I asked Step-Ladder, ''What caused the Pocketman to smash his drum?''

''Dunno exactly, something about somebody in his family dying, and they wouldn't let him go to the funeral.''

''And now he's in the cooler,'' I mused, remembering how I had done the same thing when my dad died. ''You do your thing here, but keep tabs on me every few minutes, OK?''

I tiptoed up to the head of the tier and peered down onto the main floor where the screws were gathered around the keeper's desk drinking java. All of the activity was now out in the yard and in the gym, with only a few odd cleaners left inside mopping and sweeping floors. Do-Die was down there, but instead of rapping to the guards, he was manoeuvring himself into position to steal one of the bulls' lunchboxes.

''Good luck, pal,'' whispered January Jones as I squeezed up against his cell bars in the first cell on the top tier. He was only a few feet away from the gun cage and would keep six by holding his mirror through the bars. That way he would be in a position to warn me should the man suddenly show up. Again I had no trouble unlocking the heavy barred gate. Once through, I quickly locked it behind me. Straight up above me in the ceiling was the trap door, which was secured with a big old-fashioned padlock, and below it the short ladder leading up to it. From my lofty perch I could see half of the dome floor, but not the half where the screws were, which meant they couldn't see me either. Only a few feet away January watched with interest as I stealthily climbed the few feet up the ladder to the trap door. Crouched under the ceiling, I palmed my set of lock picks (also made in the machine shop) and, feeling terribly vulnerable, started working on the tumblers. Hurrying would only cause greater delay, so I forced myself to be icy calm, but still my hands trembled and perspiration started dripping into my eyes. I hadn't included these things in my practice sessions with a similar lock. But the practice did pay off. In less than five minutes I was able to disengage the tumblers and snap open the lock. I gave January the thumbs-up sign and, scrambling through the dark opening, I disappeared from sight.

As I crouched under the slanted roof, an eerie realization hit me. I was way out of bounds, was in fact standing on the roof of my own cell, and I could be walking into an ambush. I had no doubt that if this was the case the guards would shoot me dead, having no way of knowing if I had a gun or not. The attic stretched far ahead of me as cold and damp as a mummy's tomb, with ribbons of winter sunshine stabbing through cracks in the structure illuminating the interior. Everything was dusty and old, apparently undisturbed for the past 140 years. Bloated rats with long yellow teeth stared at me with bloodshot eyes from the overhead crossbeams. Bats hung from the ceiling. Decay was everywhere. Now that my ears were adjusting to my new environment I could hear tiny animal movements, causing me to wonder if rats ate bats. Lighting up a candle pilfered from one of the chapels, I held the flickering light close to me as if to draw warmth and security from it, and moved forward. While standing on the ceiling of January Jones's drum, I considered doing a tap dance, but immediately rejected the idea as being too risky. Cautiously ducking the overhead beams and cobwebs, I moved in the direction of the rotunda, the hub of the huge wheel. I suddenly came up against the smooth circular sides of the rotunda and was dismayed to find that there was no visible opening or ladder. Slowly and carefully, one hand gripping the candle, the other sliding along the wall, I probed for a way up to the top. Suddenly my feeble light illuminated a small hatchway in the wall. I grasped the handle with one hand and pulled mightily, and the door swung open with a squeal of protest, revealing an inky blackness. I was greeted by a piercing screech and a flutter of mighty wings. My own scream of terror superseded the first as I dropped the candle and staggered backwards with my fist up. Trembling more with anger than with fear I stood stock-still as the sounds reverberated throughout the series of long attics, pushing the owl or hawk on to greater speeds. Gathering my wits about me, I worried for a few minutes about whether the ruckus had been heard by the screws far below. If so I was certainly up shit creek without a paddle. My heart slowing down to a trot, I relit the candle and crawled cautiously into the chimney-like opening, where metal rungs were embedded in a concrete sleeve. I was in a shaft a little more than two feet square. Way up at the top I could see the light of day. The wind surging down the shaft sounded eerily like a wolf howling, but assured me that I was on the right track. After a long climb I was able to poke my head through the opening. It gave access to a tiny circular catwalk with a narrow safety railing. By looking straight down through the open grate of the walk, I could clearly see tiny figures gathered around the bell on the dome floor. I could even make out Old Brew Nose among the other staff, which made me gulp in apprehension and pull my head back in.

I suddenly realized that I had been prowling around up there in the dark attics for almost two hours in a dream-like trance. Covered with cobwebs and spiders, chills running up and down my spine, I told myself that I'd better not stay any longer. I had the information I needed: it was indeed possible to escape across the rooftops from up there. I should hurry back to my cell before a head count was conducted, or I'd be stuck up there. I took very deliberate steps as I searched for the way to the trap door by candlelight, telling myself that the weird sound I heard was only the wind doing strange things and the glowing eyes were those of tiny animals. I blew out my candle, lifted the trap door, and slowly eased my head out. January Jones excitedly waved me back. Just before I pulled my head out of sight I spotted a uniformed guard turning onto the tier to take up his position near the locking wheel, which was less than ten feet away! It was unusual for him to be there that soon, so I figured it must be because Mr. Bristow was on duty, and he was a stickler for following proper procedure.

Minutes later I was still racking my brain in the eerie darkness for a solution to my problem when suddenly I heard a great commotion coming from far below. I eased the trap door open and heard loud shouts of: "Stop that naked jailbird!" It was the enraged voice of Old Brew Nose trying to stop some con from doing something that wasn't permitted. Whatever was going on was sure causing a major distraction—enough to draw away the screw near the trap door. I could hear January's hoarse whisper urging me to come down as quickly as possible, and I did so amid a lot of whoops and hollers, through which could be heard the authoritative voice of the chief keeper bellowing: "Lord Jesus—stop that maniac!"

With trembling hands I snapped the huge padlock back into place, scurried down the short ladder, unlocked the gate to the gun cage, let myself out, then took up a position with the other inmates (all of whom had their backs to me) at the guard railing to see what was going on. "Go, man, go!" shouted the cons around me as a huge hairy figure with an enormous pot-belly streaked naked up the maze of stairways pursued by a horde of uniformed guards and with Mr. Bristow in full hue and cry downstairs by the bell directing the chase. "After that fuckin' jailbird, men! Run the son of a bitch into the hole!" Never had I seen the keeper so excited. He was beating on the bell with his precious cane, getting all red in the head. In any event he was unable to stop the hairy creature with the pillowcase over his head from streaking through the milling throng, some of whom deliberately impeded the pursuit by blocking the stairways. Roars of encouragement spurred the two enormous buttocks on to even greater speed until finally the guy just disappeared into the maze of tiers. Meanwhile one of the screws in pursuit got his balls in a knot when somebody in the crowd swiped his cigar, and threatened blue murder if he didn't get it back.

With the chase off and the quarry hopelessly lost, the chief keeper rang the bell for silence. Then, struggling to regain his lost dignity, he ordered everybody to parade back to their cells for lock-up, count, and supper.

As usual between 5:00 and 6:00 p.m. the water boys made their rounds of the tiers. Dragging his steaming pail of water, Step-Ladder hunkered down in front of my drum and said with wonder in his voice: "Boy, can that cowfucker ever run, eh?" Motioning for him to pour me some hot water so that I could wash off the affects of the attic, I mumbled something about how fortunate the streaker's timing was for my hasty exit. "Don't you know?" he grinned. "That was Do-Die." I was humbled, truly humbled, that Do-Die had stuck his neck out like that for me, and I said so.

"Sure, sure," said Step-Ladder, his head bobbing up and down vigorously, "and when it's time to bust out he'll just jump the fence and leave the cows behind."

"You mean bulls," I corrected.

"Yeah, yeah," said Coolidge as he shuffled away in a cloud of steam.

So now Do-Die was the apple of his eye because he got clean away with his crazy stunt to help me. That meant that my muddled friend would do just about anything that Do-Die might suggest, maybe even going so far as to use my trap door to hide their brews. I reminded myself to warn the two of them not to do that.

Billy Knight found absolutely no humour in the streaking escapade, claiming to his friends that it could have triggered off an unorganized riot. He decided to advance his plans for the forceful takeover of the institution before something else unforeseen happened. Billy's militant mood was greeted with reservations, if not downright hostility, among certain circles in the prison population, especially from those with the most to lose, like the short-timers who feared that a violent upheaval would interfere with their plans for parole. Many feared the outcome of a riot would be quickly forgotten headlines and gruesome retribution by vengeful guards, not penal reform. They claimed that their few personal belongings would be destroyed and that they would be kept incommunicado from their loved ones for weeks and months under constant dead-lock, eating cold sandwiches. Even worse, an upheaval would give the screws a perfect opportunity to lord it over us, since we would be locked up separately and the guards would no longer have to fear a unified attack. Moreover, the guards would collect danger pay and overtime wages while sitting on their fat rumps playing cards. The more volatile prisoners said they didn't care what happened afterwards, that it was better to fight and die than to live under such punitive conditions.

The one person who might have alleviated the crisis was the warden, but like many other directors in the federal penitentiary system, he had been reduced to a pencil pusher. He was engulfed in great mounds of frustrating red tape, sticky stuff that ensnarled everything it came into contact with, including the cons. The wardens were terrified of making wrong decisions that might bring the wrath of policy makers down on their heads. Paranoid and indecisive, they were constantly glancing over their shoulders at the shadowy figures lurking there, waiting for the big error in judgment that would lose them their positions. Wardens made as few decisions as they could possibly get away with. They feared many people: the commissioner, the regional director, the press, the cons, and the screws. If they favoured the inmates, the guards would get jealous and go on strike, crippling the institution. If they favoured the screws, the cons would go on a hunger strike or tear the joint apart. Under such drastic circumstances most wardens considered it wise to side with the guards. Consequently, the deeply entrenched old keepers and hard-line guards ran the prison their way. They were, as a group, victims of their own twisted paranoia, sworn to a secret oath the day they don their uniform, exchanging unlisted phone numbers and immersing themselves in an attitude of ''us against them.'' ''Them'' is anyone who is not a custodial guard. They have a favourite all-encompassing word to rebuff anyone from examining the inner workings of the penitentiary system: *security*. Somehow it's a magic word that requires no explanation: "Sorry, you can't go in there, security reasons."

The blue-collar staff at the regional headquarters, the flagship of the thirteen Kingston area institutions, cut themselves off from the guards turning keys in the federal prisons. Also making a great distinction between themselves and the turnkeys was the massive national headquarters, a mind-boggling array of planners and specialists who further alienated the screws. Everybody wanted to be a criminologist, but nobody wanted to be called a guard; not even the screws, who referred to themselves as "custodial officers." With fifty-three federal institutions spread out across the country, the penitentiary system boils down to big business. Apart from providing thousands of jobs for people who would otherwise be unemployed, it feeds money into city and neighbourhood coffers. But more than anything else, these human warehouses act as deterrents to those who might think twice about walking a straight line. The average prisoner is constantly uptight and cynical when told that he is going to be cured of his unlawful nature while incarcerated, knowing all too well that the end result is a waste of human resources and public money. The cons feel that they are simply cannon fodder for the penal system and those who live off its avails, none of whom are going to lose any sleep worrying about the mind-boggling recidivism rate.

The con is a product of the system, and when he witnesses on a daily basis all the infighting, throat-cutting, and petty bitching of his immediate keepers, and sees first-hand the policy makers scrambling madly to fortify their positions on the way to the top, he quickly loses respect for and faith in those entrusted with his rehabilitation. Most prisoners soon learn that if they want to salvage their sanity and re-educate themselves they have to do it alone, and in spite of the system. All this serves to bolster the inmate group identity, to solidify a jungle subculture as the only meaningful community, and to prevent the prisoner from developing a sense of independence and individuality without which rehabilitation becomes an unattainable goal.

Kingston Penitentiary at this particular time was kept more repressive, dehumanizing, and security-oriented than any other penal institution in Ontario, in order to illustrate vividly the differences between the three classifications, maximum, medium, and minimum security. In medium and minimum security prisons the prisoners were treated more humanely and given more freedom, were in fact encouraged to develop a certain sense of individuality and personal worth, so that upon their release into society they could better shoulder their new responsibilities. On the other hand, the maximum security nightmares were used exclusively to warehouse, punish, and coerce the felons into brute obedience, with a possible transfer to a medium security institution dangling in front of each individual like the proverbial carrot.

As for the few token trade and academic courses available inside maximum security penitentiaries, they might as well not exist for all the good they do. They affect only a small minority of prisoners. In fact the administrators find most of the programs a pain in the butt and can barely disguise their contempt. The real problem is that the prison staff, as well as the prisoners, are captives of a system where everybody is mired in an atmosphere of frustration and despair. The job is a grind and the challenges are few. Until the day comes when the guards are motivated to think along the lines of rehabilitation and to accept the prisoners as *people* with behaviour problems, there will never be any fundamental change for the betterment of everyone concerned. If the guards demonstrated as much interest in the welfare of the prisoners as they do in their own self-interest, then perhaps the prison administrators would start treating them as partners in a joint enterprise, rather than as potential saboteurs. If the keepers of men would accept the challenge of working with humans, become involved with prison reform and the planning and evaluating of new programs, instead of opposing them, they would discover that instead of just pushing buttons and turning keys they could have a respected profession.

Immediate changes, such as purging those hard-line screws who were hired on decades ago, are required. Still others inside the penitentiary system should be subjected to stringent psychiatric tests to weed out the unstable ones. There should be higher educational standards for applicants, improved initial training, and better working conditions to attract a higher quality of custodian. Since everybody is aware that prisons contain some of the most confused and bitter people in the world, coupled with the fact that many of those people will one day be released back into the mainstream of society, it is plain common sense that the desired outcome should be rehabilitated offenders rather than avenging monsters. The way the system stands now, putting a felon in prison is like putting an alcoholic to work in a distillery.

9

WEDNESDAY, APRIL 14, 1971. To the guards on the evening shift it was a day no different than any other. By the time the first half of the evening recreation period had come to an end, nothing out of the ordinary had been noted. This was very satisfying to the night keeper, who was convinced that the real control of a large maximum security institution came from the dreary and predictable fact that everything happens, day after day, in exactly the same way. Little did the keepers of the big house know that at that very moment a small group of numbered militants was preparing to blow its collective top. Billy Knight and his five co-conspirators were counting on precisely this reliance on routine to overpower the sleeping giant. If Billy was to succeed in overpowering the night shift with his meagre force, all the breaks would have to be entirely in his favour, with no room for hitches. Almost as important would be the number of guards taken hostage, because without at least a handful of screws in their possession to be manipulated as a buffer against rescue forces, they could not maintain control of the main cellhouse for very long.

On the evening in question there were some seventy-eight inmates released from their cells to play cards in the auditorium and to watch television. This was the largest number of prisoners permitted by the night shift outside the security of their cells at one time. An equal number had already come and gone between the hours of 6:00 and 8:00 p.m. This second group from the first and second tiers was scheduled to return to their cells at 10:30, whereupon a count would be taken and the institution dead-locked for the night. There weren't very many guards on duty that night, which was not unusual since there weren't many cons loose. Some guards were manning the gun towers and the arsenal at the front gate; others were patrolling the ground perimeter. The hospital and the hole, the segregation and the psychiatric units inside the east cellblock didn't need much manpower because all their clients were under lock and key. The screws that Billy and his gang were interested in were the two separate units inside the dome and the auditorium, all unarmed except for the man locked inside the gun cage in one corner of the gym floor.

A few minutes before 10:30 the television sets were switched off as preparation was begun to usher the prisoners back through the passageway to the dome and onto their tiers for lockup. In accordance with established practice the return would be signalled from the centre of the dome by a loud clap of the bell. Standing near the bronzed monster was the night keeper, Ed Barrett, at 57 a grizzled hard-liner who had been a screw for the larger part of his life. With him was his four-man crew, Donald Floyd, 45, Douglas Dittrich, 41, and two relatively inexperienced guards, Joseph Vallier, 47, (a retired veteran with twenty-five years' service in the army), and Kerry Bushell, 24, who was just getting into the swing of things. Bushell had only two years of service, and in the penitentiary business that made him a babe in arms.

At precisely 10:30 Barrett rang the bell. He pulled down hard on the chain, shattering the silence inside the cavernous cellblocks. As the harsh sound reverberated down the shadowy hallway, his four men were already moving away from the bell to their designated positions. Donald Floyd was the only one not to take up a stance at the entrance to an empty tier. Instead it was his job to man the locked dome barrier at the entrance to the tunnel and to control the flow of inmates, permitting only one tier at a time to pass through. Looking like a gnarled hockey player, the blond Floyd had the reputation of being loud and blustery with the cons. His swaggering manner irked just about everybody, even his co-workers. Although the bell was heard in the gym, it was also Floyd's duty to go down there and tell the keeper in charge which tiers to send through first. As he strutted along the passageway, Floyd's footsteps sounded loud in the hollow confines as he neared the lighted auditorium.

Standing on the opposite side of the sliding gate were the gym keeper and his staff of four. William Babcock was another old hard-line screw with more years in service than a retired monk. He was a muscular man with a weather-beaten face acquired in the old days when he ramrodded inmate crews in the limestone quarry outside the walls. It was his job to maintain order and discipline on the gym floor where the card tables were clustered and inside the darkened TV rooms where fights often erupted. Fifty feet across the floor from the sliding gate was his real power — a shotgun guard inside an elevated cage. If that wasn't enough muscle Babcock just had to pick up a phone and yell for help, and heavy artillery would roll in from all directions. Babcock also had under his wing a recreational officer in gym pants and two uniformed guards helping to control the flow of inmate traffic.

Gripping the gate leading into the auditorium, Floyd signalled to Babcock that the main cellhouse was prepared to accept the first movement of prisoners down the passageway. Floyd then unlocked the gate from inside and, sliding the barrier open, turned over the key to a tall boyish-looking guard by the name of Terry Decker. It was now this young screw's responsibility to remain on that side of the gate while Floyd returned to a similar barrier leading into the dome. Floyd only went far enough down the passageway that he could see both Decker at one end and his boss Ed Barrett at the other in the dome. He then gave the thumbs-up signal to Decker that the movement could begin. The actual first movement was unleashed by William Babcock, who by manipulating a manually operated light indicator directly above the exit signalled range 2-H, which in turn indicated to the milling crowd of cons gathering around the gate what order they were to leave the gym in. Now that the prisoners had no choice but to head back to their cells, they all seemed to be in a big rush to do so, especially those who were anxious to hear the last of the hockey game. Others were eager to catch the eleven o'clock news so as to stay in tune with the outside world. They were all shoving and pushing so eagerly that Decker and Babcock were hard-pressed to keep the flow of prisoners moving in an orderly manner. The confusion fit Billy Knight's plans perfectly.

Prison life is so impersonal, with so few names attached to the faces, that more than half of the lineup for 2-H could belong to other ranges without causing too much suspicion. Neither Babcock nor the young guard Decker noticed the six impostors in the lineup as they shuffled and traded places with other cons, sometimes whispering threats and stressing the inmate code of obedience in order to do so. Billy wanted at least a dozen cons filing through the gate ahead of his gang so as to keep the dome guards occupied with their duties as he launched his attack on Decker. He was relying heavily on the expectation that once he got the ball rolling, those prisoners remaining inside the auditorium would eagerly join in the takeover.

Ironically, the one thing that Terry Decker did notice as the bogus occupants of 2-H squeezed past him was a flapping shirt-tail on one of the prisoners.

Jabbing a finger at Billy Knight, the young guard ordered: "Tuck that shirt in!"

For a split second Billy was speechless, then turning livid with anger he viciously punched Decker in the stomach. "That's the last order you're going to give!"

Decker was pummelled some more as he staggered backwards down the dimly lit hallway clutching his belly, a look of horror spreading across his face. Charles Saunders, one of Billy's staunch supporters, wrestled the keys from Decker's grip before he could regain his composure. In the milling crowd Billy continued propelling young Decker further down the tunnel out of sight. It was crucial that the four remaining rebels reach the dome barrier before Floyd caught wind of what was happening and locked it.

Occupied by the milling cons inside the auditorium, William Babcock did not notice that a crisis had erupted only a few feet away until he spotted Decker's hat lying on the floor, right next to the open barrier. To the old veteran, an officer's cap lying on the floor was a sure sign of trouble. Excitedly he shouted to a tall, lanky screw a few feet away on the gym floor: "Pattison, take the gate!" Then he added in a voice that was beginning to crack, "Don't let anyone through!" Everybody inside the gym was caught flatfooted, the cons even more than the screws. They just stood there numbly staring at the open gate. Even the shotgun guard inside the barred cage a few feet away was slow in levelling his weapon in support of his boss, who was now yelling to all the cons: "Everybody up against the wall!" Dismayed and leaderless, the inmates slowly followed Babcock's direction while cocking their ears to the savage sounds coming from the tunnel where Billy Knight and his five wild men were busy disrupting the order of the institution.

While Saunders kept Terry Decker pinned to the concrete floor midway down the passageway, Billy was busy rushing onto the main floor of the dome, where he found one of his younger musclemen already fighting with Donald Floyd. Kicking the screw's feet out from under him, Billy shouted to Brian Dodge, "Finish him off quickly and lock him up in F-block!"

Two more of his soldiers, Robert Adams and Allan Lafrenier, were in combat with Ed Barrett in and around the bell, wrestling and pulling at the keeper's tunic while shoving him toward the north wall of the dome. It was not until Adams threatened to discharge foam from a fire extinguisher into the night keeper's face that Barrett finally gave up resisting. He was immediately dragged unceremoniously toward F-block and pushed inside where Floyd was already sprawled on the range. With keys gathered up from the floor, Leo Barrieault, the surly sixth member of Billy's team, locked the gate and mumbled, "The shoe is on the other foot now."

Everything happened so quickly that the three guards up on the second tiers were unaware of what had just taken place below as they busied themselves with the process of admitting the dozen inmates who had preceded Billy's rush into the dome. Suddenly Joseph Vallier, a short chubby screw with a kindly face, caught some of the action through the balcony railings. Turning his attention to the handful of cons coming his way to be locked into their respective cells, he tried desperately to read from their faces what kind of mood they were in. Deciding that they didn't want to get involved, he ordered them to proceed to their drums, saying, "You lads don't want no part of this." Just then he was grabbed roughly from behind by Leo Barrieault, who had climbed up the side of the tier. "Don't try anything, little man, or I'll break your neck!" growled Barrieault, whereupon Vallier ceased to resist.

At the head of the same tier was Douglas Dittrich, a tall lanky guard with a surprisingly high-pitched voice. He was similarly manhandled and rendered passive by Brian Dodge. The third guard, Kerry Bushell, who was manning the locking wheel on another tier, was simply talked down to the main floor by Billy Knight, who convinced him that they were outnumbered. Not knowing for sure how many prisoners were involved in the bingo, Bushell decided it wasn't his job to be a hero.

Six guards — Barrett, Vallier, Floyd, Dittrich, Bushell, and Decker — were now locked up inside the barrier on the bottom tier of F-block, effectively cut off from the dome floor and the telephones. Gripping the bars of their cells were the inmates of that block staring curiously at their vanquished keepers. Dittrich took the opportunity to ditch the keys for all the second-tier cells out the cellblock windows. Ed Barrett had also managed to hang on to some keys, which he too threw to safety. Their actions slowed down the release of the prisoners from the cells.

Billy was relieved to see that the inmates whom Joseph Vallier had been trying to lock inside their cells on 2-H were finally joining in the rebellion after much exhortation. Some of these cons were urged to stand guard over the screws in F-block while Billy and his gang rushed furiously around the tiers to free the rest of the prison population still under dead-lock. A wall safe on the dome wall behind the keeper's desk was broken into and the keys gathered up to open what drums they could. Billy knew that he desperately needed lots of manpower fast if he wanted to maintain his takeover, so he and Saunders rushed toward the gate that gave access to the auditorium passageway, intending to lead the cons out of the gym. At this gate they were astonished to find the white-haired Raymond Pattison grimly holding the barrier shut with both hands.

"Back off, you pigfucker!" roared Saunders as he and Billy started kicking furiously at the hamlike hands of the guard, who was known for his incredible stubbornness.

Pattison howled in pain and was forced to let go. Deciding that retreat was the better part of valour, he hightailed it down the passageway shouting, "They're coming! The bastards are coming!"

In a high state of excitement the gun cage screw pointed his shotgun at the dark exit. Babcock, who was now armed with the sentry's revolver, also turned his weapon away from the sixty-four inmates lined up against the gym wall and aimed it in that direction. The scene was deadly quiet as Billy appeared on the other side of the sliding gate.

"Let's talk," Billy said softly to the keeper.

"Anything I've got to say to you will come from the mouth of this gun," replied Babcock in a grim voice.

"We've got full control of the dome and six hostages," replied Billy in that strangely reasonable voice. "Better listen."

"Have your say," said Babcock, confused by the magnitude of what was taking place.

Gripping the bars, Billy nodded toward the prisoners lined up against the gym wall and said loudly, "I want you to release my brothers. Let them join me in my peaceful protest. Then you and your staff can leave by the back door of the gym.''

Shaking his revolver threateningly, Babcock grinned and said to Billy, ''We have the artillery, so why should we move?''

Billy replied, ''If the auditorium is left empty it can be used as a rendezvous point to negotiate the release of the hostages and to discuss our grievances.''

''Tell them to go to hell,'' interjected Pattison, standing behind his keeper and rubbing his painful fingers.

Silencing his angry co-worker with a hard stare, the keeper wasn't about to oblige Billy one way or another, so in a monotone Babcock simply replied, ''Go away, Knight, just go away.''

Billy turned and walked quietly away into the tunnel, locking the last barrier behind him. The look in his eye said that he'd be back soon.

Minutes earlier the screw in the gun cage had called the emergency operator stationed inside the front gates to tell him that there was a riot going on in the main cellhouse. The operator in turn called the deputy warden at his home to advise him of the situation. A mild-mannered man who would later play a significant role in the crisis, Doug Chinnery was at first incredulous. ''They've taken over the dome!'' cried the voice in his sleepy ear.

''Aw, c'mon,'' Chinnery laughed. ''You can think of a better one than that.''

High up on the fourth tier of B-block my own reaction to the sounds drifting upwards from the dome floor was a little less incredulous. I had pushed my chess set aside and was gripping my cell bars, my ears cocked toward the unaccustomed sounds. In prison you can't see far, so your ears become all-important; you become extremely tuned in to the heartbeat of the joint. The beat that I was listening to now was definitely off-beat, and the hairs on my arms were beginning to stand on end. There was yelling and running, not the usual horsing around that occurs sometimes when the guys file back to their drums from the gym. These sounds had an urgency and desperation to them that I had never heard before. But what really raised the hackles on the back of my neck was a sound that I took to be a key sliding across the dome floor. The grunts and curses could have been a drunken con being bum-rushed to the cooler, but what about the key sound?

I was startled suddenly by the hoarse voice of my chess partner. "C'mon Rog, I'm waiting for your move." January had my queen pinned and was thirsting for the kill. You'd think that with a twenty-year stint for bank robbery he wouldn't be in such a hurry, but that was his combative nature.

"Sssshh," I hissed, "I'm hearing things."

With an evil cackle he retorted, "You're not only going to be hearing things, you're going to be talking to yourself after you see my next move."

"I mean it! Listen for yourself," I answered urgently.

His jailhouse instincts took over and he got real quiet. Suddenly he exclaimed, "Well, partner, I don't know about you, but I'm getting dressed." A moment later I heard the sound of his cot being fastened to the wall.

I followed suit and a moment later I was sliding my sneakers on. All my primitive instincts were telling me that I should be on my toes and ready to respond to whatever it was that was threatening me. The intensity picked up minute by minute. Soon we could hear the sounds of running on the second tier below us. From the cellblock windows we could also see blurred figures pausing and whispering furtively to the occupants of cells on the third tier. Suddenly everything flared up and the whispers became hoots and yells, the footsteps thundered like hoofbeats, and there was a pounding of steel on steel as the sounds became more and more savage. Stress and danger were making the rebels revert to their most primitive instincts; the hunted were now hunting.

Billy Knight was a busy man, dashing from wing to wing and shouting orders like a general. "Brothers!" he shouted into the hollow blocks, "Our time has come to shake off the shackles. We've taken control of the dome and got six hostages, and you'll all be released from your cells as soon as we get all the keys."

The keys never did show up for the top ranges, but some did for other ranges, enough to free more than a hundred men. Among the rampaging prisoners were individuals with good buddies still under lock and key, friends they were used to having at their sides. Armed with four-foot pipe wrenches, pry bars, and lengths of steel pipes looted from the plumber's room, these prisoners set about freeing their comrades. They expended a great deal of time and effort twisting the locking bars to pretzels in order to get the cell doors open. Other prisoners spent their rage destroying all the hated symbols of authority. The first item to go was the dreaded "metallic stoolie" at one of the dome exits. The metal detector was used unsparingly by the screws as a means of hassling and humiliating those convicts they didn't like. Rarely did the machine actually detect hidden shanks or contraband, as we were always alerted by the grapevine whenever it was in operation. But the guards would create an opportunity to skin-frisk a guy by raising the sensitivity level until even the fillings in your teeth would set if off. To the dozen cons who attacked the walk-through detector it was a dream come true. Ripping and tearing at the gallows-like instrument with inhuman strength, the inmates literally pulled it apart with their bare hands. Afterwards, like wolves, they ran off in different directions with the parts of their prey to ravage it further.

The prisoners still locked up inside their cells shouted encouragement to those outside and clamoured to be sprung from their cages. Judging by the rate at which the doors were being opened, some were beginning to think that it would be daybreak before this could be accomplished. Some of the inmates with nothing better to do began smashing their cells; others, using their bedlegs, took to digging the bricks out of their cell walls with the intention of turning that particular tier into one long dormitory! The uproar got louder and louder until it was almost necessary to plug your ears. Confusion reigned supreme as Satan's hand descended on the caged men, releasing them from their bondage and inciting them to wreak havoc on their hated prison. January and I had to holler in order to hear what the other was saying. He kept asking me if I could see anyone we knew in the window reflection. If I did spot anyone, he urged me, "Tell them to get the hell up here and let us out!" Suddenly two mighty tough characters rounded the corner onto our tier and slid to a stop in front of my cell.

"C'mon, knucklehead," growled the ape-like creature to his willowy sidekick, "put some muscle into that pipe wrench."

"Quit pounding on the handle," wailed Jezebel, gingerly blowing on her manicured nails. "It's hurting my fingers."

"You'll have more than that hurting if you don't put a lid on it," roared my old friend Hugo as he hammered away at my door handle with a steel bar.

January joined me in egging on the two misfits, knowing we'd then direct our energy to freeing him too. My two friends worked furiously to bend the locking bar far enough for me to swing my gate open. By this time three more cons had showed up and were using their combined strength to free January. Finally I was out! "I owe you one," I said to my two beaming friends as I rushed off toward the stairway, pushing my way through the mass of prisoners running around like chickens with their heads chopped off. I was in a big hurry to do something I'd been dreaming of for decades — destroy the gong in the centre of the dome. It had penetrated my skull for so many years and been the subject of so many nightmares that I wanted the glorious pleasure of destroying it before someone else did. Halfway down the stairs I spotted another con, Mike Logan, in the process of taking a chair to the bell. "No! No!" I shouted down to him. "Save me a piece of the action!"

Rushing headlong toward the bell, I could feel a sort of insanity building up inside of me. I was intoxicated with the thought that there was no one to order me about. Other convicts whom I had come to know as quiet and passive were also displaying that eerie glint in their eyes. Lips pulled back in a snarl, I snatched a steel club from someone's hands and bounded across the dome floor. Drunk with power, I ripped the buttons off my denim shirt, its tails flying as I joined Mike in a combined attack on the bell. We whooped and hollered each time our mighty blows brought a clang of protest from the brass monster. Its pitch almost drowned out the noise around us until a tremendous blow from the fire extinguisher ended its bullying career. As Mike continued to smash away at the pedestal, I pursued the brass splinters as they careened across the concrete floor. Pouncing upon the largest piece, I raised it high over my head and threw it with great force across the keeper's desk, where it crashed through the glass-encased count board containing all the names and call locations. It landed with a terrible racket and sent the call location stickers flying off in every direction, but still the greater part of the bell refused to shatter into smaller pieces. Enraged at the thought that the screws might later want to patch the thing together again, I scooped up all the parts, then, hurrying through the boiling crowd to the far end of C-block, I shoved the fragments far down into the bottom of a garbage bin. The only piece I kept was the little brass ball that was attached to a short gold chain — the pull lever that was used to ring the bell. Triumphantly I hung it around my neck on a leather thong.

The bingo had been under way for almost an hour, and a lot of the guys were still occupied with smashing open the cell gates and also destroying the locking mechanisms so they couldn't be used against us again. Very little plumbing was broken inside the cells, though, because the cons had learned from previous disturbances that they'd be left to rot in their drums once the officials regained control of the prison, and it was better to have plumbing that worked than a pan to wash in and a slop bucket for a toilet. Most of the prisoners were convinced that we were only being given enough rope to hang ourselves with, that the warden was bound to use his massive fire power to regain control of the prison, and that it would be accomplished by bloody daybreak. Although my numbered friends knew only too well that in any prison riot the convict ends up suffering the most, it didn't seem to matter at the time. Perhaps we all suffered from defective reasoning — we couldn't seem to apply past experiences to present reality. We had a paradoxical trust in each other, trust in the fact that at face value none of us could be trusted. That most of the rioters were desperate men was evident from the terrible destruction being inflicted upon our dreaded bastion. That the majority were from deprived backgrounds, from a world of broken promises, was also clear. We all had a inbred instinct to snatch what we needed, even if it meant reaching into hell. The impending move to Millhaven had whetted fear, fed the flames of hatred, gnawed at the phobias festering in our minds. It was a process that became a steamroller with catastrophic results.

Billy Knight and his ever-growing band of rebels did not believe that the prison uprising would be over by daybreak. In fact they were still organizing their strength, getting their priorities straight, fortifying their position. Very little attention was paid to the hostages for the first little while. Some of Billy's lieutenants delegated certain inmates to organize some of the younger, more energetic cons into work gangs. Their job was to pound the heavy metal barriers from their hinges, gather up other heavy objects, and barricade the half-dozen exits against any attacks from outside.

Half of the cells inside the dome were still dead-locked. There had to be a better and quicker way to spring the guys from their cells. Having spent a lot of time studying the locking mechanism at the end of each tier, I suddenly realized how easy it would be to neutralize the gears inside the control boxes. Armed with a heavy hammer from the plumber's room, I went up to 4-C and simply pounded off the four nuts that held fast the key plate. With the inner workings of the gutbox exposed, I concluded that it was only a matter of reaching inside with my fingers, grasping the flywheel tightly, then pulling the guts out. I learned the hard way that when doing this one should duck. I didn't, and the powerful spring that flew out like a jack-in-the-box split my upper lip and cleanly knocked out one of my teeth! But at least now all the remaining drums inside the dome could be unlocked in minutes by spinning the locking wheels which could now be neutralized.

As more and more prisoners were released from their cells to join in the riot, there was a noticeable tremor of relief, a sense of safety in the increasing numbers, for we were armed only with primitive clubs and spears, puny trinkets of war in the face of an enemy armed with machine guns. When human flesh is crowded together in great numbers, generating massive energy, the combined roar and crunch can make even a soldier armed with a stengun shudder with an awful dread. One incident of pure muscle power is etched forever in my mind. A mob of prisoners rushing headlong down a dimly lit passageway was suddenly brought to a halt by a huge locked gate, but the combined weight of the hostile crowd pushed forward until the barrier exploded off its hinges and crashed to the floor twenty feet away.

Everybody was aware of the fact that having busted loose from our cages we were now official targets for the enemy, that we had by the very nature of that act given those with guns the legal status to shoot us. The only way to shake off the sense of impending doom and fear of reprisals was to let yourself go berserk, turning that fear into a working anger. As we were a little older and more jailwise than most of the guys, it occurred to January Jones and me that, while the destruction of the dome was going on, some thought should be given to things like grub and java. By one o'clock Billy Knight was starting to convince a lot of the cons that the bingo would last for days. "We've got hostages, men!" he kept shouting to large groups. "We're not going to release them until our demands are met, and that, my brothers, will take days of hard talk." If the present situation was going to last for several days then my old buddy and I were determined that we wouldn't be without at least coffee supplies, both of us being caffeine addicts. We quickly flagged down some recruits to help us batter down the kitchen barrier.

The entrance to the well-stocked kitchen was directly between B- and C-blocks. With January, Hugo, Jezebel, and two hotheads in tow, I instigated the raid on the kitchen, after biting down on a rag to stem the flow of blood from my lip and the cavity where my eyetooth had been knocked out. Together we raised a heavy steel barrier waist high, backed off to the centre of the dome floor, shouted for a path to be cleared, then charged toward the solid oak door like a demon train. Our legs pumped like crazy as we got closer and closer. Suddenly from the tiny barred window a shotgun appeared and — *boom!* The blast from inside totally disintegrated the four tiny windows. My merry band of outlaws hastily dropped the barrier and scattered.

An awesome silence descended upon the dome floor and all movement ceased, except for the tinkling of glass falling from the shattered window frame. Then, as eyes fixed rigidly on the opening where the gunsmoke drifted lazily into the tense atmosphere, Billy Knight took the opportunity to slither along the dome wall until he was right next to the damaged door. Breaking the eerie silence, he shouted to the guard who had fired the first shot of the riot that none of them was harmed. "If there are any more shots fired we'll start cutting off some fingers!" Suddenly a barrage of debris pelted the doorway from the upper tiers, along with threatening insults and a thunderous metallic pounding.

As all hell broke loose once again, my raiding party took the opportunity to gallop away. Jezebel was in tears, complaining that the makeshift battering ram had fallen on her foot. Her outburst got very little sympathy from Hugo, who pointed out that it was her own fault for leading instead of following. January was furious at the screw's audacity in blasting away at us like that without warning, saying he'd be willing to kick his coffee habit for a chance to wring the hacker's neck.

"It's okay, old buddy," I said in an effort to cool him off. "I know a couple of other spots where we can get coffee."

Curious at the lack of official activity, a lot of the guys were peering out of the broken windows in the various wings to see if they could spot the riot squad and the army pouring in through the gates. But except for a few screws running around the lighted compound, the exterior was strangely quiet. There was one brief flurry of panic when guard Raymond Pattison showed up on the other side of the barrier inside the keeper's hall. Flustered, he angrily pointed his shotgun at a surprised throng of convicts on the dome floor, all of whom immediately froze in their tracks. Although everybody knew that he was perfectly capable of blasting away, two spunky cons who had not been directly involved in the opening stages of the riot charged right up to the screw and, ignoring the shotgun aimed directly at them, shouted indignantly through the bars: "Get the fuck out of our face, you stupid son of a bitch, or we'll chop your friends up!" The guard backed slowly and uncertainly up the passageway until he was out of sight.

Around midnight the six hostages who had been huddled in fear at the far end of F-block were led out into the centre of the dome by Barrie Mackenzie and his followers, big tough convicts sworn to protect the hostages against inmate reprisals and to murder them if a rescue attempt was launched. Surrounded by these pirate-like figures, the screws must have thought their last moments on earth had arrived. Even though they were surrounded by hellish noises, jostled, and insulted, some of them still had the guts to complain when they were relieved of their wallets and valuables. Kerry Bushell grabbed the wrist of a very dangerous inmate who was in the act of plucking the cigarette package from his shirt pocket. Laughing cruelly, the con waved a sharpened screwdriver around threateningly. Bushell wisely released his grip and allowed the inmate to take the smokes. Terry Decker, who was sporting a black eye, told one of the mutineers he got it by running into a door. "You remember to tell the warden that when you're free of us," retorted one of the leaders with a smile and a wink. The dozen cons guarding the hostages had their work cut out for them. Some of the prisoners wanted to kill Floyd and Dittrich, two very unpopular bulls who were disliked for their treatment of prisoners. There was no real plan as to what should be done with the hostages that first hour. As the mob was getting bolder and their jostling of the hostages more violent, someone suggested herding them into the service duct (a utility corridor between G- and H-blocks) for the time being. It was a spooky area where all the plumbing was exposed and the guards could prowl along narrow catwalks to observe the prisoners in their cells through peepholes.

Now that all the cell doors had been opened, a new element was entering the arena: powerful individuals with strong personalities were starting to get involved. The direction and politics were taking on new shapes. First there were Barrie Mackenzie and Brian Beaucage, two powerful and natural leaders, hard men who for the moment were going along with the play. But those of us who understood prison politics felt that it wouldn't be long before those individuals would be flexing their muscles, might in fact become a rival force competing for power. There were other loosely-knit groups, some members of which were borderline psychos whose minds were becoming overloaded from the excitement and the scent of blood, men who could quickly resort to primitive tactics. Still others, gripping makeshift clubs and spears, dressed like pirates, and vibrating with hostility, had encircled the hostages, and were nudging, ogling, and sniffing the scent of fear from their hated keepers; these men had to be watched closely.

Almost from the beginning of the riot about a dozen of the toughest prisoners had delegated themselves as guardians of the six hostages. They knew the value of healthy pawns, knew that without them the authorities were certain to machine-gun their way inside the main cellhouse, a dreadful outcome that would leave a lot of people dead. It was a tough assignment they set up for themselves, yet they did it with a tenacity that was awe-inspiring. They also took on the added commitment to kill the hostages should the dome be invaded by outside forces. There was no bluffing from this group, no bravado, just an awesome singlemindedness.

The most noticeable of the above "police force" (as they came to be called) was Big Wayne Ford. He was serving a life sentence for murder and tipped the scales at 280 pounds of muscle and tattoo. He had a massive head that was shaved bald. His ominous look was enhanced by the gold earring he wore in one ear and by the fact that his original crime had made headlines. Although Wayne was still a boy at the time of his trial, the judge had labelled him a psychopath. In reality Wayne was a gentle giant and a bit of an intellectual, a man who throughout the duration of the riot would provide a cool and temperate voice. He had only one thought in mind, the protection or total destruction of the hostages, depending on who was threatening to take possession of what he was guarding.

It was Wayne who smashed the lock from the barrier leading into the service duct and who urged that the hostages be herded inside for their safety. It was also Wayne who volunteered (along with three others) to lock himself inside the duct with the hostages, explaining to the guards: "Nobody is going to get at you; we'll protect you as long as you don't double-cross us."

When the insurrection began, as the Parliamentary Investigation Committee report indicates, Warden Arthur Jarvis was working late in his office across the street in the grey limestone administration building, and was notified within minutes by the guard on duty in the North Gate that a disturbance had occurred. He was very shortly thereafter advised that control of the main cellblock had been taken over by members of the inmate population. In compliance with the Commissioner's directives, the warden immediately ordered all off-duty guards to return to the penitentiary for immediate assignment. He further notified the duty officer of the Canadian Armed Forces Base at nearby Barriefield and requested that the army be maintained on stand-by in the event that they might be required at the penitentiary. He further notified the Regional Director and the Commissioner of Penitentiaries in Ottawa.

Within the hour the Penitentiary Armoury, located within the North Gate, had been opened, and as the guards arrived at the institution they were armed and posted around the perimeter of the main cellblock, with particular attention being paid to the entrance to the building and to the entrances inside the building leading to areas not controlled by the prisoners.

Regional Director John Moloney, who was in charge of all the staff in the area institutions, arrived shortly after 11:30 p.m. Upon receiving a preliminary report from the warden in the administration building, he proceeded to the keeper's hall, where he was able to look into the main dome area through a small barred window.

The Regional Director, who had a shock of white hair and an equally white mustache, had worked his way up from the guard ranks. He watched in awe as groups of prisoners, seemingly possessed with superhuman strength, ripped a four-hundred-pound steel gate from its supports on the fourth tier, then wrestled it over the guard railing to let it fall crashing to the dome floor far below. Other heavy objects were used to barricade the few entrances to the dome in the hope that they would slow down any attempts to rescue the hostages.

Meanwhile Billy Knight had proceeded down the winding hallway to the barrier leading into the lighted gym. Again all eyes were turned on him, including those of the sixty-two cons now standing rigid against the auditorium wall. Talking through the barrier to William Babcock, Knight asked if the man had changed his mind about releasing his numbered friends.

"No!" retorted Babcock. "And I've got nothing further to say to you."

Billy lost his temper. "You've warehoused us, you've tried to destroy our minds, but you'll never contain our anger!" With that outburst off his chest he settled down and said in a reasonable voice, "Tell the warden I want to talk to him. He'll be safe in the gun cage; we can negotiate from there."

It was after 1:00 a.m. when Billy returned to the dome with the intention of addressing the inmate population and gathering from them various grievances that could then be relayed to the authorities. Billy also wanted a free vote on a resolution to either end or continue the mutiny. On entering the dome he was surprised to learn that the Regional Director and the warden had held an impromptu meeting with a few of his followers through the barred window in the door leading to the keeper's hall. The inmates explained to Moloney that there was no cause for alarm, that everything was under control, that no one was hurt, and that the hostages were safe as long as the riot squad kept its distance. Brian Dodge then took the opportunity to request a loud-hailer to better communicate with the prison population, explaining that the bullhorn would ensure that everybody would hear what it was they were voting on. After complying with this first request from the rebels, the Regional Director and the warden then retreated under armed guard from their exposed position to await further developments.

While Billy was calling for a general assembly, the six hostages were hustled from the service duct, stripped of their hated uniforms, and dressed in ill-fitting prison garb in an effort to confuse any rescue attempt. From there they were pushed through hundreds of hostile prisoners who jostled them every inch of the way up the winding stairway. Crude weapons were pressed against their backs to thwart any rescue attempt by snipers now known to be positioned on top of the auditorium roof. The Regional Director was also on the roof, his eyes glued to binoculars as he tried desperately to see through the grimy windows what was going on inside the main cellhouse. A lot of the prisoners were clamouring for revenge, some shouting that at least two of the screws should take a plunge off the fourth tier.

Yankee, a lanky cowboy from Georgia, and quick-tempered to the point of being off his rocker, was especially vocal as he blocked the way of one of the hostages. He jabbed a bony finger at the screw and, mimicking their ways, he yelled: "Button up that shirt, boy! You been here long enough to know the rules; next time I catch you you're gonna take a nose dive over the railing." The guard replied with a very wise "Yes sir."

It took a lot of aggressive behaviour on the part of Wayne Ford and Barrie Mackenzie's crew to keep the hostages in one piece as they herded them up to the top tier of E-block. Upon arriving on that upper range they were immediately locked up in cell 10 with a padlock and chain, there being no other way to secure the door as the locking mechanism was now destroyed. The inmate police force then set up a barrier around the cell, bristling with primitive weapons, determined to fight anyone to the death to protect their valuable cargo.

Just as word was being passed around for the population to gather in the centre of the dome for a meeting, Billy was informed by one of his men that the warden had been seen entering the gun cage inside the auditorium. Handing the bullhorn to Robert Adams, who was the youngest member of his original attack force, Billy pushed his way through the milling mob while brushing off anxious questions from his fellow cons. Gathering all his energy for the confrontation with Warden Jarvis, his heart beating wildly, Billy passed through the dome barrier into the darkened hallway that led to the gym gate. Billy was aware that he was now dangerously out of bounds, that he was pushing his luck, was in fact a perfect candidate for a bullet from an angry screw. By this time more and more guards armed to the teeth with guns could be seen pouring into the prison compound from the front gate.

Suddenly the warden's attention was drawn to the exit gate. Billy Knight turned a long key, boldly slid open the heavy gate, and strode onto the gym floor, blinking under the bright lights. He gave the peace sign to the prisoners gathered against the auditorium wall and, ignoring the revolver Babcock had pointed at him, marched up to the short steps leading to the barred gun cage. With a wave of his arms, he first of all alleviated the warden's fear as to the state of the hostages. He then gave a brief summary of what the riot was all about, explaining that the situation would remain non-violent as long as the riot squad made no attempt to quell the disturbance. He further informed the warden that the presence of additional guards brandishing guns and fire hoses in a most aggressive manner had been observed by the inmate population and that the prisoners were getting "very concerned."

"One of your trigger-happy guards fired a wild shot a little while ago," Billy went on to say, "and if one of the inmates had been killed, then it goes without saying that at least one of the hostages would have met a similar fate."

Warden Jarvis cried out, "Knight, I'm warning you, if any harm comes to those men I'll hold you directly responsible!"

Billy thumped himself on the chest and shouted back, "You count us like diamonds and treat us like animals, then expect us to abide by your rules — no way!"

"Knight," said the warden, gripping the gun cage bars and calming himself, "what exactly do you want from us?"

"For a start we want positive results in our desire for decent living conditions." Billy reached out and, tapping his fingertips against the warden's white knuckles, added solemnly, "It's all up to you — the fuse is ignited."

As a first step, Billy requested that the guards be removed from the recreation hall, that the gun cage also be cleared of screws, and that the auditorium be used as a negotiating place. The warden accepted the request (a decision that was later questioned by a Commission of Inquiry) and in response to his orders, the keeper and his men left the hall through an exit door to the yard. The officer in the gun cage also vacated his position. About twenty minutes later the predictable occurred. The inmates who had been in the auditorium were no longer there, having decided to follow Billy Knight back into the dome. Sixty-two new prisoners had joined the insurrection.

The warden, the Regional Director, and other senior penitentiary officials used the keeper's hall during the initial stages of the riot as a centre of administrative activity. The first twelve hours were a mass of confusion. There was no riot plan for the staff to adhere to, other than ordering all off-duty guards to return to duty.

Nor was there any clear direction as to who should be running the show, the warden or the Regional Director, a situation that caused even more confusion. The Commissioner of Penitentiaries in his Ottawa headquarters was kept informed of events as they developed. The question that worried the officials the most was what kind of weaponry the inmates had. They were worried that maybe we had guns and might be planning a jailbreak amid the confusion. In fact nothing could have been further from our minds. Planning to escape during a riot just wasn't feasible because of all the extra security around the perimeter — that is, unless you were going to use the hostages to bluff your way out. The best time to bust out is when there is no heat. Besides, the guys were too busy trying to reduce the main cellblocks to rubble, hoping that a parking lot would emerge from what was now a human warehouse.

CHAPTER 10

THE BINGO had been under way a few hours when suddenly the dome area went quiet and it was announced that a general assembly would be held. The ringleaders took up aggressive positions along the railings on the second tier, directly in front of the radio room, while hundreds of convicts looking like tattered zombies stared up from the cluttered main floor. Others gazed hungrily down from the maze of circular galleries, all trembling with suppressed excitement and hoping for some kind of enlightenment. Deep down we truly felt that many of us were going to die before the rebellion was over, probably with a bellyfull of buckshot, but damned if it didn't feel good to strike back. Like lost souls we looked up at the individuals who were leading us for a sense of direction, a light at the end of the tunnel, someone who could present our grievances to the authorities.

Gripping the railing with fire in his eyes, Billy Knight loomed like a minister in a pulpit, relishing his moment of glory as he spewed out fancy quotations on the hand-held bullhorn. For the time being the numbered men whom he addressed were desperate enough to believe what they heard, might even be reckless enough to do what they were told, but deep down everybody wanted to run and hide with their fears. It soon became clear that Billy just didn't have the bared-teeth, bare-knuckled charisma necessary to instill total confidence in the prison population. He didn't have a strong assertive voice or a powerful presence, essentials without which he could not hope to remain king of the castle. The prisoners prowling the concrete jungle studied his every move and, like beasts of prey, could only fear and respect that which was stronger than they. For the moment Billy had proven himself by shooting from the hip, but gradually his long-winded speechmaking was creating the impression that he was really much more comfortable shooting from the lip. The old-timers knew that he

121

didn't have enough muscle to quell any sudden challenge to his leadership, and that the pecking order would turn on him if he slipped and gobble him up as if he had never existed.

Surrounded by his lieutenants, Knight went on and on vaguely outlining the reasons for the riot and what he hoped it would accomplish. He stressed the need for non-violence, a proposal that drew grudging acceptance from the mob, who showed their approval by thumping the railings mightily with their iron clubs, creating a sound that made me think of jungle drums. Although his robot-like voice lacked emotion, Billy seemed fired up by the reluctant roar of approval and, focusing on some sore points, he promised with clenched fists that past injustices would be rectified. "Have courage, my brothers, and remember that when a people have nothing to lose but themselves, only a coward would deny them the right to rebel." It was almost as if he was addressing a press conference as he went on to explore some of the prison reforms he wanted to see implemented. "You warehouse a man and you destroy him, but show that same individual direction and you can contain him. They should give us the opportunity to earn at least minimum wages in the prison workshops and in that way aid us to get established upon our release. For those of you who have families on the outside, those wages could be directed to your loved ones to keep your family together. That, my friends, would be motivation, paying off our debt to society while at the same time supporting our dependents in the outside world."

Billy Knight went on expounding his ideas from his lofty pinnacle, foolishly blind to the negative whispers and silent manoeuvres around him. Some of the snarls were coming from hotheads who were short on talk and quick with their fists, men of action who didn't like to be reminded about paying their pound of flesh to society. Certainly they were not followers, and they felt that Billy had dragged them into a no-win situation against their will and personal beliefs, placing their lives in jeopardy. Any individual who dared to take on this great responsibility had better make a lot of sense! One of these individuals with a mercurial temper was a handsome twenty-three-year-old convict by the name of Brian Beaucage. Muscular and athletic, he seemed to operate on the principle that he either liked or disliked you according to your face. He obviously found Billy's profile entirely to his disliking and was itching for the opportunity to re-arrange it.

Maybe sensing that his talk had to get rougher, Billy brandished a short iron club and went on to say, "By sunrise we'll have direct communications with the outside world, including the warden's office. And either we get penal reform or else we turn this shithouse into a parking lot!" This was the kind of rhetoric that always drew an ear-splitting response with much shouting and beating on the railings with clubs.

"Let one of the screws do a four-storey dive and the pigs will get the message!" roared an angry voice from the mass of convicts.

"Brothers! Brothers!" pleaded Billy. "It's our turn to tighten the screws and set the record straight. Don't blow it with an irrational act. Blood will flow before I fail you, that I promise, but right now we have to rely on negotiations."

It was at this stage that some of the strong personalities in the crowd started heckling Billy, making negative remarks about the way he was conducting the bingo. Startled by the fierceness lurking behind the snide remarks, Billy stuttered, then regained his composure and continued in an anguished voice, "Let's not give the pigs the satisfaction of finding a reason to brandish us as animals to the world. We need the public's moral support, and we won't get it by creating a bloodbath. We have to convince the people out there that we don't mean to be a threat, that what we're striving for is for the good of everybody, that this is a peaceful demonstration by an oppressed few." The latter part of his speech gained him grudging support by most of the population, a captive audience willing to give him the benefit of the doubt, at least for the moment.

As Billy was retreating into the radio room one of his followers took over the bullhorn and urged the ragtag army to continue wrecking the prison, especially the locking mechanisms so that the cells would be unfit to house us once the bingo had ended. In reply to the request there was a loud ripping sound that brought a hush over the dome. As all eyes turned upwards toward the third tier, a voice cried out "Timber!" Two massive locking wheels that secured the cells had been laboriously pried loose from their moorings and the whole thing was now slowly pulling out from the wall. *"Timber!"* cried the voice again. The mechanism crashed straight down through the gallery floor with an incredible noise and came to rest amid a pile of rubble and dust two tiers further down. Walking sheepishly to the edge of the gaping crater to peer downwards and make sure no one had been killed were my two lunatic friends, Step-Ladder and Do-Die, still gripping wrecking bars and grinning like fugitives from a funny farm. The two looked absolutely villainous decked out in makeshift pirate garb. Step-Ladder was wearing a screw's cap (minus the badge), and strapped to his waist was a leather harness laden with tools. His pants were rolled up above his knees. Do-Die was wearing a cut-down version of a keeper's tunic and had a red bandanna wrapped around his sweaty brow. Slung over one shoulder was an army canteen filled with home brew. Just as Step-Ladder was getting set to crawl timorously out of sight, there arose from the silent crowd loud applause and bar-thumping in recognition of their patient labour. A large piece of plywood was used to cover the open hole so that no one would accidentally fall through. Still later that same crater was camouflaged with a blanket and set up as a trap in the event of an attempt to rescue the hostages.

Step-Ladder, Do-Die, and a handful of old cons now took it upon themselves to renovate the joint. Never in their entire life had they worked as hard as they did destroying what had been their home for so many decades. On tier after tier they combined their energy to systematically demolish the travelling bars embedded in the concrete above the cells. The damn things stretched for hundreds of feet and were the size of railroad tracks and every bit as heavy. On each tier about twelve hours of steady digging and prying with primitive tools were required before these bars could be sent crashing to the floor far below. Each time this was accomplished the old-timers would be rewarded with a deafening cheer. Their single-mindedness gave the younger prisoners the inspiration to do no less in their own tasks.

Inadvertently Billy Knight ended up with one very gruesome responsibility he hadn't planned on: keeping alive fourteen child molesters and rapists in the protection unit. Pushed down to the very bottom of the prison social structure, the deviants were segregated from the general population for their own safety on the bottom tier of D-block, where they had their own workshop and exercise yard. Shunned and despised by their fellow inmates, every one of them was high on the extermination list, especially since the average prisoner was a parent himself with his children's pictures proudly displayed in his cell. The prison population thought it was horrifying enough to have lost their personal freedom, but the final insult was to have been locked up in the same prison with this group, whom the inmates dubbed ''undesirables.''

Immediately after the takeover of the main cellhouse, Billy Knight had made it his business to secure the keys leading into 1-D where the undesirables were caged. Some of the hotheads were enraged that access to the deviants was denied them and demanded hard and fast answers from Billy, who reiterated that a bloodbath would be detrimental to everything the prison population was fighting for. Enlisting the reluctant support of Barrie Mackenzie and Brian Beaucage, Billy was able to keep the wolves at bay, at least for the time being, but everybody could feel the ill wind blowing in that direction. In fact two violent cons were slow in getting the word, and shortly before 1:00 a.m. they climbed down into the protection unit from the top tiers and smashed open the first cell, which housed James Ball. The young muscular inmate had switched off his cell light and taken refuge under his bunk screaming: ''God have mercy on me!'' With grim determination the two prisoners dragged him out from under his cot while beating him with iron bars and calling him a rat, a stool pigeon, and a loudmouthed punk. Ball had brought the beating upon himself: in the days preceding the bingo he felt protected enough to hurl back verbal insults to the cons living on the three tiers above him. One thing the inmate code demands is absolute deference from the diddlers and stool pigeons.

About an hour after the first encounter, Billy Knight's orders were again ignored. This time three different angry cons showed up at the door of Ball's cell, and again beat him to a pulp. Further down the range another group of rebels was systematically terrorizing the undesirables by watering them down with a powerful fire hose, causing the occupant of each cell to scramble madly beneath his bunk for protection. Gasping and looking like drowned rats, they were saved from further harassment by Barrie, who showed up to cool down the situation through the use of commonsense diplomacy.

Ball's cries for help at first could not be heard by Billy Knight, because the bingo had reached a crescendo with lots of yelling and banging going on; but now with flashlight in hand he went from cell to cell checking on the undesirables until he came upon the crumpled form of Ball curled up on the floor in a pool of blood. Most of the red stuff was flowing from gaping wounds in both his wrists. In desperation Ball had slit his wrists in a bid to take his own life rather than be beaten up a third time. Knight immediately posted a guard on the inmate and rushed to the dome phone to dial the prison hospital number. ''We have an emergency situation here,'' said Billy to an astonished orderly. ''An inmate in protection has slashed both his wrists.'' The stunned orderly requested that Billy call back in three minutes. ''We'll try to work out some kind of transfer arrangement with the brass.''

Half an hour later James Ball was carried out of the dome on a stretcher by two prisoners as far as the hospital gate at the far end of A-block where the screws had set up a kind of fortress. Assurance was given by the warden that the prisoners could approach the fortified position and return safely with impunity. Ball was then deposited unceremoniously on the hospital doorstep by two brave individuals who immediately scooted back to the safety of their manmade hell. The warden was pleased to have an eyewitness to question on the actual conditions inside the cellblocks. For the next little while the residents of 1-D were spared further physical attacks, but they were not spared from verbal abuse hurled down to them from the upper tiers. In graphic detail the undesirables were told what they could expect when the blood started to flow for real.

On the extermination list was a tall, stooped sexual offender dubbed ''The Camel'' who worked in the machine shop. In his late twenties, the Camel was serving a life sentence for raping two very young girls. When the bingo broke out he had somehow been living quietly in the prison population, having already served many years of his sentence. During those years he had survived several beatings and a stabbing, but had stubbornly refused to be locked away for his own protection. That stubbornness was coming back to haunt him now that there were so many convicts prowling the tiers thirsting for victims. Early in the riot somebody mentioned his name and cell location, which was halfway down the fourth tier in E-block, and the Camel barely had time to jump off his bunk before two convicts rushed into his drum and knocked him down. With the help of a third party the two dragged the lanky rapist struggling and screaming from his cell. With great effort the three cons tried mightily to throw him over the railing to his death far below. The Camel had developed great strength in his hands, which he now used to grip the railing, stubbornly refusing to let go even when one of the men bit and kicked at his fingers. Finally in exhaustion the three cons gave up and settled for punching and kicking him until he curled up in a ball.

Later one of the inmates was asked why they changed their minds, and they replied: "Because he was screaming too much."

Billy Knight and Barrie Mackenzie got word of the attempt on the Camel's life and rushed up to his cell, where they found him huddling in terror and crying out: "Why me? Why me?" Both his eyes were swollen and he was bleeding from facial lacerations. Billy and Barrie then decided that it would be better for him if he were locked up in one of the protection cells in D-block. The Camel took violent exception to this suggestion, his instincts telling him that he had a better chance of surviving the riot hiding in the maze of wrecked cellblocks. He had concluded that the undesirables on 1-D were probably all earmarked for slaughter anyway. Thus it was necessary to drag him forcibly, screaming all the way, down to 1-D where he was dead-locked in an empty cell.

The occupancy of a drum on 1-D was considered *prima facie* evidence that the guy was a skinner. However, not all rape cases get a great deal of publicity. In some instances there is no mention in the media. Thus a lot of newcomers entering the joint claim they are shaking time for armed robbery or some such crime, anything at all not to be labelled a "rapo." There were others whose degree of guilt was so uncertain that they were excused pending more evidence and were permitted to mingle unmolested among the prison population. But now in the turmoil of a violent bingo these same individuals no longer had immunity. Thus many of them were hiding out in the devastated cellblocks praying fervently that they wouldn't be ferreted out by roving wolf-packs thirsting for blood. One rapist who ran and hid was Ralph Lake, a thin, wiry sadist in his late twenties who had a compulsive habit of hurting whoever he came into contact with. Ralph was the clerk in the mailbag department and was roundly disliked by most of his co-workers. He managed to survive in the population only because of the "wolf" who was protecting him, a big, brawny, shaggy shop mechanic with a belt full of tools named Harold St. Armour. Because he was able to move around a lot, Harold took advantage of his relative freedom to become a jailhouse bookie and merchant. He was valued as a good connection; scratch his back and he'd scratch yours. As an individual he wasn't very well liked and was thought of as a "joint man," but because he provided a valuable service, he was allowed to do his thing.

Not long after the bingo got under way Ralph Lake had been set upon by a prisoner who worked in his shop, struck over the head with an iron bar, kicked about the face, and called a stoolie and a skinner. He managed to break away and, eluding his pursuer, ran to St. Armour's cell on a top tier. Armed with a homemade shiv and a club, St. Armour strung blankets across the open face of his cell front and declared the place off limits. In fact this tactic was becoming more and more popular with a lot of the inmates who tossed their iron cots over the railings and placed mattresses around their cells, thus creating a small island of privacy. If you didn't want your head chopped off you simply did not go around poking it through one of those blankets unless you were invited. So for the moment characters like Ralph Lake were safe.

Two notorious drag queens wasted no time in setting up business on the first floor of B-block by closing off the front of their drums with blankets. They even went so far as to knock down the brick wall partition that separated their cells to enlarge their sleeping quarters, dragging in mattresses from nearby empty cells and then painting their light bulbs red! A sign hanging out in front of their drums declared that this was a "Liberated Zone"! Contrary to vicious rumours later circulated by the frustrated guards, no youthful offender was muscled or forced to submit to sexual activities. That's not to say that a lot of the younger prisoners weren't scared about being raped. To be on the safe side a lot of the weaker cons asked some of the tougher ones if they could cling to them for protection, thinking that it was better to submit to one guy rather than to an imaginary wolf-pack. In fact if some creep tried to ruin some straight kid it wouldn't be tolerated; it would be inconsistent with the general code of inmate behaviour. After all, how could the prisoners justify torturing skinners and diddlers for their nefarious crimes and yet condone rape among themselves? Remaining anonymous, the cowardly guards would later whisper to the media gathered outside the prison walls describing what they said they had seen through the broken cellblock windows. They painted gruesome pictures of youthful prisoners tied to what remained of the bell platform being repeatedly raped by long lines of hardened cons. The screws also vividly described savage tribal-like dances by sinewy cons wearing only jockstraps on long tables set up in the centre of the dome. That much was true. Some of the guys, stoned on pills or tanked up on brew, were dancing wildly on top of tables to the blare of rock music coming from the radio room. But it was simply a way of clowning around and letting off steam while the crowds cheered them on.

A lot was later said in the media about the massive destruction done to the three chapels at the far end of F-block, creating the overall impression that Satan himself had orchestrated the orgy of destruction and blasphemous impiety. In reality the heavy oak benches, wall partitions, and marble slabs were needed to barricade the exit doors in the churches and throughout the cellblocks through which the enemy could mount a surprise attack. True, there were many gripes against the religious order of the institution for the various restrictions they placed upon the population over the years, especially the Catholic church for its narrowminded position on the censorship of reading material. We were even refused subscriptions to *Playboy* magazine because, it was claimed, the articles and pictures would rot our minds and lead to masturbation. The archaic rules of the institution directed that any screw discovering an inmate masturbating in his cell should cause the inmate to be reported and summarily punished, which was one of the reasons there were peepholes at the back of our drums. Another gripe was the insistence on the part of the churches that there be no recreational activity on Sunday mornings in order to encourage the inmate population to attend church or else remain locked up for the duration. Most guys would do anything to get out of their cells, even bite the bullet and attend church, nevertheless begrudging the fact that they had to do so under those circumstances.

The raid on the Catholic, Protestant, and Jewish chapels commenced around two o'clock in the morning when Billy turned the keys over to the fearsome Elliot twins, Hal and Al, both of whom were serving life terms for the brutal murder of a rival motorcycle gang member. (It was said that they quartered the guy by tying chains to his legs and driving off in opposite directions.) Their job was to round up a crew and haul down some heavy oak benches from the chapels to reinforce the barricaded entrances around the dome. It was potentially a dangerous assignment because the chapels were situated at the upper far end of F-block behind a locked barrier at the top of a metal staircase that gave access to the three chapels. Inside, everything would be dark, and somewhere there was a fire-exit door which the riot squad could use to gain entry into the chapels. Thus, when the Elliot twins turned the key in the gate and with flashlight in hand cautiously stepped through the darkened entrance, they half-expected to be greeted by a hail of machine-gun bullets. But somehow the guards had failed to take control of that important area. When the twins realized with relief that the chapels were empty, they bellowed out to the dozen misfits hugging the stairwell below that the place was up for grabs. Like bulls in a china shop the motley crew charged through the opening in three different directions, lighting up candles as they forged in deeper, their shadows dancing crazily on the white walls and ornamented windows. As for the Elliot twins, their larcenous hearts were set on smashing open the padre's filing cabinet that contained all the sacramental booze!

Meanwhile January Jones and I had come to believe that we were in for a lengthy siege, and so had been foraging for supplies in other parts of the cellhouse. Both the kitchen and the hospital were too well fortified for us to give any thought to plundering in that direction. Nevertheless, we had not given up our quest for coffee, and when some young bucks stormed past us blurting out that the chapels were being raided I let out a cry of glee.

"January, ol' buddy, if there's one crew in this joint that stocks up on kitchen supplies, it's sure to be the chapel orderlies!"

"I'm way ahead of you," shouted January as a gang of cons stumbled past us carrying heavy oak benches. "Let's boogie on down there!"

Passing through the maze of cellblocks we could see marauding rebels scurrying around like an army of demented ants armed with all kinds of primitive weapons, including molotov cocktails created from flammable cleaning solutions. Some had big goofy grins on their faces like little kids caught plundering the cookie jar; still others seemed totally lost amid the havoc as they peered anxiously through the cellblock windows into the dimly lit compound, expecting to see god knows what. A lot of windows had been broken the first few hours of the bingo, and now a bitterly cold wind howled through them, chilling everybody to the bone and causing some of the inmates to build small bonfires to stay warm. Sloshing through the water and debris that were building up on the floors from broken water mains, January and I reached the bottom stairs leading up to the chapel area just in time to be greeted by an alarming sight. Rumbling toward the upper entrance with the speed of a churning locomotive was the mighty church organ, pushed along by a horde of drunken rebels. Even more startling was the sight of Hal Elliot sitting astride its mahogany back whooping and hollering! As its wheels clattered across the hardwood floor the whole upper structure trembled, sending me and January leaping to safety beneath the metal stairway. The musical monster then smashed right through the guard railing, yawned dizzily in space for a brief heartbeat, and plunged downwards just as Hal managed to grab an overhead beam. Its final musical note resounded throughout the prison as the organ smashed to pieces on the concrete floor far below. Left dangling high up by the ceiling was one very sober bald con begging for his brother to pull him to safety.

"Rog, ol' buddy," said January as he brushed off splinters, "there's just too much heat around here. What do you say we split and come back later, OK?"

Sliding around the still vibrating organ, I nodded and we cautiously made our way back to the central part of the dome to see if we could tap into any new rumours that might be circulating.

Most of the lighting system within the areas controlled by the convicts had been deliberately knocked out so as to conceal our movements from the uniformed spies lurking on top of the prison walls and the gym roof. The brass was continually trying to get a positive fix on the six hostages in the hope of using massive firepower to rescue them, but they were frustrated by the action of the inmate police force, who made sure that the hostages never remained in one spot very long. Also the guards were now decked out in inmate clothing and were almost indistinguishable from their captors. Guard Donald Floyd complained continually about a weak heart, claiming that it was a matter of life and death that he be released to the prison hospital for immediate care. Laughing unsympathetically, the cons would toss in a handful of aspirins to the screw and say, "Now you know how it feels to be given an aspirin when you're dying!"

Around 3:30 a.m. there was a great hullabaloo as scouts posted at the broken windows spread the alarm that the army was coming! Everybody immediately stopped what they were doing, grabbed their weapons, and rushed to the cellblock windows to see for themselves this new deadly threat that was descending on us. With their boots crunching down on the gravel and the lights gleaming off fixed bayonets, the doughboys marched in smartly and encircled the entire cellhouse. Their massive weaponry brought home the stark reality of our situation: some of us might die before the bingo ended. Military vehicles could be heard entering the front gates, and somebody started the rumour that the army was bringing in tanks. It soon became obvious that at least for the moment the military was going to settle for digging in and maybe doing a little bit of sabre rattling to scare us into giving up. By this time the joint was crawling with screws, police, army personnel, and a lot of dishevelled brass from Regional Headquarters and other area institutions, all asking how such a thing could possibly have happened in Canada's toughest penitentiary. As a show of force the mainline screws interspaced themselves between the army boys, ten feet apart, a brown uniform alternating with a blue one, creating a human chain that stretched all around the dome. Punching windowpanes out from the cellblock windows, some of the more vocal jailhouse sages started hurling playful taunts at our new keepers.

"Go home, army, it's not your war!"

"You guys ain't fussy about the company you keep!"

"The Bible says the lowest of the low is the keeper of man!"

"How about sharing what you got in them canteens?"

The ribbing would fly right and left and a small cheer would go up each time a rigid soldier cracked a smile. A few soldiers even gave the high sign with their thumb and finger, a gesture that could get them in hot water with their commanding officer. Barbed wire was strung out between the enemy camps; portable spotlights were set up, and heavy machine-gun placements were established behind barricaded sandbags at the various entrances, especially at the door leading into the hospital from A-block. Snipers also took up position with infra-red telescopes along the prison walls, rooftops, and the nearby water tower. Heavy explosives were strategically placed along the cellblock walls so that at a moment's notice the enemy could blast their way inside the dome. It was for this reason that the guys living on the lower tiers tied mattresses to their cell fronts, anticipating such an attack and wanting to avoid stray bullets and grenade fragments. A lot of prisoners willingly shared their drums with friends, convinced that there was safety in numbers. It gave them the opportunity to put at least one man on point while the others slept, ready to give the alert should the action start. Still others chose to drag their mattresses down to the main floor of the dome where they could stretch out and be closer to the unfolding events.

By 4:30 a.m. the chapel area was declared off limits and the barrier at the top of the stairs was dead-locked. It couldn't be defended properly by the rioting rebels, and anybody entering this area could easily be interpreted by the screws as trying to escape, it being so close to the outside wall. Nevertheless, I managed to get my hands on the key and a keeper's flashlight to illuminate the way, explaining to Billy Knight that January and I would do the honours of obtaining some lamp fluid that I ''knew'' was in the Jewish chapel. The contents, I pointed out, could be used to make additional firebombs. Like two thieves in the night, January and I once more pussyfooted to the darkened stairway leading up to the chapel area and with great trepidation turned the long key in the lock. The interior was in total darkness. We advanced cautiously, half-expecting to be greeted by a wall of gunfire with every tentative step we took.

''Do you hear anything?'' whispered January.

''No, do you?'' I croaked, shining the beam of my flashlight around the inky interior.

''Guess not,'' January replied as the light illuminated the exit door leading to the outside fire escape, which was barricaded from inside with heavy pieces of furniture. Suddenly I gave a gasp of horror as a headless statue jumped into focus.

''Christ, that looks real,'' muttered my sidekick.

''What kind of shithead would do that to a lady?''

''We've got them all in here, Roger, you know that,'' said January.

Entering the Catholic chapel we were greeted by an awe-inspiring scene of even greater destruction that chilled us to the bone. Nothing was left intact. It was as if a stampeding herd of demons had trampled everything into kindling sticks. The massive pews had been either smashed or carted off to reinforce the barricades in the dome, as had the marble altar; littering the floor were hundreds of Bibles, candles, and priest's frocks. Still trembling from the sight of the headless statue, I pulled open the top drawer of a filing cabinet and was greeted by the missing head. That time I gave a yell that could be heard all over the place!

We didn't hang around very long, but when we did leave we had plenty to carry — a small cache of precious coffee, canned milk, sugar, eggs, butter and bread, even a small hotplate and water kettle. Just for the hell of it we lugged off the padre's old-fashioned radio. That way we could search the airwaves and hear what was being said about us. But before collecting all this stuff, we first had to locate the jug of lamp oil in the Jewish chapel in order to keep the militants happy. Everything was a mess, but January did manage to locate the flammable liquid beneath a pile of mopheads in a closet. I then made the nearly fatal mistake of coming up too quietly behind where he was kneeling and popping open a can of Pepsi that I had found among the food supplies. First there was a long shuddering scream, then a tremendous swipe at my head with the iron bar January had in his hand, which in turn slipped and plunged straight through a stained-glass window — just as the prison had quieted down!

Crouched low with the candlelight illuminating his weathered features, January looked like a crusty old cowboy, albeit a mighty scared one, as he whispered, "We're a goner!"

Together we scrambled madly out of the chapel area, locking the gate behind us and plunging carelessly down the metal stairs toward the light coming from the dome. Here we dropped off the jug of lamp oil, then headed up the maze of cells with our goodies.

Early morning fog was starting to roll in through the broken windows, and indeed everything had quieted down. Much of the initial fury had been spent on smashing breakable things. What was left needed more planned exertion to destroy. The only scurrying to be seen inside the cavernous cellblocks was of cons trying to borrow, beg, and steal blankets to keep warm. The scene resembled a costume party as the prisoners came up with all kinds of bizarre clothing, even cloaking themselves in priestly frocks with a few rips here and there to accommodate their weapons. Several groups had taken to building small campfires in front of their cells, so we decided to do the same. But rather than just warming our hides, we used the flames to heat up coffee and to cook a gourmet breakfast. Soon the delicious aroma of eggs cooking was drawing mooches to us in droves, all acting buddy-buddy while extending their metal cups for us to fill with steaming java. "Guess we're going to have to hit the trail again, partner," said January in a western drawl as he pointed to our rapidly dwindling supplies.

Just then Step-Ladder and Do-Die drifted up to our fire sagging with fatigue and also mooching coffee. Like haunted desperados they laid down their tools, and Step-Ladder blurted out hoarsely, ''The whole cowfucking place is coming apart!'' His beer-bellied sidekick just nodded his head as he sat with his back against the cell bars, then after a moment added, ''We've got a home brew fermenting right inside the bell platform, and I'd like to see Old Brew Nose try and get his hands on it.''

It was a fantastic sight to see those previously well-behaved old cons taking a perverse delight in breaking the chains of obedience and orderly conduct that had stifled them for so many years. They were now letting it all hang out, including their shirt-tails, and damn the ironclad rules.

There was a subdued silence throughout the cellblocks as the sun started breaking over the walls, illuminating the incredible destruction. Pirate-like figures bundled up in blankets were everywhere, some lying down wherever they chose, others clustered together in cells, still others shuffling around through the debris as if the only reason they were still walking around was to save the funeral expenses. No one dared sleep for fear of an attack, and as a result paranoia permeated every inch of the conquered territory. It was now the warden's turn to make a move, though throughout the night awkward attempts were made by both sides to open a channel of communication. Billy Knight and his lieutenants kept the phone inside the central dome intact and used it briefly to obtain information and to give the enemy instructions. The calls were not regulated at all and led to confusion because various inmates were taking it upon themselves to make calls, sometimes to the warden in his office, other times to whoever was in the keeper's hall. Thus the brass, not knowing where the blower was going to ring next, were kept on point and ready to scurry madly about. One argument that raged for hours inside the administrative offices centred on who exactly was in charge of policy making, the warden or the regional director? As a result Billy was getting all kinds of inconsistent answers that made him look foolish, and by sunrise the prison population was demanding some concrete answers to the mind-boggling rumours that were circulating. There were also many disjointed demands and requests from both camps, our side demanding food and medication, theirs some solid proof that none of the hostages were dead or injured. On the official side nobody was willing to give any hard answers, claiming that they were waiting for instructions from the Commissioner's office in Ottawa. The warden flatly refused to provide us with food and coffee, but he did agree to dispatch an inmate orderly from the joint hospital with prescribed medication for those prisoners suffering from chronic ailments such as epilepsy and bad hearts. "But," he added, "as an act of good faith you should permit me to speak to one of my men on the telephone, to hear from him firsthand that the hostages are safe and well treated."

This request was followed by a great deal of bar pounding and shouts for everyone to gather in the centre of the dome to witness the occasion. Brandishing our weapons, we all lined the circular galleries and cluttered the stairways until the selected guard, Ed Barrett, staggered into sight on the top tier of B-block, supported by two brawny cons and looking ludicrous in baggy inmate clothing. He was led blindfolded down the winding stairs to the rhythmic tempo of bar music in the form of an eerie death march. Like the devil's heartbeat, the spine-tingling tattoo reverberated everywhere, drifting out to the soldiers and the guards like a deadly chill, then floating over the walls to touch the curious civilians lining the streets. Barrett was worried that his legs might give out under him, as he was half-convinced that he was being led to some grisly slaughter. He shuddered each time he felt a hostile prisoner brush past him. Still unable to see, and with his prison shirt buttoned up to his neck, he was herded across the dome floor to a wall phone and handed the familiar receiver. The rhythmic beat ceased and everybody watched as the keeper talked rapidly to the warden at the other end of the line in an emotional voice, saying that the hostages were safe, that for the moment they were unharmed, but that he firmly believed they would all die if the inmates' demands were not met. At that point Billy snatched the receiver away, told the warden to think about what he had heard, and hung up. As the hostage was led away to join his comrades the prisoners resumed pounding the railings with their iron bars until the cellblocks seemed about to explode with the sound.

At 8:00 a.m. the warden called the dome and he and Billy Knight agreed to have their first official meeting in the hospital boardroom at 10:30 that same morning. Billy took the opportunity to inform him that an inmates' committee had been selected to represent the prison population and that he was to be the spokesman for this small group.

Shortly before that meeting was to take place Billy again called Warden Jarvis and insisted that he be permitted to speak over the phone to Jerry Retzer, a popular news reporter on the staff of a Kingston radio station. After discussing the matter with the Regional Director, who was always at his side, the warden agreed to allow Billy to communicate with Retzer. Hanging up the phone resignedly, Arthur Jarvis removed his horn-rimmed glasses and allowed his eyes to fall on the sculpture on a bookshelf above his desk of a small man looking up at a bird on his hand with an inscription reading, "Go ahead, everybody else does."

As a result of the above decision Billy and a few of his closest advisors spoke over the dome telephone with Retzer, informing the reporter that the insurrection was not intended to be violent, that its purpose was to enable the prisoners to air their grievances. Assurances were given this time to the outside world that the guard hostages were not harmed, and were in fact being protected by an inmate police force. Retzer was informed that the inmates had chosen a committee to meet the administration later in the morning, and that they wanted Retzer to be present. The broadcaster volunteered to attend, and said that he would bring a tape recorder to the meeting and would inform newspapers and television stations in both Kingston and Toronto of the situation.

Suddenly a new voice with a heavy American accent came on the blower. It belonged to Emmanuel Greenberg, who stated that he had been elected by the inmate population to be their legal advisor. In that capacity he informed Retzer that the population desired that the Inmates' Committee meet with a citizens' committee to which the prisoners could present their combined grievances. Greenberg was the forty-five-year-old American millionaire I had met in the Don Jail, a stockbroker serving time for fraud. In his new capacity as jailhouse lawyer, he submitted a long list of prominent citizens in the media, political, and legal fields, hoping that these outstanding individuals might volunteer to come to Kingston. When the Regional Director heard about this new twist he made an immediate telephone report to the Commissioner of Penitentiaries.

That one phone call to Jerry Retzer in the outside world really got the ball rolling; the cat was out of the bag and the media's ear around the globe was tuned in. The Kingston riot had become a stage play for all the taxpayers to watch, a glimpse into a murky world which up till then the average citizen had chosen to ignore. They preferred to play the ostrich, to bury their collective heads in the sand and pretend that society's offspring did not have to live that way.

The meeting took place at 10:45 on Thursday morning inside the boardroom of the hospital. In attendance were Regional Director John Moloney, Warden Arthur Jarvis, acting Deputy Warden Douglas Chinnery, Billy Knight, Charles Saunders, Emmanuel Greenberg, and seven members of the media. It was an extraordinary meeting. The tension was heightened even more by the bright television lights and flashing cameras. In the background a veritable arsenal of weaponry was bristling as the three rebellious prisoners were escorted into the whitewashed room and seated at a conference table directly across from the prison officials.

Immediately Billy Knight made a statement that the inmates were "tired of being zombies" and that this was "a last-ditch stand against the inhumanities that the prisoners would face upon a forced transfer to the Millhaven complex." Before the prison officials could comment, the media took it upon themselves to engage the three riot leaders with questions; they later prompted the crusty old Regional Director to describe the meeting as a "press conference." Emmanuel Greenberg then submitted a written memorandum stating that they were only asking for five points to be discussed at this time, explaining that distrust and a feeling that "we cannot get through to the people in the prison administration" had led to the formal request for the formation of a citizens' committee to negotiate a peaceful settlement. After discussing the need for food and medication Billy Knight let the other shoe drop: "If your people try to force their way into the dome from anyplace, they will do so at the peril of the hostages. We do not wish to harm anyone; our only desire is to be heard. As for further negotiations, we all must wait until at least four members of the noted citizens' committee volunteer to meet with us."

As a result of the turn the meeting had taken, and in an effort to terminate it, the Regional Director advised that the written demands of the inmates would be considered. These were on the subject of the administration of justice, the parole act, and prison life in general. He then rushed off to brief the politicians in Ottawa, who in turn suggested that as a matter of "convenience" just two prominent citizens of the Commissioner of Penitentiaries' choice be convened to meet with the inmate committee. John Moloney immediately phoned Billy Knight in the dome to relay the suggestion, saying that Billy should put the proposition to the inmate body for a general vote. Astonished that Ottawa should think along such narrow lines, Billy flatly refused to give the idea any consideration.

The Regional Director again contacted the Commissioner of Penitentiaries and stressed that if they wanted to get the negotiations under way an immediate attempt should be made to contact the civilians requested by the riot leaders. However, radio news and press reports had already carried the list of names that had been given by telephone to Retzer, and as a result the first volunteers were already flying to Kingston aboard an army helicopter. The first two arrived at the deputy warden's office at about five o'clock that afternoon.

Meanwhile the afternoon newspapers and radio reports carried banner headlines concerning the life-and-death struggle going on inside the walls of Kingston Penitentiary. They also carried off-the-record complaints from disgruntled prison staff. "Publicity stunt," decried one high-ranking officer, referring sarcastically to the prisoners' refusal to negotiate directly with "untrustworthy" penitentiary staff. He went on to say that the request for a citizens' committee was a "slap in the face." Another frustrated and angry guard stepping through the front gates of the prison cried out to the media gathered there that six of his co-workers, "my gang, my friends," were being held captive and there was nothing he could do about it. Puffing nervously on a cigarette he added with a furtive look around him (paranoid that his supervisors might see him talking to the press) that it was "the do-gooders who got us into this mess, all those damn reformers and civil rights people who seem to forget that we're not dealing with boy scouts, that this is a maximum security institution filled with killers and thieves. I wish people would remember that we know how to deal with the prisoners, that's our job, that's what we've been trained for. Rehabilitation? We'll rehabilitate them, but we might have to hurt a few of them a little bit."

CHAPTER

11

BY MIDDAY on the second day of the bingo, the frantic tempo had slowed down to the point where most of the guys were actually spooked by the silence. Some felt that our lack of activity might be interpreted as a sign of resignation and weakness. For this reason, every hour on the hour, the riot leaders would gather everybody up to the railings fronting our cells and the circular dome and get us to pound out a rhythmic tattoo. The eerie sound brought a chill to my spine as hundreds of grim-faced convicts beat louder and louder until the grey fortress quivered in terror. We were too hoarse to holler any more and our bodies sagged from fatigue and hunger. Sleep for periods of more than an hour was impossible because of the enforced participation in the drumming. One radio report quoted the warden as saying that he decided to provide the inmates with sandwiches because "lack of food increases the blood sugar, and that brings on increased excitement."

It was well known that the fearsome Elliot twins were massive eaters and extremely impulsive. Perhaps driven by hunger, they reneged on their new responsibility of guarding the screws and switched instead to the alarming act of snatching one of them from the locked cage. The two drunken hulks dragged Donald Floyd screaming and kicking along the narrow top tier to the front of B-block, then grabbed the guard by the throat and bent him slowly over the top railing until the screw was staring bug-eyed onto the dome floor far below.

"It's the deep six for you, pig!" roared Hal, grinning broadly at the curious faces staring up from the floor below.

"Out of the way! This pig is going to make a big splash!" bellowed Al, delighted at the panic that he and his brother were causing.

Just then a powerful hand reached out of nowhere and gripped

Hal's shoulder tightly. "Where's he going?" Barrie Mackenzie demanded.

"Into the pool," replied Al, with a crooked grin that displayed missing teeth.

"Yeah, if we ever get the bastard's hands loose from the railing," panted Hal as he tried to break Floyd's grip.

"We just drained the pool," replied Barrie with a boyish grin that masked his violence, muscles tensed for action.

Missing Barrie's silent gesture to Big Wayne Ford, Brian Beaucage, and other members of the inmate police force to move in even closer, Hal just chuckled and dug thick knuckles into Floyd's back to stifle a plea. But Al got the drift and, not wanting a busted melon, turned to his brother and said: "It's true, Hal, ain't no water down there."

Survival instincts jumping to the fore, Hal got the dig, smiled innocently and said, "OK, we'll wait until the tide comes in."

Floyd was then led back to the cell, where he gratefully joined the other hostages. A semblance of sanity once again prevailed. Chains and padlocks now gave additional security to the hostages, and the key went into Barrie's pocket. Previously the inmates could roam onto the hostages' tier at will to view the guards locked behind bars and maybe drop a few wisecracks. That dubious privilege was now curtailed. The range became off limits except to the riot leaders and the inmate police force.

Later, on Thursday afternoon, the inmate population was summoned to the dome and told that a TV reporter from Toronto would be touring the dome area and talking to the hostages to see whether the situation was under control. Henry Champ thought that at thirty-one he was too young to die, but nevertheless at the suggestion of Billy Knight he volunteered to enter the section of the prison under siege. The penitentiary officials made him sign a document stating that they were not responsible for his actions or his safety and that he was entering the section on his own initiative. The army and guards were secretly delighted to be getting an eyewitness account of what the inside now looked like, including the inmates' defence system against any rescue attempt. The militants thought Billy was unwise to allow an outsider in, but Knight was worried about public opinion and the vicious rumours being circulated to the news media by anonymous guards.

Moving through the hospital doorway, Henry Champ carefully stepped over the machine-gun placement and entered A-block. Midway down the tier, which contained twenty-eight cells, the reporter had to climb awkwardly over a massive barricade of iron cots and broken furniture while directly above him hooded militants were poised to rain down a storm of metal and firebombs. As soon as he was in the clear, he was met by Billy Knight and Emmanuel Greenberg, who shook his hand warmly as they led him into the central dome. At first there was a deadly silence as the rebels took the opportunity to size up this stranger in their midst, but after a little while they decided they liked this square-jawed guy. Champ took in the condition of the ghostly figures moving about in the shadows and decided that they were men who would fight blindly out of pain and rage.

Displaying a nervous smile, the reporter nevertheless started replying to the questions coming from all around him. One of his first priorities was to hear firsthand that the hostages were all alive and well, but the militants wouldn't let Champ into their area for fear that he would later tell prison authorities exactly where the hostages were being kept. It was agreed that one of the hostages would be brought down to meet with the reporter inside the security of the radio room, where Champ could ask whatever questions he wished. The cluttered radio room on the second gallery fronting the dome floor was equipped with sophisticated radio and television gear and was where Billy had set up quarters. It also provided some privacy because the steel gate at the entrance could be pulled shut and locked.

To meet with Champ they chose Ed Barrett, the man who had been in charge of the night shift when Billy Knight took over the prison. Blindfolded and with his hands tied behind his back, the burly guard was escorted down the winding stairways, past hundreds of silent prisoners, and into the large radio room where he came face to face with Henry Champ. Obviously happy to be still alive, he informed the newsman in an emotional voice that he and his fellow hostages had not been unduly harmed, that they were being well treated, and that the convicts had even formed their own security committee to protect them from hostile factions. Then with a sad smile (having been a screw longer than Roy Rogers was a cowboy) he added in a choking voice: ''Now we are the prisoners.''

Champ was also given a tour of 1-D, where he spoke to a few of the undesirables. He was visibly shaken by the experience, perhaps convinced that he was seeing them alive for the last time. As he moved freely through the wrecked main floors, the reporter heard complaints about being overguarded in a fortress everybody knew was escape-proof and about being bored and having little recreation time. But the big beef was about the uncertainty facing the population upon transfer to the Millhaven complex. Everybody complained that surveillance was already too strict and confining and that the goon squads enforcing the rules were becoming a law unto themselves. We asked for a light at the end of the tunnel, a little hope, and a chance to better ourselves. Champ later reported that the inmates were acting in a democratic manner and had set up ''more committees than I can count.'' He reported that there was a committee to scrounge for food, one to handle the radio system, one to draw up a list of predominant grievances, and many more. ''Most of the windows were smashed in the initial stages of the riot and they [the inmates], realizing it was solely their fault, are not complaining, except for a request to the warden to turn up the heat as far as it would go.'' He couldn't guess, he said, whether we had food stashed, but he did notice a group of convicts scurrying about with half a loaf of bread and a can of peanut butter.

Henry Champ's sincere concern for everyone's safety was so obvious that the population soon warmed up to the outsider's presence. They pounded him on the back by way of friendly greeting until they realized that he received each blow as though it were a knife thrust. After that they settled for giving him the peace sign or just shaking his hand and imploring him to do his utmost to air our conditions to the public. Some of the inmates asked him to let their families know that they were okay.

After the reporter left, things got quiet again. One of the radio operators strung several large speakers around the dome, and some wiseacre requested that Elvis Presley's ''Jailhouse Rock'' be piped through the speakers. With the music blaring, the younger guys got right into it, clapping and singing, urging the operator to turn the sound up louder and louder, especially the part where Elvis is bellowing ''And here comes the warden with his tommy gun!'' The words roared out through the cellblock windows, over the walls, and onto the streets . . .

Meanwhile the selection of prominent Ontario individuals to form a citizens' advisory committee was finally carried out from a master list submitted by Billy Knight. It was agreed that the first five persons to respond to the urgent plea would be chosen to act as negotiators for both sides. It was further agreed that more than five people on the committee would only lead to confusion. At five o'clock that Thursday afternoon three men all dressed in black suits arrived at the deputy warden's office inside the walls of Kingston Penitentiary to be briefed.

Ron Haggart, a well-known columnist from a Toronto newspaper and a commentator on public affairs, was a handsome and distinguished man who was not afraid to stick his neck out.

Aubrey E. Golden was a barrister and solicitor with vast experience in labour negotiations. He too was tall and distinguished-looking, and his receding hairline gave him the appearance of a seasoned politician.

Professor J. Desmond Morton, Q.C., was still my lawyer, and still ready to do battle in the name of fair play. The little Irishman, though recovering from a serious heart attack, disregarded the arguments of his doctor and his family to race to the prison to offer his services after hearing his name mentioned over the radio.

The Warden and Regional Director gave the three men a brief outline of the facts as they were known. No restriction or limitation or authority was imposed on them, as there had been no specific discussion of the role that the Citizens' Committee was to be permitted to play. However, it was understood from the first that the Committee had no authority to bind the government or the Department of the Solicitor-General to any settlement or course of conduct. The Committee members thought of themselves as a "third force" who could not lean heavily in either direction. Later, after several meetings with the inmates, they began to develop a sense of the real role that had been imposed on them. One of the members summarized it this way:

> Although the Committee never did sit down and formally spell out to each other what we considered its status to be or what its role was, I think we all accepted the view that, having been requested to act by both the Government and the prisoners' committee, we had an independent status, that we were not a mere agent of either the Solicitor-General or the prisoners' committee. Again, while

we didn't spell it out, I think we saw from the beginning that our role was to exercise our best judgment in doing everything that was reasonably possible to bring the riot to a speedy termination and prevent loss of life or injury to the guards who were being held hostages and to the prisoners themselves.

Very shortly after their arrival within the penitentiary walls, the first of the three members of the Citizens' Committee proceeded to the hospital wing, where he met Billy Knight and Emmanuel Greenberg. Also in attendance were the prison officials, monitoring everything that was said. The stakes were so high, and the tension so heavy, that the first session was simply used as an icebreaker. The warden did announce that within the hour Billy Knight's group would be provided with sandwiches and milk to be distributed to the inmates, providing that the hostages be given their share of food. This was good news for Billy. His credibility had sunk to the point where factions were starting to form against him, and for once he could return to the population with something positive.

The food containers arrived around six o'clock and were deposited by the screws at the entrance to A-block, a few feet from the machine-gun nest. Watching from the dome barrier leading into no-man's-land were some very tired characters, hungry and shivering inside their tattered clothing. With great interest they watched Ralph Lundrigan, a male inmate nurse living in the hospital, drag the containers over the barricades and into the waiting hands of the food committee. At one time Ralph had the reputation of being one of the toughest and strongest cons in the joint, but now, in his late forties, his hair turning white, and a life sentence to contend with, most of the fire was gone. He now concentrated on being a diplomat, shuttling back and forth between both armed camps, regularly visiting ill patients, and making up a list of necessary medications to be submitted to the hospital officials.

Long tables with white bedsheets draped over them and fancy candles from the chapels set on top were erected in the centre of the dome for the food distribution. The guys were excited at the prospect of getting some grub, and while music blared over the loudspeakers one big lug with a hairy torso jumped up on one of the tables and did a fancy jig. Other guys clapped their hands and urged him on to even greater antics. Some of the prisoners didn't move off their mattresses — not for food, not for anything — because they were stoned out of their minds from sniffing glue and popping pills.

In charge of the food distribution was Dave Shepley, a gregarious, chunky guy in his mid-twenties who was serving time for armed robbery. Popular and always thinking positive, Dave was usually good company, but at this stage of the bingo hardly anybody was really themselves, including Dave, who kept swinging between good humour and rash anger. Dave seemed to have control of the bullhorn most of the time, trying to keep the guys on an even keel, continually passing on tidbits of news, good and bad. Standing in the centre of the dome, he took it upon himself to make sure that the food was allotted fairly, with each guy getting precisely his portion, no more and no less. Actually it was starvation portions (one baloney sandwich each), and some of the greedier prisoners did their damnedest to score at least a second serving.

Dave Shepley had many friends, but two of his closest buddies were Ziggy and John, young cons serving short sentences, both as lively and playful as bear cubs and forever getting into jackpots. On this day Ziggy was crashed out on a mattress against the dome wall, having popped too many pills to try to escape the terrible reality of the riot. An incident was about to happen that probably affected Dave Shepley's course of action during the remaining hours of the bingo. Dave had made it his business to remember who had already passed through the long meal line for sandwiches and to discourage those who tried to get seconds.

John McBride was one of those who waited a long time in line before he picked up his baloney sandwich. He quickly ate his portion and shortly afterwards discovered that his best friend, Ziggy, had passed out without getting any food. He got back into line and within half an hour was again facing Dave Shepley at the table. He explained that he had come to pick up Ziggy's sandwich. Dave laughed and said, "No way, John, you already went through the line."

John exploded, "The sandwich is for Ziggy, not for me! Do you take me for a goof?"

Dave's nerves were just as frayed as his friend's, and so he responded with anger of his own. "Yes, I think you are a goof!"

John stepped around the table, not really in control of his actions, and threw a wild punch that caught Dave on the jaw just as he was about to say more. Dave stood there, stunned that his skinny friend would take a poke at him in the midst of a prison riot. For long seconds everyone nearby also froze. Suddenly John's arms were pinned behind his back by two of Dave's soldiers. John stared in horror at the knife in Dave's belt, panic racing through him as he realized that he was helpless to get at his own. Just as Dave was clearing the cobwebs from his brain and John was preparing to die, Brian Beaucage shouted down from the second tier in front of the radio room, "Let the kid go!" These were the most beautiful words John had ever heard. His arms were released and he was now free to get at his weapon. Staring hard at Dave, John gulped and apologized sincerely to his old friend. Dave replied that it was okay, that they should forget what had happened. John saw that for now it was over, but for the duration of the riot he made sure that he kept his eyes open.

It turned out that John had broken Dave Shepley's jaw. Somebody got on the hotline and it was agreed that Dave could make his way down the bottom tier of A-block to the hospital for repairs. After they wired up his jaw, the warden suggested that he was free to remain as a patient in the hospital. Dave flatly refused, declaring that it was his wish to return to his friends. (In the dying hours of the riot Dave Shepley became a murderous force, a deviation from his usual friendly self. With this drastic change in mind, John McBride later said to me: "I've always wondered, did that broken jaw cause Dave to work out like he did, his way of showing the population that you couldn't fuck with him?")

By nine o'clock Thursday evening a full Citizens' Committee of five members was meeting with five members of the Prisoners' Committee for the first time, again in the hospital treatment room. The two new civilian representatives were from the Toronto area. Like the other three, they dressed in black. The oldest of the five was Arthur Martin, Q.C., an imposing figure of a man whose heavy jowls gave him the stern appearance of a Kremlin leader. He had engaged almost exclusively in the practice of criminal law for thirty-three years and was a prestigious figure in the Law Society of Upper Canada. As the hours dragged on, he became a highly persuasive devil's advocate by continually warning the riot leaders that the government was pointing a cannon at their heads, that they should be reasonable in their demands, and that they should try harder to end their occupation of the main cellhouse.

The fifth committee member was William R. Donkin, a barrister and solicitor and the area Director of Legal Aid for York County. Donkin was a bearded, agreeable man who would patiently listen to the inmates' complaints about the legal aid system, giving them the impression that they were winning points.

The Citizens' Committee determined that the most useful approach in the initial meetings would be for them to hear out the inmates' grievances. The beefs were wide-ranging but generally fell into two categories. The first was a criticism of the administration of the criminal justice system, including the operation of the courts, the back-room torture tactics of the various police forces, and the punitive nature of sentencing.

The second category of grievances related to the administration of the penitentiary system in general, and to Kingston Penitentiary in particular. Emmanuel Greenberg, who could spew out verses of law like a Shakespearean actor, but who was relatively new at shaking time, complained about the prisoners' isolation from society and the illogical nature of that isolation in view of the need to integrate the inmate more effectively into society upon release. Complaints were put forward concerning systems of mass punishment whereby the privileges of all would be reduced because of their abuse by a few, the use of segregation and disassociation in the prison system, the muscling of prisoners by the guards, and the lack of meaningful or useful work. The Inmates' Committee further expressed its concern about the effect of long sentences, especially the difficulties of adjusting to outside life upon release from the penitentiary. Billy Knight hammered home the point that life inside the penitentiary was unnecessarily degrading and humiliating, and that the riot was the prisoners' only means of impressing upon the community outside the walls the dehumanization we suffered.

At the conclusion of the first meeting of the Citizens' Committee the five civilians agreed to relate the prisoners' grievances to the Commissioner of Penitentiaries in Ottawa. It was also agreed by the warden that they would all meet again the following morning at nine o'clock.

It was almost midnight when the Inmates' Committee returned to the dome and called a general assembly to advise the population as to what had taken place. They were appalled to find that while they were gone a mini-riot had erupted, caused by the sudden appearance of hundreds of extra soldiers. Bristling with weaponry, the army looked very aggressive as they took up offensive positions and reinforced the platoons already encircling the main cellhouse. Initially panic had spread because the prisoners were convinced that the army was about to storm their fortified positions. In blind anger and frustration the inmates went on an orgy of destruction, some smashing what was already broken while others manned their own self-defence system on the top tiers. Do-Die and Step-Ladder made an effort to rewire the heavy-duty electrical systems to the entry gates with the intention of electrocuting any invasion force, but all they managed to do was blow the fuses in G- and H-blocks and start a small fire, almost frying themselves in the process!

The army's sabre-rattling also triggered off a hostile reaction by a fiery breakaway group of convicts determined to kill at least one of the hostages. Armed with spears and iron bars and led by a hulking newcomer, they charged through the crowded stairways until they came face to face with the dozen inmates guarding the hostages. The eyeball-to-eyeball confrontation lasted about five minutes, but the police force was just too tough and stubborn to be out-manoeuvred. Finally the hotheads realized that they were flirting with their own certain demise if they didn't smarten up and back off. That was a close call and spooked the moderates in the population, who feared that things were getting out of hand.

Barrie Mackenzie, who was taking a more and more active role in the direction of the riot, also half-believed that the army was about to attack. He shouted angrily into the dome phone to the warden that the troop movements were endangering the lives of the hostages. Ron Haggart took over the blower and, acting as an intermediary, handled his first crisis by convincing Barrie that the soldiers were merely additional reinforcements arriving a little too enthusiastically. The fact that Haggart was a civilian made all the difference, and a bond of trust began to develop between the two strong personalities.

Minutes later Billy Knight called the prison population to the centre of the dome for a general meeting. Soon hundreds of villainous-looking characters were lining the railings. As he stood in front of the radio room on the second floor it became obvious that the strain of leadership and lack of sleep was taking its toll on his iron nerves. His voice had never been very strong, but now it was reaching a high pitch, cracking every once in a while. I'm sure many took that as a sign of weakness as he pleaded for common sense to prevail. When he spoke he was surrounded not only by his own lieutenants, but also by threatening figures who were not happy with his leadership. If what he was saying made good sense, Barrie Mackenzie and others like Brian Beaucage would nod their heads in silent agreement.

"Those of you who are running around setting off fires are toying with our lives!" hollered Billy. "If the cellblock goes up in flames we'll all be trapped!"

That got strong nods from everybody. A committee of inmates was detailed to keep an eye out for flash fires and to bust heads if necessary. After Billy's talk, Dave Shepley took possession of the bullhorn and, bouncing around the main floor like an angry bull, harangued the population about the "undesirables."

"How come these creeps get a share of our grub? We ought to drag them out here in the middle of the floor and beat their canary brains in! That would convince the doughboys not to try and rush us."

That kind of talk scared the rational cons, who knew only too well that such a radical statement could easily be turned into a bloody reality. If the army did witness such carnage it would give them the excuse they needed to crash in with guns blazing.

"No, no, no! Dammit, no!" shouted Billy Knight, as he rushed down the stairs to Shepley's side and placed a restraining hand on the arm holding the bullhorn. Whispering urgently in Dave's ear, he somehow managed to cool him down.

Friday morning around 2:00 a.m., January Jones and I were on the prowl again for more coffee, but this time we were tiptoeing along the top tier of D-block like thieves in the night, searching for a bricked-in-window that I remembered was at the end of the range. When we arrived at the blank wall everything was dark and spooky. There was no action at all in the area. But when the tower spotlight silhouetted us we ducked behind the railings, not wanting to be a target for a sniper. By the light of a church candle I could see the square outline of what had once been a window. With heavy tools we quickly broke through the plaster and pulled loose the bricks. Facing us were rusty iron bars, and far below on the main floor was the hobby craft office bathed in a dim light. The prisoners who worked in that department were the most active hustlers in the joint, often trading favours with the kitchen crew for coffee and steaks. We had to approach the place from an upper tier because the main entrance was via a steel gate outside the cellblock.

"Go for it!" January whispered as I punched out a dusty window pane. Even as the pieces fell all the way down into the cluttered office we were arching our necks for a look. "There's a goldmine of goodies inside that filing cabinet, ol' buddy!"

"Shit, cool it, January," I whispered, alarmed at how loudly his voice carried into the office below. For long seconds we waited with bated breath for some kind of reaction to the sounds of the breaking window. Finally, letting out my breath, I handed my tools to January and said, "It seems clear. Gimme the cord and hook; I should be able to pull out that drop drawer."

I had just manoeuvred the heavy fishing line through the bars when an ear-splitting explosion sounded and a high-powered rifle bullet smashed out a window pane right beside our faces. We both went sprawling on our backs and immediately scrambled into an open cell for cover. Still on hands and knees, our faces covered with powdered dust, we stared blankly into each other's eyes and then smiled as we both came to the same conclusion. Holding a trembling hand before me I laughed nervously and croaked, "For two guys struggling so hard not to get involved in this fuckin' cherub, we're sure getting shot at a lot."

"Rog, ol' buddy," replied January, picking glass out of his hair, "I think it would be wise if we got the hell out of here."

Halfway down the tier we were met by Brian Dodge and other riot leaders who wanted to know what had happened. "I dunno," said January, shrugging. "We were minding our own business when some asshole took a potshot at us."

"Yeah, it ain't safe to walk around here anymore," I added, gingerly touching the cuts and bruises I had accumulated.

A hothead to start with, Brian was really getting upset, especially since the brass had been specifically warned that the hostages would lose fingers if any more shots were fired by the screws. They're playing fucking games with us, and it's Billy's fault for giving in too much." Then Brian added bitterly, "I'm not going to drag ass any more. Maybe I'll pigstick one of them hackers myself."

With that chilling prediction he and his gang rushed down to the main floor to place yet another angry call to the warden, "a final warning" as he put it. The warden defended himself by pointing out that it was the army that fired the shot, not one of his men. But Brian Dodge had made his point. Not long after the riot, the guards broke his back in retribution.

"What a drag," I said to January. Not only did our caffeine raid fail, but we were now out of a home. The fourth tier of B-block was out of bounds because the hostages were being guarded there by the inmate police force.

"That's okay, partner," said January as we headed back to the lighted dome. "We'll bunk down on 4-G toward the rear. That way we'll be high enough and far enough away from the exits not to get Pearl Harboured when the army decides to attack."

The last drum on 4-G was empty. We gathered up a few metal bunks and mattresses and barricaded the front of the cell against stray bullets and grenade fragments. We then sprawled on the floor on top of more mattresses to get some shut-eye. Both of us were bone weary, and my missing tooth was hurting me a lot. An hour later January got irritably to his feet and slammed the cell gate shut.

"Can't sleep with the damn door open . . . "

CHAPTER 12

BY EARLY FRIDAY MORNING everybody was gearing up for a long siege and erecting more and more booby traps along possible invasion routes. It was bizarre how methodically the die-hards were preparing to fight a battle they couldn't possibly win, but the one overriding goal seemed to be to take as many of the enemy to hell with them as they could.

We were also arriving at the point where we were inflicting more violence on each other than one army could. There were many fights as the fuses on short tempers ignited. More and more cons checked into the hospital. Fortunately a lot of the beefs were neutralized by the intervention of those with clearer heads. The only way to stay afloat in that quagmire of lunacy was to keep busy at all times and to think positive, no matter how negative the situation appeared. One dangerous and unpredictable segment of the population sought relief through intoxicants, popping pills and sniffing glue, anything that would draw a curtain across their conscious minds. One young prisoner put on a dazzling display while stoned out of his mind on hobby craft glue. Dangling from a top tier with one hand while chanting demon talk, the boy threatened to plunge to his death if somebody didn't give him drugs. Death was narrowly avoided only when three members of the prison police force snatched him to safety. Immediately afterwards Barrie Mackenzie confiscated a large pail of glue and poured it down a drain, restoring some sanity to the highly charged atmosphere.

The bingo was now considered a hot item by the news media. Reports of it were being heard around the world, and more and more foreign correspondents were rushing to the scene for direct coverage. For the past twenty-four hours reports had been filling the airwaves that included vicious anonymous lies deliberately leaked to the press by off-duty guards in an effort to sabotage any prison reform that might come out of the riot. Some of the fabrications were so venomous that it's a wonder the press accepted them as truth, such as the rumours that depicted mass gang rapes of young prisoners who (they said) were tied to what was left of the bell platform. These reports had the effect of transforming dormant prisoners into a cyclone of destructive activity, so that each time a particularly vile rumour was aired over the radio, the guys would go on an orgy of destruction. Do-Die and Step-Ladder, for example, did some unique renovating of their own, punching through all the cell walls on one tier in an effort to create one long dormitory. That took a tremendous effort, as the walls were made of brick and two feet thick. They then carefully carted the bricks up to the top tiers and stacked them like cannonballs to be used later as weapons.

No rapes occurred during the riot. Any convict caught committing such an act would have been torn apart by the prison population in much the same fashion as an undesirable would have been treated. Certainly there was some illicit sex during the bingo, but only among willing parties and almost exclusively in the privacy of a cell. Not even the most blatant drag-queens were bold enough to be seen committing lewd acts in public. There was one minor exhibition by a hairy drag-queen who strip-danced on one of the long tables in the dome. "She" spotted Step-Ladder passing by and suddenly in a fit of passion swooped down off the table and scooped up his emaciated form in her big hairy arms. She was rewarded by a fierce screech of indignation as Coolidge zipped straight up through the muscular embrace to grab hold of the overhead tier. Wiggling his skinny butt furiously until he was able to squeeze through the bottom railing, he scooted off into the labyrinth of cells, followed by thunderous catcalls and applause.

Do-Die and I later found him hiding in total darkness in one of the service ducts mumbling and chanting to himself. It was sad to see him so uptight, pawing at imaginary cobwebs, saying that he was going to remain hidden until the riot was over. That's exactly what he did, and no matter how many times I came back with provisions to see him, he just wouldn't budge, saying that the webs were ensnaring him so tightly that he couldn't move very far. I knew that he had taken a fancy to the brass ball I had hanging around my neck from the remains of the bell, so I gave it to him for good luck.

At nine o'clock on Friday morning when the prisoners' committee returned to the meeting room in the hospital, Emmanuel Greenberg no longer occupied a seat as "legal advisor." He had been unceremoniously deposed only minutes earlier. The American mafia figure may have been streetwise, but he sure wasn't jailwise. He came within an inch of having his head caved in for his self-serving manoeuvres with the enemy at the expense of his fellow cons. Somebody had tapped him lightly with an iron bar and suggested that he fade into the brickwork, where he should remain quietly for the duration of the riot. Emmanuel was happy to oblige.

The meeting started off with Billy arguing once again for total immunity for those involved in the riot. He pointed out that the immunity from prosecution would extend only to the acts associated with the original assault and kidnapping of the guards, but would not include any harm done to the hostages following their original capture. Arthur Martin, who was acting in the capacity of chairman, had already spoken to the Commissioner of Penitentiaries at 2:00 a.m. about the demand for immunity for the leaders of the riot. The reply was a resounding *"No!"* However, the Commissioner said there would be flexibility shown regarding the prisoners' grievances. When informed of this decision, Billy and his lieutenants got very upset. After putting their heads together they issued this threat: "Without assurances of total immunity we won't be able to guarantee the safety of the hostages."

Alarmed, Mr. Martin promised that he would talk once again with the Commissioner on the subject of immunity. Professor Morton pointed out that they were only intermediaries and as such had absolutely no authority to dictate any deals or course of conduct to the government. Mr. Donkin gave his personal promise that the full resources of the legal aid system would be utilized to ensure that if any inmate was charged as a result of the insurrection he would be properly defended in a court of law.

At that point Billy Knight leaned across the table and uttered a surprise announcement. "As an act of good faith, we are prepared to release one hostage."

Visibly delighted with the breakthrough, the Citizens' Committee roundly applauded this announcement and the apparent extent of inmate cooperation. Knight's decision would also give the five civilians credibility and respect, especially from the hardline guards who wanted to go into the hornet's nest with guns blazing. Billy and his lieutenants were escorted back to the hospital entrance to gather the population together for a vote on which hostage was to be released. The Citizens' Committee rushed off to inform the prison administration of the good news.

That same Friday morning January Jones, Do-Die, and I decided that we should keep busy by going up to the attic by way of the trap door. Our objective was the tiny circular catwalk just below the dome's skylight where we hoped we could appease our curiosity as to what was going on outside the prison gates. There was absolutely no other way to see over the prison walls. I warned my pals that it would be dangerous — we would be out of bounds and our presence up there could be mistaken for an escape attempt. There was little doubt that if that occurred the other side would shoot first and ask questions later. Nevertheless we all thought it was a good idea to probe around up there. This time we didn't stick to my previous method of entering the attic through the trap door by laboriously picking the padlock; we simply smashed it off with the iron club I carried.

"Shit to hell, man!" spluttered Do-Die, remembering my barb about his not fitting through the sawed bars. "I told you I'd be making it up there one day . . . belly and all!" With that shout of triumph Do-Die shook his shaggy head and, taking a deep breath, he wiggled clumsily through the narrow opening with our help.

This time we had candles to illuminate the way, but we still got entangled in thick cobwebs as we cautiously made our way toward the circular wall of the rotunda. Do-Die kept tripping over things and banging his head loudly, then cackling in glee. Half expecting the army to come down on us like gangbusters, we spooked each time a snaggly-toothed rat scampered between our legs. Do-Die must have been high on something because he kept exclaiming at the weirdest things until January grabbed him by the arm and shook him into a grudging silence. It got even scarier as we approached the tiny opening in the rotunda. Because I knew the way I went up first, followed by January, then Do-Die. Having to hold onto the candles made climbing up the metal rungs awkward, especially as there was very little room to move around in. It was somewhat like being inside an oversized stove pipe. When I climbed out onto the narrow catwalk at the very top of the rotunda just below the glass skylight, I did so very cautiously. My heart was in my mouth as I cursed myself for being a reckless fool. The bottom of the catwalk was an open metal grate so that I felt strangely as though I was suspended in mid-air. I was also perfectly visible to those standing around on the dome floor far below. By the time all three of us were standing on the catwalk and gripping the flimsy railing, we had become the centre of attention for all the cons on the circular galleries who were pointing excitedly toward our little group. It was intoxicating to be so dangerously out of bounds.

Affixed at intervals around the circular catwalk were a dozen huge spotlights which illuminated the entire dome area. Gripping our iron bars we set out to smash the bulbous monsters so as to make it more difficult for the enemy forces to see what was going on inside the cellblocks. Each blow brought a small explosion, and it was with fierce satisfaction that we watched each one go suddenly blank. The guys on the dome floor had to scurry wildly out of the way to avoid the falling glass. Manning the bullhorn, Billy Knight barely got our attention in time to plead with us to save at least one of the huge spotlights so the dome area wouldn't be in complete darkness. When the spotlights were put out, the overall effect was eerie, as imposing shadows danced everywhere. The one remaining spotlight stared down at the microscopic inhabitants like a baleful eye.

From the narrow catwalk we needed only to stand on tiptoe in order to see through the tiny barred windows. The view from our lofty perch was breathtaking; we could see every inch of the prison grounds, including the army field kitchen, a military helicopter landing near the northeast gun tower, and hundreds of soldiers surrounding the main cellhouse, with still more crouched on top of the many walls. Beyond that forbidding enclosure we could see all of the city of Kingston, while behind us stretched the waters of Lake Ontario. It was a vast panorama that caused the three of us to gape in wonder. Keeping our heads low for fear of being sniped at by the army, we took note of what was happening in front of the prison gates. We could see hordes of people in what appeared to be a carnival atmosphere, a sight that brought home to us the realization that this was one hell of a bingo! The news media were everywhere, even perched in nearby trees, all striving to get that exclusive shot. Included in the milling crowd was a youthful group of demonstrators, both male and female, brandishing banners that stated: "We Support the Prisoners' Cause."

It took a lot of guts and conviction for them to back us up like that, especially in the midst of the enemy, including a confused crowd that was continually being fed ugly rumours by the screws. We decided to show our appreciation by making banners of our own and hanging them out the window.

From outside the prison walls, the rotunda had the appearance of a flying saucer, especially with its tiny circular windows. Certainly we felt like aliens when we returned one hour later carrying slogans painted on white bedsheets. Tagging along with us were another dozen villainous-looking characters trying to get in on the action. To unfurl our banners we had to climb up onto a narrow shelf that would leave us exposed to snipers. Four of us did so cautiously, keeping our eyes on the grassy knoll outside the prison gates for a hostile reaction among the throngs of uniforms gathered there. Slowly I extended a long metal conduit through the bars. Just as the sheet started to flutter in the brisk wind, two little boys high up in a tree on the lawn of the administration building pointed excitedly in our direction, only to be harangued by a policeman who ordered them to come down. Suddenly we were the focus of massive attention as my banner unfolded completely, revealing a peace symbol along with the words "Thank You for Your Support." Do-Die simply hung his sheet declaring in bold letters "The Devil Made Me Do It!" to the iron bars. Then came January Jones's tongue-in-cheek inscription, "Under New Management." Somebody else kept his opinion to one crisp word — "Justice" — and above it was a drawing of a skull and crossbones. Immediately dozens of news photographers with telephoto lenses aimed and took pictures that were to make the front pages of newspapers all around the world. In fact there were no less than sixty media representatives gathered on the grass knoll all dying for a picture.

Shortly after noon the prison population was assembled around the dome and informed by Billy Knight that the Inmates' Committee had decided it would be wise to release one of the hostages. The majority agreed that this would be a solid diplomatic move and would help to dispel some of the ugly rumours being fed to the media by the screws.

"Who will it be, boys?" Barrie wanted to know.

"Let it be the young hacker!" piped a voice from one of the circular galleries above.

"Yeah, the one with the shiner," added another.

"They're talking about Decker," whispered Billy to Barrie, who was standing next to him.

"Sounds good to me," replied Barrie. "Let's put it to a vote."

Thus it was that Terry Decker, the screw who had originally ordered Billy Knight to tuck in his shirt, who in fact provided the spark that ignited the riot, was voted the most liked of the six hostages and won his freedom.

All of the hostages had come to dread the sudden unlocking of their cell door, thinking each time that it was the moment when one or more of them would be stabbed, clubbed, or given a four-storey nose-dive. When big Wayne Ford approached one of the two cells where the hostages were being detained, roughly removed the chain and padlock, then ordered Decker to step forward, all six hostages stopped breathing.

When told that he was being set free, Decker's first reaction was that the whole thing might be a hoax, a pretence for some of the others to get at him.

The young guard's knees were shaking visibly as the inmate police force surrounded him with their weapons, two of them gripping his arms firmly to keep him upright. In a haze Decker was then led to the end of the long tier, in the direction of the circular galleries, convinced that if death was in store for him it would surely take place at that point. With great relief he safely passed that corner and was gently pushed down the winding metal staircase past hordes of silent prisoners. He was then blindfolded for the remainder of the journey so that later he wouldn't be able to describe our defences to the enemy. At the barrier leading into no-man's-land, Barrie Mackenzie took over the responsibility of directing him past the mass of obstacles and into the anxious hands of the Citizens' Committee. There followed a great flood of emotional tears from his co-workers. Everybody was throwing questions at him about the safety of the remaining hostages.

"Where did you get the black eye?" the authorities wanted to know.

"I walked into a door," was the deadpan reply. He instinctively knew that he should not worsen the situation or rock the boat in any way, that the lives of his comrades depended on what the press would report concerning his release. Asked how he was treated during the takeover, he replied with emotion: "Much better than could be expected under the circumstances. In fact they treated us with respect, calling us Sir, Boss, and even Mister. For every sandwich they got we received two; same thing for the coffee.'' Asked if the prisoners would resort to murdering the hostages if they felt that they were being double-crossed, Terry Decker answered flatly, ''Yes. They have nothing to lose.'' He went on to describe the mood of the convicts as one of fierce determination with no sign of surrender.

Grilled in detail by the warden's staff, police, and finally the army, Decker was then permitted to telephone his young wife, who hadn't slept for days, to inform her that he was free. He was told not to talk to the press and was given a packet of money — overtime pay, it was called. Then he was hustled through a side gate of the prison in order to avoid reporters who had not yet been told that a hostage had been released. Within the hour he, his wife, and his three-month-old baby were fleeing the city and the media for an unknown destination. When the reporters realized their quarry had fled, they were livid. The deputy director of information for the Solicitor-General's department simply informed them that one of the hostages had been released unharmed and had left the city for a paid vacation. Regional Director John Moloney was already mad at the news media covering the riot for surreptitiously using the penitentiary's internal telephone system. Mr. Moloney claimed that some of the reporters were telephoning directly to the convicts in the dome and interviewing whoever answered. On one occasion a bored reporter sitting in the warden's empty office picked up the phone when it rang and found himself talking to Billy Knight! The subterfuge was finally discovered when a misdialled number got the Regional Director himself on the blower. Moloney immediately threatened to evict all reporters from the administration building, which had been functioning as a press centre since the start of the rebellion.

Right about this time a news blackout was imposed. The army and prison authorities would no longer give regular press conferences. This grim situation lasted until the bingo came to an end. Even the prisoners had by then settled into a surly silence, a sort of wait-and-see lull, with no more booing, hissing, or jibing at the screws and the army through the cellblock windows. The silence was so heavy that it reminded one of an old western movie in which the deputy says, "Sure is quiet now, Sheriff," and the sheriff replies, "Yeah. Too quiet."

Desperate for any news at all, the media members took to ambushing lone guards reporting to and from work, pushing a smoke at them while drawing them into a corner. Only the most bitter screws would talk, and demanded anonymity. "You would never believe what's going on in there," said one guard while puffing furiously on the reporter's cigarette. "Unbelievable atrocities." When we heard all the ugly lies of sodomy and mutilation over the radio a lot of convicts became so enraged that they wanted to cut the tongues out of the hostages so that their comrades really would have reason to wag theirs. Some prisoners voiced regrets at having voted for the release of one hostage as an act of "good faith." However, the level-headed cons were just plain saddened by the unfairness of it all. (After the bingo ended, the Regional Director felt it was his duty to meet with representatives of the local media to "clear the air" concerning the news reports of castrations and sexual assaults that supposedly occurred during the riot. "The reports just were not true," said Mr. Moloney. "Regrettably of a lot of misinformation was given out by our own staff.")

In the meantime, outside the prison walls the media were still scrambling for something to report. In fact the photographers were so desperate they even took pictures of a carload of fried chicken that arrived abruptly at the front gates. Military vehicles came and went. One contained fierce-looking German shepherds in cages, snarling at the rush of photographers trying to get closeups.

As for the penitentiary brass, the Deputy Solicitor-General, Ernest Coté, and the Commissioner of Penitentiaries, Paul Faguy, decided for the moment to remain in Ottawa, while remaining very close to the emergency telephone. Because there had also been some hot and heavy debates taking place in the House of Commons as to where the blame should rest, the acting Prime Minister, Edgar Benson, was also being kept informed. In fact two members of the Citizens' Committee, Arthur Martin and Ron Haggart, had left shortly after noon that Friday to fly to Ottawa by army helicopter for a hurried meeting with the Solicitor-General and his staff, including the Deputy Solicitor-General, the Commissioner of Penitentiaries, and the Deputy Commissioner of Penitentiaries. Their talks took place around four o'clock in the afternoon at national headquarters. Mr. Martin did his best to persuade the brass that in light of the particular circumstances of the case, and given that Kingston Penitentiary was about to be closed as a maximum security institution in any event, the granting of immunity from prosecution would not really create an unfortunate precedent. After some discussion, Mr. Martin concluded that the bigwigs were prepared to accede to the prisoners' request regarding complaints, but they would not agree to the request for immunity. He stated that if the convicts would withdraw their request for immunity, a foundation for a peaceful solution to the prison rebellion existed.

Before leaving Ottawa, Mr. Haggart telephoned his three colleagues at their hotel rooms in Kingston, informed them as to what had happened, and suggested that a third meeting with the inmate committee take place that evening around midnight. In the meantime helicopters kept landing on the prison grounds, while at the nearby civilian airfield troop transports were busy shuttling in more and more soldiers from Petawawa. These were special riot-trained troops from the 3rd Battalion, Royal Canadian Regiment from Camp Petawawa, brought in to relieve the 1st Canadian Signals Corps from the nearby Kingston Armed Forces Base.

Late Friday afternoon the prisoners' committee, dismayed and angered by the media reports of violent acts, murder, and mayhem, requested that Professor Morton make a firsthand assessment of the true situation inside the cellblocks. Billy Knight, talking over the blower to the frail little Irishman, asked him point-blank if he had it in him to volunteer to come inside and determine for himself whether there was any truth to the horror stories. Drained emotionally by two sleepless days of tense negotiations, and still shaky from his recent heart attack, the professor hesitated just long enough to bite down on his unlit cigar, then declared in a strong courtroom voice, "Yes, by god, I'll do it!"

The Regional Director was against the idea, saying that the situation had deteriorated drastically and that the atmosphere had become too charged to permit a civilian to enter the lion's den a second time. But he too was curious and so gave the green light to go ahead.

Billy Knight and Barrie Mackenzie took the professor into custody midway down no-man's-land, lit up his cigar for him, then led him into the centre of the dome amid hundreds of curious convicts. He was soon sufficiently at ease to ask to see one of his clients: me, the man for whom he'd promised he'd win an acquittal. But although Billy's soldiers searched thoroughly for me, I was nowhere to be found. The overturned beehive had become completely congested, and what had once been uncluttered tiers and cellblocks was now dark tunnels of debris and pitfalls. For the short duration of Professor Morton's visit, I was busy exploring the darkest recesses of the attics in C- and D-blocks. January and I were still trying to get at that coffee stash inside the hobby craft area, only this time from a little higher up. Thus it was that I missed out on my lawyer's visit to the dome area.

To the hundreds of rebels who watched his every move as he toured the devastated cellblocks, Professor Morton became an "OK guy." Speaking freely to those gathered around him, he told the prisoners that he would reassure their families, and the families of the hostages, through the media that they were all safe. His visit included a look into the block where the fourteen undesirables were still being protected by the riot leaders. As he spoke to these men some of them expressed fears that they would be set on fire inside their cells and burnt to death. Professor Morton assured them that nothing of the kind would happen, that they were safe. "I managed to calm them down," he later said. "I told them that there was no danger. . . . At that point in time they were safe. "Unfortunately that changed for reasons unknown to me." Like Henry Champ before him, Professor Morton was not permitted to visit the tier where the guards were being held captive. Instead, one of the hostages was brought down to the bell platform wearing a blindfold, and blurted out that for the moment they were all safe.

Shortly after Professor Morton emerged from the dome, he got together with Ron Haggart, and together they drafted a press release intended to provide reporters with a firsthand account of the existing situation within the penitentiary. In this way they hoped to allay the rumours and gossip broadcast and published through the news media. Mr. Haggart put his off-the-record view in these words:

It has been expressed to us by the inmates that they were anxious that people should understand that things were under control in the institution. They were first of all anxious that their own families should understand that they were not in danger, and also they were anxious to convey the impression that the institution was peaceful and being maintained in an orderly fashion.

We thought it would be useful to reassure the inmates inside the cellblock that they were not being regarded by the outside world as animals. There was apprehension expressed to us by the inmate committee that the outside world considered all inmates to be the same and that they were irresponsible people.

The following draft was prepared and referred to authorities in Ottawa:

"Very useful talks have gone on between the two committees and are continuing," Desmond Morton, spokesman for the citizens' committee, said this afternoon. "I am very hopeful of reaching a satisfactory solution."

Professor Morton personally toured the cell blocks this afternoon and is reasonably satisfied with the conditions there.

The following was the joint statement prepared by the Inmate's Committee and the Citizens' Committee:

The hostages are safe, in good health, and are not being threatened with violence. They are being fed regularly and receive their food first, in larger quantity than that now being received by the men.

The inmates have organized their own police force which provides security within the area. The police force is also responsible for safeguarding the hostages. The hostages have been able to send out signed letters to penitentiary officials assuring that they are being well treated.

Complete order is being maintained. There are no sex attacks. Even personal property in cells is being protected. There is little fighting among the inmates. There is fair discipline within the area. No harm is being caused by, or threatened to, persons who were locked up in protective custody by the administration prior to the disturbance. Professor Desmond Morton spoke to these men and confirms this. Those who might have caused harm to themselves have been handed over to hospital authorities.

Representatives of both committees wished to assure wives, close relatives and friends of those in the institution that there is no cause for personal anxiety. As they have repeatedly mentioned, there is no attempt being made, or even suggested, to break out of the institution.

Medical services and sanitary conditions are as best as can be expected under these conditions. There is no immediate health risk. The inmate organization is doing its best to keep sanitary conditions as good as possible.

Although proper meals are not possible, no one is going hungry. The administration is delivering sandwiches regularly which are being distributed equitably by the men following an organized procedure.

The above brief was not approved. In its place the department of the Solicitor-General released its own shortened version:

Three members of the Citizens' Committee entered the area occupied by the inmates at Kingston Penitentiary today to listen to their representations. The Committee Members, in reporting on their meeting, also said they were informed by the Inmates' Committee that no harm has come to any of the inmates in protective custody. This information has been passed directly to the families of the hostages. The Solicitor-General realizes that the families of the inmates are also concerned about the situation and is therefore releasing this information although it cannot be confirmed by the Canadian Penitentiary authorities.

The Solicitor-General, Jean-Pierre Goyer, now sensing a note of resignation coming from the prisoners' camp, thought it politically wise to get more and more into the picture. If the convicts were on the verge of throwing in the towel to the Citizens' Committee, it just wouldn't look good to have a peaceful settlement brought about by five civilians. So late on Friday Mr. Goyer, bowing to parliamentary pressure, guaranteed in the House of Commons that he would personally terminate the riot "one way or the other" by no later than Monday at noon.

CHAPTER

13

WITH FRIDAY FADING into uncertain darkness, Kerry Bushell, one of the five remaining hostages, found himself celebrating his twenty-fifth birthday as a prisoner of the riot. It was a truly humbling experience for the guards to observe the convicts from the other side of the bars, to watch them giving orders, to beg them for the opportunity to step out of the guarded cells to stretch their legs for ten minutes. The five hostages who were being held in the last two cells on 4-B were experiencing firsthand the claustrophobia of being locked away in a tiny steel cage for days on end and the loneliness of being separated from family and friends. One member of the inmate police force guarding them was Ted Woods, a blond Apollo-like man, who was serving a life sentence for murder. Armed to the teeth with primitive weapons, he gripped the bars of keeper Ed Barrett's drum and said with a crooked smile, "Before this is all over I hope you and your men get the full drift of what doing time is really like." Pointing to the lidless toilet, he added, "Having to squat over that shithouse in full view of your cellmates, little things like that which you took for granted in the outside world. I just hope you and your staff learn that the people you guard inside the cages are not pawns, they're human beings."

Sitting in a nearby chair was a hairy brute called the Russian. He interjected, "Teddy is here for life, so don't feel down, boss. After all, you and your men will soon be getting out of here 'one way or the other.' "

Each time a barbed comment was thrown at the hostages they would collectively cringe, having quickly learned never to antagonize their keepers. They were learning what it was like to have to bite back an angry retort. That verbal give-and-take was reserved exclusively for those in the free world.

"Besides, you people should be thanking us," chimed in another wiseacre. "I heard over the radio today that each of you bulls has already earned more than six hundred dollars in overtime pay!''

"Yeah, you just sink your teeth into that good news while you feel the walls of the cell closing in on you,'' said the Russian.

The guards were also getting a firsthand knowledge of what it was like to have pangs of hunger ravage their insides, subsisting on two baloney sandwiches a day, wishing that there was more to eat. Some of the old sages cackled that it was good therapy for them, that all new screws should go through this humbling experience as an introductory course on man's inhumanity to man.

Meanwhile the hostages either whispered quietly among themselves about their chances of survival, or played cards to while away the time. Always they tried to bolster each other's spirits as best they could. Joseph Vallier, a relatively new guard with twenty-five years of army experience behind him, took on the responsibility of pacifying his captors' paranoia each time the military enraged them with new manoeuvres. Although he claimed to be scared to death, saying he had "never prayed so much in my whole life,'' he nevertheless kept the rebel leaders informed as to what the army was most likely to do and not do and thus kept a lid on their tempers and paranoia.

Around one o'clock on Saturday morning the five-man Citizens' Committee met once again with the four-man Inmate Committee to discuss the Solicitor-General's reply on the subject of immunity. Mr. Martin informed the prisoners that Ottawa indicated that there would be no problem agreeing to most of their requests, but that the concession of immunity from prosecution would clearly not be granted. Billy Knight was already upset that the news brief presented jointly by the committees had been shot down. Now there was the bad news that immunity from prosecution was also being denied.

"It's an act of bad faith!'' raged Billy about the bullying tactics that seemed to be coming out of Ottawa. "Goyer's news release was just totally and absolutely useless.''

Barrie Mackenzie, who wasn't facing any criminal charges arising from the prison takeover, shouted Billy down: "Dummy up, just dummy up, we're getting tired of your bullshit!''

Norm McCaud, a 38-year-old counterfeiter serving a long term, pointed out that it was clear that no immunity would be granted. Therefore he now leaned toward settling for the proposal put forward by Mr. Martin, which was agreed to in principle in Ottawa, that if the prisoners surrendered peacefully, their combined grievances would be presented to an appropriate Board or Tribunal, with the participation of the Citizens' Committee, if necessary, and with legal counsel. "We've gone as far as anyone could possibly expect us to go," said McCaud in a firm voice.

Just before the meeting ended around 2:30 a.m., Billy reluctantly gave in. Rubbing his tired eyes and trembling with fatigue, he said in a voice long ago gone hoarse, "So be it, we'll take our chances in a criminal court. All we ask is that the Solicitor-General give us his word that we will not be mistreated."

The five civilians thought that the prisoners were being overly paranoid; they were convinced that such unlawful vengeance was beyond even the lowest guard.

"Believe us," said Charles Saunders in a gloomy voice. "Some of us have reason to fear that we might be murdered, or at the very least savagely beaten, once the guards get their chains on us."

"If a satisfactory solution to the prison population's grievances can be obtained in exchange for the hostages," added Billy Knight, "we would still demand some kind of assurance against physical reprisals by the guards."

Barrie Mackenzie then put forward the suggestion that if they did release the screws, it should be on a pro rata basis. In other words, for every hundred prisoners herded out of the dome to the yard to be searched and reclassified, one hostage would be released when proof was obtained that none of the inmates had been molested.

"That," said Mr. Martin, "is a most reasonable request."

At that point Ron Haggart stopped taking notes and added, "You understand that because the main cellhouse is totally destroyed, you can all expect to be transferred to area institutions."

"Yeah, like Millhaven," added Barrie with a short laugh.

"Because so much uncertainty awaits us," added Billy as he pushed himself tiredly to his feet, "we're going to have to do a lot of convincing to get the diehards to release the hostages and lay down their weapons."

"Put it to a vote," said Mr. Golden.

"It won't be that easy," said Billy, pleading for understanding. "A majority of one vote will not be sufficient. Things do not work that way inside. Without a substantial majority of inmate votes, a settlement cannot be achieved."

"He's right about that," said Barrie as he pocketed Ron Haggart's package of cigarettes.

At this time the Citizens' Committee was convinced that a formula for the peaceful termination of the bingo had been achieved. They were quite certain that the prison population would not only find the terms satisfactory, but would also work out the mechanics for releasing the hostages so that safe passage for all concerned could be assured. Thus the chairmen for both camps called the meeting to a close. By this time everybody concerned was on the verge of collapse from the incredible tension and lack of sleep. As the prisoners filed back to the tomb-like silence of the dome for an inmate vote on whether to fight or give up, Mr. Martin was rushing off to the administration building across the street from the penitentiary to report what had happened to the Regional Director and the warden, both of whom were also on the verge of collapse.

After talking to the Citizens' Committee, Mr. Moloney made notes which set out the following items:

1. No immunity from prosecution.
2. Nobody will go back to government for a rebuttal.
3. No bargaining about who is to come out or where they are to go.
4. As the first hundred prisoners are going out the hostages will be released from time to time.
5. Right to present grievances with assistance of counsel and right of Citizens' Committee to observe if required.

These notes were then read to the Commissioner of Penitentiaries over the telephone, who indicated to both the Regional Director and Mr. Martin that the arrangements were entirely acceptable to the administration.

By then it was after three o'clock in the morning. Arthur Martin and Aubrey Golden, convinced that the institution would soon be back in the warden's hands, decided to leave immediately for Toronto. The remaining three civilians elected to stay and make certain that the transfer of the hostages went smoothly. As the three drove slowly toward their nearby hotel rooms they tuned in to a late newscast and heard the Solicitor-General being quoted as saying that he was dealing with the problem by not making any concessions to the rioting prisoners and that the presence of the armed soldiers was scaring the life out of the inmates. It was a dumb statement. Certainly it caused Ron Haggart, Desmond Morton, and William Donkin to roll their eyes in dismay, knowing that the inmate population was sure to be listening to the same news bulletin.

14

THE NEWS BROADCAST had indeed been over-heard by the rebels. Around four o'clock that Saturday morning the radio speakers inside the dome were suddenly turned off and the cons were roused from their cells and told that a meeting was going to take place. Some of the guys had withdrawn out of fear, like soldiers in a foxhole, not wanting to budge. However, aggressive leaders bristling with clubs and spears pounded on the steel cages to encourage them in no uncertain manner to make a showing. Because of the radio report there seemed to be a small minority whose mood was turning blacker by the hour. Stir-crazy and not responsible for their actions, they were ready to take on the army. Slowly the convicts straggled into the circular dome in groups and pairs. No one came alone. Fear had pushed everyone into the buddy system. The crafty wheelers and dealers who now saw their ship sinking banded together for greater strength in cells near the exits. These were the cons who were in key positions to grow fat on the normal daily grind. They liked their jobs and thus had been opposed to the takeover of the institution and the rocking of their boat. Nevertheless they were too crafty to verbalize their disagreement outside of their own little circle. Instead they concentrated their energy on finding a quick way to surrender should their ship be torpedoed. Stationing himself on the second range in front of the radio room and using the bullhorn to amplify his hoarse voice, Billy Knight called for silence and complete attention. On one side of him were Barrie Mackenzie, Norm McCaud, and his five original co-conspirators. On the opposite side was the surly crowd of Dave Shepley, Brian Beaucage, the Elliot twins, Yankee, and many more hotheads. Billy had just started his speech by saying that the negotiations were proceeding well and we had nothing to worry about when Brian Beaucage flipped out.

"You're full of shit!" he roared, grabbing Billy by the throat.

He swung a short metal bar at his melon, and missed by hitting an overhead beam instead.

"Go easy!" shouted Barrie, as he wrestled Brian's hand away from Billy's throat.

Trembling with suppressed rage, Brian stared hard at his friend, then said in a tight voice: "He's just so full of shit, gambling our lives away like that." His temper once again getting the better of him, Brian suddenly snatched the bullhorn from Knight's trembling hands, saying, "You've had it, you're through talking."

"Aw, c'mon, Brian," cried out Barrie in disgust, "go easy, man, there's enough heat already." With those words he reached past Billy and gently retrieved the bullhorn from his buddy and handed it to Norm McCaud, not having any faith in his own oratorial capabilities.

Just then there came a chorus of voices from the circular galleries requesting that Billy Knight have his say. Norm McCaud handed back the bullhorn to Billy who, taking strength from the supportive voices, continued shakily. "We've lost our civil rights and now we're on the verge of losing our human rights . . . ." He went on to make a not very memorable speech, and from that point on it was obvious that Billy was no longer in the driver's seat.

Throughout a leaderless Saturday morning and afternoon incoherent speeches were made by Barrie Mackenzie's loosely knit group, but they amounted to nothing. No real attempt was made to secure a vote because nobody wanted to stick their necks out and vote in favour of giving up to the authorities. Meanwhile Dave Shepley, Brian Beaucage, and their breakaway group regarded the meeting with increasing hostility, each individual brooding, sulking, and becoming awesomely dangerous. They were hurting from years of oppression at the hands of the guards, and their memories were making them unpredictable. Unlike the average convict in the prison population, who let the screws push him around in order to be left alone, rebellious individuals like Dave and Brian were incapable of letting themselves be abused by the guards. Their insubordination earned them a lot of cooler time, clubbings, and tear gas while bound hand and foot in chains. When the officials spoke of only 25 percent of the prisoners being active participants in the riot, they were talking about these individuals who could fluctuate between good and evil, depending on how they were being treated at the moment. What was building up inside the dome was a mass suicide pact orchestrated by the insane element, men who hoped that their one-sided battle with the army would be emblazoned in banner headlines around the world. Their self-destruction was intended to show the world that the prison system as it stands is dreadfully wrong and totally incompatible with rehabilitation.

Barrie Mackenzie, who had no axe to grind with anybody, simply wanted a peaceful solution to the bingo so that people wouldn't die. He wasn't the type to make fancy speeches or dream up specific grievances; nevertheless he found himself more and more at centre stage. His position was akin to that of a passenger aboard a hijacked airliner who finds both pilots zonked, and being a man of action instinctively takes control of the plane and undertakes the monumental task of trying to land it with instructions from the tower. But he has to contend with the small band of hijackers who say they'd rather crash in flames than give themselves up to the authorities. So how does he handle the situation? The easy way out would be to wash his hands of the whole mess, but that's not his nature, so he stubbornly plows ahead while desperately trying not to make anybody mad at him.

Later on Saturday afternoon nerves were becoming so frayed that good buddies turned to punching each other over the smallest of disagreements. The prison hospital treated three inmates for an assortment of cuts and bruises. There was also a great deal of distrust building up. Some con was feeding information to the authorities by dropping kites out of the cellblock windows near the chapel area, but his identity was never discovered. Some of the guys thought the information leak might be coming from Ralph Lundrigan, a hospital orderly who was acting as medical and food intermediary between the authorities and the prisoners. He was warned that his life would be in peril if he made another trip to the dome, and that the best thing for him to do would be to stay in the hospital from then on.

Some of the "silent majority" were of the opinion that if a secret vote could be taken about 80 percent of the cons would opt to end the siege and take whatever knocks were coming to them. Barrie Mackenzie and Norm McCaud agreed that this was certainly the case, but that the radical element would insist on an open vote, knowing only too well that nobody would want to be openly branded "chicken" or worse yet risk the disfavour of the diehards. Barrie chose his words very carefully so that he could never be accused of influencing anyone.

"I'm not here to tell you guys what to do, but if you decide to pack it all in and let the hostages go, then you got my word that I'll be the last man out, with the last screw."

The guys went off in small groups to discuss what had been said, but nobody wanted to say openly what he felt. Thus the issue of the vote remained a question mark. Finally it was dark and most of the prisoners settled down around the dome to watch the hockey game on television. Some of those who didn't take an interest in hockey playoffs took on the duty of scouting, peeking out through the grimy cellblock windows at the enemy troops, gripping spears and clubs just a few feet away from army demolition experts who were planting heavy explosives against the outside walls. It was through observations like this that we were able to conclude that if the army did attack, they would not come through the barricaded exits as we had assumed. Instead they planned to blast straight through the two-foot-thick walls. It was obvious to us that the stone fragments would create disorder and casualties, and for this reason we avoided the targeted areas like the plague, except for checking them periodically and piling more and more mattresses against the planned point of entry.

Now that most of the "renovating" was over, there wasn't a hell of a lot we could do to keep our minds off the revenge we knew was waiting for us at the hands of our keepers. I for one kept nudging myself to stay awake and on point, telling myself that in sleep there was danger. I was also aware that lack of sleep brought a new danger — hallucination and impaired judgment. Maybe that's why everybody's hands were trembling so violently and they were yelling and jumping at unexpected sounds. Pushed beyond human endurance, guys resorted to sniffing industrial glue, their faces pushed into a plastic bag, inhaling deeply until their eyes turned into their skulls so that only the whites showed. They were the worst sight of all, snapping and growling at each other like wild animals. Others dulled their fear and resentment by other means. Step-Ladder still refused to come out of his cave. As he muttered and chanted to himself, Do-Die and I brought him blankets and the odd sandwich, imploring him not to remain there in case the army attacked.

"Cowfuckers!" was his only reply.

January and I just prowled around, our experienced eyes not missing a trick. With such a variety of characters, it was interesting to see how our numbered friends reacted under stress. It was like a wild party where everybody seemed to be taking note of tidbits of scandal to be whispered over at a later date. A few prominent characters within the prison hierarchy who were known as outspoken opponents of institutional sex were caught red-faced in homosexual acts. Almost everybody had their cell doors blocked off with blankets for privacy, and nobody entered without announcing themselves. In one case a guy rushed up to the cellblock to tell his good buddy something. Knowing that his friend was an avowed "straight," he didn't hesitate to pull the blanket aside without knocking, and . . . lo and behold! Although sworn to secrecy, he couldn't help telling another person, who in turn told another friend, who in turn . . .

By late Saturday afternoon the three members of the Citizens' Committee who had stayed behind were sufficiently alarmed at the deteriorating turn of events to place a call to Toronto urging that both Arthur Martin and Aubrey Golden return immediately to the penitentiary to negotiate further. Coinciding with their arrival that Saturday evening were additional reinforcements of army troops, bringing the overall contingent to more than five hundred soldiers. This hammered home the point to Mr. Martin that the government was running out of patience. In fact he was briefed along these lines by the penitentiary brass shortly after he returned to the prison. He was informed that the time available in which to negotiate a settlement had been shortened. The impression given was that a secret deadline had been fixed by the authorities.

The Inmates' Committee was in and out of the hospital wing all that day, advising that a settlement proposal had not yet been accepted or rejected by the inmate population. When it became clear that Barrie Mackenzie and his men were having a great deal of difficulty in getting that green light, both committees got their heads together and decided that it might be best to ask the warden and the Regional Director to join in the talks. Around this time Mr. Moloney was getting calls from the Commissioner and Deputy Solicitor-General, who expressed concern that new settlement proposals might be drummed up in an attempt to renegotiate the release of the hostages. During the last of the telephone calls the

Regional Director was given specific instructions from the politicians in Ottawa. These notes were then passed on to the Citizens' Committee and were as follows:

1. Remind the Citizens' Committee they are not to negotiate in any way, shape, or form.
2. The administration wants to know what are the proposals of the inmate population.
3. No more information or point of clarification is to be discussed.
4. The Minister wants to know first before any answer is given.
5. The Minister wants to know what they are going to do with the hostages.
6. Then we will discuss ways and means.

The pressure was on! Members of the three groups racked their brains for ways of persuading the prison population to accept the meagre proposals. Meanwhile Barrie continued to ride the fence, while fearing that the army might attack without warning.

Shortly before midnight a meeting of the three groups was interrupted by an urgent telephone call from the dome area. The few crisp words whispered to Barrie Mackenzie were enough to cause a noticeable tremor in his hands as he slammed down the receiver. Without explanation the three convicts hurried out of the hospital, past the machine-gun entrenchment, and into the dark cellblocks.

The members of the Citizens' Committee later testified that it was obvious some kind of disturbance either had begun or was about to break out in the area held by the prisoners. As a result the Regional Director and the warden got sufficiently alarmed that they immediately conferred with senior army officers as to the feasibility of an armed assault in the event of any indication that either inmates or hostages were being injured or killed. They were informed that it would not be possible to assault the prison successfully before daylight. The Regional Director then advised the army to prepare for any eventuality. He also requested that the warden order the morning shift to report for duty at 6:00 a.m. instead of 8:00 a.m. That order was given.

Mr. Moloney then reported by telephone to the Commissioner of Penitentiaries in Ottawa to advise him of the alarming developments in the main cellhouse and to inform him that negotiations appeared to have become stalemated. The Regional Director was then advised that the Commissioner of Penitentiaries, the Solicitor-General, and senior members of their staffs would proceed immediately to the prison by helicopter.

Meanwhile, in the dome, the shit had hit the fan. The latest rumour was that there would be no concessions, and that we had the choice of giving up the hostages and surrendering in one hour or the army was going to come in with guns blazing. Before the population could vote on whether or not to throw in the towel, a handful of screws did a very stupid thing. They axed a hole through the thick wooden door leading to the auditorium passageway so that they could be in a position to use a fire hose if fire broke out. The result was pandemonium. Some of the prisoners were actually leaning against the door when the pounding started, and they shouted the alarm: *"The army is coming! The army is coming!"*

The militant prisoners stopped whatever they were doing and headed for the top ranges, vehemently urging others to join them there in order to fight a bloody battle. Windows and lights were smashed, and more and more mattresses were fastened to the upper railings to be used as shields. Most of the prisoners rushed up to the top tiers, thinking that it was safer there if the army did burst in with guns blazing and no questions asked. The thought of screws with guns was terrifying because they were not known for their restraint or cautious gun-handling. Also they would be more than a little bit pissed off at anything wearing a prisoner's uniform.

At this moment Barrie Mackenzie, Billy Knight, and Norm McCaud rushed into the dome, only to be stopped in their tracks by the sight of all those hostile prisoners gripping spears and clubs, prepared to roll down tons of metal on their heads.

"What the hell is going on?" Barrie wanted to know, his words echoing throughout the circular galleries. "C'mon, I want to talk to you guys."

Slowly some of the cons filed down the maze of stairs and, still gripping their weapons, took up positions around the main floor. Still others filled the second and third galleries while throwing questions and complaints at the committee members a mile a minute. Barrie was so uptight that he almost forgot the ominous presence of the militants still on the top tiers who were glaring down with increasing hostility.

Fending off questions for which he had no answers, except to reassure the population that the army was not attacking, Barrie stood uncertainly at the railing in front of the radio room for long seconds and finally blurted out in frustration, ''For fuck's sake, you guys better get with it or a lot of us are going to die!''

''Nobody is going to give up to the pigs!'' A voice came booming down from the top tiers. It was Dave Shepley, straddling the railing and gripping the bullhorn with black gloves. ''No more talking, it's time to fight!'' Brian stood at his side brandishing a crude spear and whispering suggestions to Dave. Other men, big and brawny, grunted their agreement. ''We're calling the shots from now on,'' Dave shouted down at the upturned faces. ''Ain't nobody giving up!'' Suddenly all the guys on the top tiers started beating their clubs rhythmically on the railings. As the noise increased more and more cons joined in, until the sound of pent-up anger was loud enough to raise hairs on the backs of the necks of the army.

Unwilling to push too far in one direction or another, Barrie didn't try to sway the mob any further at this time. Instead the three committee members elected to return to the hospital wing for more talks. Their one chance lay in wrestling some kind of golden nugget from the prison officials, something tangible that might appease the militants. Overcome by it all, Billy Knight decided that his nerves couldn't take the pressure any more. He requested a sleeping pill, and permission to sleep in a hospital bed. The warden readily complied, thinking that his absence might further erode the determination of the others to stand and fight.

Still fearful that the army was on the verge of bursting in, Dave and Brian again urged the cons milling about on the dome floor to join them on the top ranges to fight. Their demand was accompanied by name-calling and threats until some of the more popular cons started slowly climbing the stairs in shame. Most reported that they were afraid not to do so. As one inmate said: ''I could see that the insane element had taken over, and I decided to go with my friends at least up to the third range.'' Another stated: ''By that time nobody had any will of their own.'' Some of the guys who were living on the third tier had started down to the dome floor, but angry club-waving made them turn around and go back up. Not everybody went up. Some just turned deaf ears to the threat, while others wandered off into cells along the bottom tiers.

After half an hour of running around the top tiers fortifying positions and tearing up pieces of white sheets, wetting them down to be used as a defence against a tear-gas attack, there was a sudden change of plans. A dozen of the militants rushed into the radio room and ordered the operator to churn out rock and roll music over the amplifiers strung around the dome. Again manning the bullhorn, Dave told everybody, "The fun is about to begin!" It was decided that the hostages and the inmate undesirables would be dragged out to the centre of the dome and tied to a circle of chairs. After that, blood would be drawn from each of them in order to show the army that we meant business and would kill if invaded. While Brian led one group to gather up the undesirables on 1-D, Dave and company went around to 4-B where the screws were being guarded on the top tier.

The inmate police force grimly refused to allow Dave Shepley and his gang onto the range. Blocking the way were the enormous Wayne Ford wielding a heavy sledgehammer inches above his bald head, Teddy Woods armed with a heavy chain, and directly behind them the crafty ex-boxer Cyril Rousseau gripping a deadly spike-studded shield in both beefy hands. Also crowding the narrow tier were a dozen more hulks bristling with weapons and ready to do battle. Ironically the opposing forces were good friends under normal circumstances, but now they were ready to kill each other.

"The hostages belong to us," growled Cyril in broken French. "If they gotta croak we'll kill them; until then back off!"

In his own stubborn way Dave could appreciate their position, but he had to give it a try anyway. "Crap! Billy Knight is no longer calling the shots, and neither are you guys, so give us the pigs."

The knuckles of the cons guarding the screws whitened as they gripped their weapons more tightly and shook their heads. "No way, pal," muttered Wayne Ford.

The argument went back and forth for a few minutes until finally Dave backed off in disgust. He and his group returned to the main floor of the dome to direct their anger at the undesirables.

The loud blare of rock and roll music camouflaged most of the screaming coming from the first floor of D-block where the thirteen rapos and diddlers were being dragged from their cells and across the dome floor with the militants punching and kicking at them every inch of the way. They were tied to straight-backed wooden chairs in a big circle amid the wreckage while hundreds of fiery-eyed convicts lining the circular galleries screamed down at them, "Kill the baby molesters! Give them a taste of their own medicine!" As their hands and feet were being securely tied to the chairs, somebody at the very top of the dome dropped a hundred-foot chain into the circle. It was used to bind the inmates' legs to the chairs. At the very centre of the circle was the bell platform, which now had an altar cloth draped over it, on top of which was an assortment of burning candles, chalices, and short iron clubs. Meanwhile the one remaining spotlight glared down from the top of the dome, illuminating the sacrificial circle. The narrow beam of light and the flickering candles created bizarre shadows. The population beat a hair-raising death march on the metal railing with their iron bars, a sound that got louder and louder as preparations were made to bleed the undesirables.

There were no plans to kill anybody, at least not at first. The idea was to give the prison and army staff the opportunity to witness firsthand through the cellblock windows how far the militants were prepared to go. Brian Beaucage and Dave Shepley assumed that the enemy would then reconsider trying to rescue the hostages and regain control of the prison. Still gripping the bullhorn in his black-gloved hand, Dave loudly exhorted the other prisoners to join him within the circle as a show of force. Only about 10 percent of the guys went down to the main floor; another 10 percent elected to remain on the top tier to fight under Brian's leadership; the remaining 80 percent remained on the second and third tiers in a warily neutral attitude.

It was approximately one o'clock on Sunday morning when Dave Shepley announced over the loudhailer that he knew there were more undesirables hiding in the cellblocks. He added with a cruel laugh, "All diddlers and finks please step forward!" As his words echoed throughout the dome and the maze of cells, those individuals who were guilty of such misconduct burrowed deeper into their lairs. From the beginning the search for undesirables had been going on in a halfhearted way, but now the pursuit became deadly serious. In the beginning there had been a reluctance to invade the privacy of a cell that was draped with blankets. But now wolf packs on the loose probed and sniffed deeper than ever in search of victims. In Harold St. Armour's cell they found Ralph Lake, Melvin Travis, and Ron McCorkel, all lurking behind a barricade of beds and furniture on the third tier of F-block. A fight ensued in which Travis and McCorkel were overpowered by the Elliot twins and company, while still others took off in hot pursuit of Lake, who had managed to escape. Like a fox pursued by the hounds he hightailed it through the crowded tiers desperately searching for a safe place to hide, but the militants on the top tiers kept pointing him out to his arch-enemy Brian Beaucage. Finally, as Ralph tried vainly to climb down a network of bars to reach another tier, he was cornered by a tough hombre called Kowalchuk. Brian immediately knocked Ralph to his knees with an iron bar, saying: "I've been waiting four years to get you, you little rat fink."

As Lake joined Travis and McCorkel inside the circle of chairs which now included sixteen battered individuals, his old man Harold St. Armour, who had wisely decided to counteract his image as a "joint man" by becoming an active militant, had to watch his "sweet kid" being dragged bleeding and screaming into the circle to be tied to a chair. It took a lot of fervent whispering in Dave Shepley's ear by St. Armour to get Ralph's punishment postponed until Harold could dig up some legal correspondence from Ralph's cell, documents he claimed would prove extenuating circumstances. Harold better not be giving us the runaround," said Dave ominously to Lake, "or we're gonna cut you to ratshit!" St. Armour then dragged Lake, still tied to the chair, to a position under a stairway and left to search for the so-called documents.

Travis, a huge muscular black man, sat bleeding in a chair in the circle. He was about to receive some mighty blows from the Elliot twins, when another black man, a young and popular homosexual, rushed into the circle to argue on behalf of Travis, claiming that there were also extenuating circumstances in his rape case.

"No way!" roared Beaucage from the top tier. "He stays right where he is!"

"Yeah," growled Kowalchuk, "this asshole forced some white broad to go down on him."

But the young homosexual stood his ground and, relying on his popularity with the militants, continued arguing on behalf of his black comrade until somehow he got his way and dragged Travis out of the circle and under the stairwell next to Lake. The gutsy black youth hoped that the mob would forget about Travis long enough for him to cut his friend loose from his chair. Travis was having a great deal of difficulty breathing because his nose was broken in two places. Ralph Lake, who had a bloody sheet partially wrapped around his head, sat very quietly with his eyes squeezed tightly shut.

Satisfied that he had enough undesirables tied to the chairs, Dave Shepley signalled for an end to the bar-pounding and announced, ''The show is about to begin!'' It was decided that the militants would start things off by breaking every nose in the circle so that the blood could be seen by the screws with binoculars on the gym roof. Dave set down his bullhorn on the bell platform and walked up to the first undesirable.

Grabbing a handful of the inmate's hair, he yanked the guy's head backwards and brought the edge of his gloved hand down hard on his nose. There was a sickening crunch and a massive flow of blood. The undesirable squirmed in wordless agony. Other militants immediately followed suit by breaking the noses of the remaining fourteen prisoners, sometimes striking many times in frustration before the bone would break. Starting off the butchery were the Elliot twins, the Yankee, and St. Armour. As things got really messy and the scent of fear grew stronger, the mood of savagery induced more and more bystanders to join in on the torture.

The cruellest of the lot were two very young prisoners, Bobby and Eddie, who had grown up in a string of foster homes and who under ''normal'' circumstances were handsome and likeable nineteen-year-olds. It was a surprise to everyone to see them manifest such a cruel streak. This was their opportunity to create a macho image in place of the ''sweet kids'' image they hated. In an effort to upstage the seasoned psychos, they added extra little touches of cruelty, like violently twisting the bleeding noses to see if they were truly broken, which brought forth anguished screams from their victims. Their combined inner hostility was awesome, repelling those who had to watch to the point that one newcomer foolishly rushed onto the dome floor yelling: ''For god's sake put a harness on those two!'' The crowd groaned as they watched the new fish put his head in the lion's mouth.

''He must be a diddler,'' shouted the Rebel as he smashed the man on the side of the head with a long iron bar. The guy screamed in pain as his glasses went flying and he tumbled on all fours into the circle with blood flowing down his face. ''Fucking goof!'' added Dave Shepley as he booted the fish squarely in the face. Cursing a blue streak, the two boys pounced on the man as he tried to regain his balance and beat him viciously with short iron bars. Suddenly the bar-pounding started up again and the newcomer took the opportunity to scramble madly out of the circle. Then, standing upright, he staggered dazedly into one of the darkened wings where he remained hidden for the duration of the riot.

That incident dissuaded anyone else who might have entertained thoughts of intervening in what was becoming a bloodbath. Not even the army with all their weapons or the prison officials with their silent promises of retribution could halt the torture at that stage. The overriding concern was for the safety of the guard hostages, and as long as they remained unharmed Satan would have his feast.

One of the Elliot twins, not to be upstaged by the two younger cons, approached each victim, saying: "You've got a real nice nose there, but it's kind of twisted, so I think I'll reset it for you." He would then pull their heads violently backwards and chop them across the nose with a short iron bar. A shaggy-looking militant carrying a wooden shield studded with sharp spikes drove the pointed ends into McCorkel's shoulders and the back of his head after he complained about choking on his blood.

It was absolutely awesome how hard the human skull appeared to be as one head after another was rocked back and forth by tremendous blows from iron bars. Still, hardly any of the undesirables cried out or begged for mercy. They were almost like zombies, and that provoked the militants into taking even mightier swings at them so that the heavy metal smashed even deeper.

Among the undesirables two in particular were high on the extermination list, their crimes so despicable that they were not expected to survive the riot. The first was Bertrand Robert, who had disciplined his children by burning their bare bottoms on a red-hot kitchen stove. The courts punished him with a six-year sentence, but his fellow prisoners had a much higher penalty in store for him. The second was the Camel, who had undergone a severe beating earlier in the bingo, and who was now tied to a chair in the circle to await further punishment for his crime of raping two little girls. His life sentence was considered too light for the damage he had inflicted on his victims.

Saying that he was fixing it so that the undesirables could "go out in class," Dave Shepley had the loudspeakers turned all the way up so that wild music pulsated throughout the cellblocks. Each of the executioners tried to be more macabre than the next guy by asking the victims loaded questions. No matter what answer they gave they were sure to be tortured, and if they gave no reply they'd be accused of being disrespectful to their captors, which would bring an avalanche of bar blows and kicks to the groin. Smokey, an old con who looked like a midget, seemed to be a favourite target of Bobby, who played games with the little man in a way that turned the stomachs of the hardest criminals watching from the circular tiers.

"Hit me again, sir," Smokey would cry out.

"Don't sir me — you bastard!" Bobby would then smash the man across the kneecaps with an iron bar.

"We're going to play a game," Bobby would say with a big grin. "Tell me, how many ribs are in your body?"

"I really don't know, sir."

"Well, take a guess — thirty-two, thirty-four?"

"I just don't know, sir," Smokey would reply apprehensively.

"Well, let's find out," answered Bobby as he pushed his painter's cap to one side and started systematically smashing Smokey's ribs, crying out in glee each time he thought he'd broken one.

Meanwhile I was manning the wall telephone about ten feet behind Smokey. Before he returned to the hospital for more meetings, Barrie had asked me to relieve one of his men who had been monitoring the life-line for twenty-four hours straight. Barrie and Norm called the dome several times between midnight and 2:30 a.m. to get an update on what was taking place. I refused to go into detail for fear that our conversations could be overheard, but I did tell him that everything was going haywire, that he'd have to see the situation for himself. In an extremely emotional voice that was so hoarse I had to strain to hear his words, Barrie shouted, "That crazy son of a bitch is going to get everybody killed! Tell Dave to come on the fucking blower!"

Because of the loud music and all the bar-pounding I had to go into the circle to tap Dave on the shoulder and deliver the message. Following him back to the telephone I had to brush past young Bobby, whereupon I took the opportunity to ask him to give little Smokey a break. He was so stoned that it took him long seconds to focus on me. "Sure, Rog, sure," was all he said. Then he swaggered over to where Bertrand Robert was tied and whacked him a terrific blow on the head. "This is for boiling your kids!"

The bloody sheet covering Smokey's head had shifted so that he was able to see me out of the corner of his bloody eye. "I'm taking it pretty good, ain't I Roger?"

Startled, I blurted out, "You are indeed."

"Think I'll make it out of here alive?"

"No, I don't think so," I replied in a choking voice.

"You're probably right," he mumbled as I walked away. "God," I thought as my vision blurred, "wipe these memories from my mind." January said he had been sick to his stomach twice and had seen others in the same condition. Most of the guys concluded that the safest place to be was right here in the dome, gripping the railings, staring down at the atrocities with glazed eyes, and pounding the railings when told to do so. If the wolf packs did find somebody hiding out in his cell they'd ask with barely suppressed hostility, "Are you with us or against us?" and explain that everybody was needed in the dome for a show of force.

As I returned to the phone I heard Dave laughing eerily at Barrie's concerns. He laughed even more when he was informed that Norm McCaud had just folded under the pressure and asked to be locked away in a hospital cell. "Don't sweat it, Barrie, there's just the two of us, and by dawn we'll all be tits up!" With those chilling words Dave returned to the circle just in time to overhear one of the undesirables request that St. Armour ask the population to vote on whether to continue the beatings or not. Dave laughed and butted out his cigar in the man's battered face.

The Camel and Bertrand Robert were treated more savagely than the others, and at one point the Camel was bleeding so profusely from facial cuts that one of the Elliot twins placed an old mop over his head to stem the flow of blood. I saw Robert swaying dizzily in his chair trying desperately to balance a burning candle on top of his head. It had been placed there by the Yankee, who told him that he'd beat his brains in if it fell off. Eventually it did, and he was struck so hard with an iron bar that his chair crashed over backwards onto the concrete floor. The Camel was also struck so hard that his chair fell over several times and his head hit the concrete with a sickening crack. The undesirables must have figured that their only chance of survival was to play dead, which was no easy task since they were being probed everywhere for signs of life. Young Eddie, a former altar boy in the Catholic chapel, particularly enjoyed breaking the undesirables' kneecaps in an effort to jolt some life back into them. When the militants started smashing the undesirables across the shins with iron bars, those of us forced to watch felt really sick because everybody could readily identify with that particular pain. At one point the Elliot twins swung their iron bars simultaneously and struck Robert on each side of his head, once again knocking him to the floor. It took him a while to regain consciousness, and when he did he kept vibrating. This bugged some of the pipe-men, and they ordered him to quit.

By three o'clock most of the undesirables seemed to be unconscious or dead. It was about this time that Barrie showed up in the dome to see for himself what was going on. The sight that greeted him made his knees sag. He flopped down in the chair I had just vacated beside the phone, muttering "Lord Jesus Christ, everybody is insane!"

Nothing Barrie could say would change the mood of the militants, who were intoxicated by the smell of blood. It was made very clear that Barrie should continue the negotiations if he wanted to, but that he had better not interfere with the torture. He could easily have retreated back to the hospital and gotten himself safely locked away from the nightmares in the dome, but like the gutsy kind of guy he was Barrie decided to stay and communicate directly from the cellblocks with Ron Haggart. These two extraordinary human beings were all that stood between the antagonists and another bloody Attica.

CHAPTER

15

"I'M GOING TO GET Step-Ladder out of that service duct," I said to January Jones as I gave up my position on the phone to Barrie, "If the army crashes in and finds him lurking that close to the hospital entrance they'll waste him for sure."

"If they do come in when you're down there, they'll do a number on you, too!" argued my good buddy.

"Yeah, maybe so, but he's going to be a sitting duck. Can you imagine him throwing 'cowfuckers' at the army? Naw, I've got to dig him out of there."

"Want me to go with you?" volunteered January, pulling a tattered blanket around his shivering body.

"No, thanks, he's too spooked to receive company."

I took a final look over my shoulder at Dave Shepley smoking a fat cigar while pouring flammable liquid over the heads of the undesirables. "Should we torch the turkeys?" he shouted through the bullhorn at the downturned faces. "No!" gasped half of the prison population in horror. Dave just laughed and shouted back, "OK, later!" Like a cave man one of the Elliot twins had a fur piece draped over his shoulder as he danced savagely to the loud music. Meanwhile his brother was busy plunging a syringe needle filled with salt and urine into the neck of one of the undesirables. From the top tier the brawny Russian yelled down, "Bleed, you motherfuckers, bleed!" The prisoners on the centre tiers whispered that the crazies were getting even crazier, that the cons guarding the screws were spoiling for a fight, and that all the inmates on the fourth tier were now operating as a unit with one thought in mind: "Kill the hostages and fight the army if they have the balls to attack."

"Roger, you're nuts too!" I thought as I entered the tunnel between A- and B-blocks, which was now in total darkness. Somewhere at the far end was Step-Ladder, less than the thickness of one cell wall away from the machine-gun emplacement at the hospital entrance. Lighting my candles I gave a nervous little chuckle and mumbled, "Fuck you too, Warden." As I cautiously picked my way through the debris I could hear a faraway mumbo-jumbo of words and suddenly relaxed when the cursing became more distinct: "Bunch of cowfuckers!"

"Step-Ladder," I whispered over the flickering light, "come here." There was a sudden flurry of activity and then silence. "C'mon, don't be horsing around or I'm going to take off on you," I said in an attempt at reverse psychology that got me nowhere. "You got Do-Die there with you?" I asked, knowing only too well that our little pot-bellied friend was too crafty to trap himself in a corner like that. Pushing stubbornly on I added, "You've got to get out of here or the army will zap you for sure when they come storming in."

"Bunch of snakes squatting over their eggs," shouted Step-Ladder unexpectedly from somewhere in front of me. I could tell that he was confused and upset and thus unpredictable. My hunch was confirmed when he struck a match to light up a rolled cigarette, displaying long scratch marks that ran from below his eyes right down to his chin that had been self-inflicted in his fear. The light from my candles showed him hunched down behind rolls of decaying tarpaper and wrapped tightly in the blankets I had brought him. "I tried burning the webs, but it don't work, cowfuckers won't fire up," gasped Step-Ladder as the match burned his fingers and the butt dangled from his lips. By then I was hovering right over him. I grabbed him by the trailing bandanna wrapped around his head and gave him a mighty tug which sent him sprawling forward on all fours. "OK, the webs are loose," I said grimly. "Now let's get out of here." The poor bastard let out an ear-piercing screech and hightailed it right back to his corner.

Nothing I said would get him to move, so reluctantly I had to give up helping my friend. Besides, I was suffering myself, not only from hunger and cold, but also from a toothless socket throbbing for attention.

It was after four o'clock in the morning when I came back to the dome to find Barrie Mackenzie whispering hoarsely into the blower to Ron Haggart in an effort to find a peaceful solution that would end the riot. They were both under enormous stress. Behind the reporter the army was massing for a dawn attack, with newly arrived politicians ready to move depending on how the dice fell. Behind Barrie inmates were being tortured, and an even greater sense of doom emanated from the top tiers as the militants prepared for a last-ditch stand. As death knocked loud and clear, Barrie must have been asking himself how in hell he ended up in charge.

Barrie asked Ron Haggart urgently, "How much longer have we got to make up our minds before the army comes in?"

Arthur Martin, who was standing at the reporter's side, whispered into Haggart's ear that Barrie should try to arrange a settlement by 5:00 a.m.

"Don't shit me, man! If those bastards are coming in the next few minutes, then say so. If not, don't make me bullshit my friends."

"I won't bullshit you, Barrie," said Haggart. "it's up to me and you now; after 5:00 I can't promise you anything."

Mr. Martin immediately went to the Administration Office to report to the Solicitor-General and his staff, who had arrived at the penitentiary and were reviewing the situation in conference with prison brass. He told the Solicitor-General about Barrie's brave efforts to swing the prison population around and to get the militants to surrender. Mr. Martin pleaded for more time, saying that he felt no drastic action should be taken right away, at least not until Barrie Mackenzie had exhausted all avenues of persuasion. Mr. Martin then got the impression that he was imposing himself and had interrupted the brass in their war games. Possibly they were planning an assault on the cellblock come sunrise. Thus, feeling that he was not a party to the feverish whispering, he withdrew from the room. But his concern that precipitate action might be taken led him to return moments later to tell the Solicitor-General that he hoped that before any aggressive action was taken a warning would be broadcast over the loudspeakers to the inmate population advising them that they had just a few minutes to give themselves up, thus allowing those who wanted to surrender to come out peacefully. The Solicitor-General advised Mr. Martin that this would be done.

Barrie was succeeding in getting more and more convicts behind his effort to convince the population to throw in the towel, all except the diehard militants who were now becoming more and more determined to resist violently. On the main floor the pools of blood around the undesirables were getting so thick that one of the rebels brought out a pail and started mopping it up. Surprisingly, when one of the younger undesirables protested that the Polack was threatening to tear away his crucifix, the Yankee came to his rescue and said: "Let it be." By this time both Melvin Travis and Ralph Lake had somehow been freed from the ropes that bound them to the chairs and had fled into the maze of cellblocks to lick their wounds.

Inside the circle Eddie was viciously wrapping wire around the forearm of one of the undesirables in an effort to stem the blood pouring from a deep slash.

"What in hell are you doing?" Dave wanted to know.

"I'm saving the asshole's life," Eddie replied with a grin.

"Fuck it, let him croak, they're all going to die!" Dave then scooped up the guy's false teeth from his lap, placed them carefully on his head, and smashed them to pieces with a short club he was carrying in his gloved hand. One of the militants then poured salt on the open wound, which brought forth howls of anguish from the victim. All of the undesirables were now trying to fake death, and most of the cons looking on were of the opinion that these guys were all dead. Outside the cellblock windows it was still dark, and the baleful spotlight continued to illuminate the gruesome stage for the devil's disciples.

"Nope, this one's not dead yet," said the Yankee as he tore a bloody sheet from the head of a rapist called Malone and pitched the liquid remains of whatever it was he was drinking into the man's face. "I need some meat to go with this moonshine." He then withdrew a very sharp knife from his belt and with crazed eyes slashed deeply into his victim's right thigh in a downward and then sideways motion until finally he gripped a large chunk of flesh in his bloody fingers. The crowd's gasp of horror superseded the long shuddering scream that burst forth from Malone's lips.

The great majority of inmates did not approve of what was going on, but they were afraid to interfere for fear that the same thing would happen to them. One prisoner, testifying in court later, stated that he made it look as if he was going along with the whole affair: "If you tried to stop the beatings, you'd end up joining the undesirables in the circle." He said that when somebody he didn't know asked him what he thought, he would reply, "Well, I think they are getting what they deserve."

Another witness stated that he had cheered in the beginning, and that he had given the thumbs down signal. He said: "I had no love for these people, but I thought they were only going to be tied up. One little guy called Smokey was shaking and begging them not to kill him as they dragged him from his cell on 1-D, but somebody cooled him down by telling him that he was going to be tied down so he could watch television. So feeling as I did when they came into the circle, I didn't mind seeing them get punched a few times."

Other typical remarks from the spectators were:

"The scene in the dome was mind-boggling, absolutely horrible, a real torture chamber that made everybody sick."

"After the beatings had gone on for a short time I took sick at the sight of it all and left for my cell. It was the worst sight I ever witnessed in all my life. I still think about it at night."

"I watched the beatings for about an hour; there was so much blood and suffering that it made me sick. I took a chance and went back to my cell where I got sick to my stomach again. After that I just couldn't go back and witness any more beatings."

"I left a few times. The torture and the sight of so much blood made me ill and I had to go for walks."

"I could not stand the sight of all that blood, so I hid in the cellblocks."

There were others, however, who obviously enjoyed the spectacle, constantly shouting encouragement to the militants, even throwing objects on the undesirables and giving the thumbs down signal when a particular punishment was suggested.

Dawn was not too far off, and the scouts were reporting increased activity on the part of the military, including lots of helicopters coming and going inside the walls. Most of the militants were convinced that an armed attack was imminent, so there was a great deal of pill-popping and consuming of anything else that would get them high. The evil that had invaded the minds of the rebels now took on even greater proportions as fear and rage made them lose touch with reality.

By now all the radio speakers had been turned off, and except for low moans and groans from the undesirables, the dome area was as silent as a graveyard. But then, as hundreds of horror-filled eyes watched, one of the Elliot brothers brandished a very sharp knife and slashed the Camel's right thigh open to the bone. The population sucked in its breath in shocked disbelief a split second before long shuddering screams erupted from beneath the white sheet that covered the Camel's head. Huge quantities of blood poured forth from the wound as his head jerked spasmodically with each heartbeat. Not to be upstaged, the Yankee rushed over to the Camel's side with a silver chalice gripped in one hand and an iron bar in the other.

The Camel's eyes glazed over and child-like whimpers came from his throat. He kept jerking up and down in his chair, his chains rattling eerily in the otherwise silent dome. The Yankee filled the chalice with the Camel's blood and toasted the man with a satanic grin: "Here's to you, sucker!" He then drank from the chalice until blood ran freely down the sides of his mouth. Wiping the gore from his lips with his sleeve, the Yankee added: "Time for you to die!" Then, as the inmate population gasped in revulsion, the Yankee beat the Camel's brains in with his heavy iron bar.

That the Camel was dead there could be no doubt. His head sagged backwards in the chair, his eyes gaping. Grey matter oozed from a hole in his forehead.

The terrible silence was shattered by young Eddie who, laughing loudly, approached one of the undesirables tied to a chair in front of the barricade leading to the keeper's hall. The victim was an old convict named Allan, who had been locked up in the protection block because he had been branded a stoolie. The militants had deliberately placed him in front of the barricade as cannon fodder, telling him that when the army stormed the cellblock he'd be the first to get a bullet. Allan had a plastic pail pulled over his head upon which Eddie amused himself by beating out a tempo with a short iron club.

"The Camel's dead, you old fucker, and you're gonna be next unless you recite the Lord's prayer, word for word!" Try as he might the old con couldn't recall all the words. "I'll give you another chance to save your rotten skin," growled young Eddie. "I wanna hear you say the alphabet backwards without a mistake."

"I can't, I never went to school." moaned Allan from inside the pail. Then, as blood dripped down the sides of his neck, he pleaded, "C'mon, guys, my head is hurting awful." With those words he lost consciousness.

At that moment somebody shouted, "Six! Sixty-five!" Everything went deadly silent as all eyes stared in the direction of the huge barricade erected in the centre of no-man's-land in A-block, as if everyone expected a horde of soldiers to come charging through the hospital entrance. In the sudden silence Barrie could be heard whispering urgently over the wall blower to Ron Haggart as a dozen prisoners hovered tightly around him to better hear what was being said.

"What the hell is shaking?" growled Dave.

Somebody waved Dave to silence and explained: "I think Barrie is getting word that the army is going to blast its way in."

"Fuck the army!" snapped Dave from the inner circle. Still gripping the bullhorn in his gloved hand, his white running shoes covered with blood, he shouted, "Any of them skinners still breathing?"

"No sign of life over here," grinned the Yankee as he smashed Bertrand Robert over the head with his iron bar, knocking the undesirable over backwards in his chair. "Least he ain't breathing normally," added the Yankee as he wiped his bloody boots across the man's head, causing his body to jerk about on the floor.

"Well, let's cut the turkeys loose and toss them back in D-block where they belong," said Dave as he looked up to Brian, who was gripping the railing on the top tier, for approval. "We're gonna need the space to fight the army."

The militants involved in the beatings ignored the drama occurring between Barrie and Ron Haggart and went on a final orgy of head-busting. With whoops and hollers the dozen executioners released their victims from the chairs they were tied to by smashing the wood to pieces with heavy iron bars. The sound of heads hitting the cement floor was absolutely sickening. The undesirables displayed awesome resiliency by playing dead convincingly under these horrendous circumstances. It was hard for any of us witnessing the mock release to believe that there were any survivors among the fourteen battered individuals, some of whom were being unceremoniously dragged into D-block with pieces of chairs and chains still attached to their limbs. Several inches of brackish water covered the floor of the protection wing from the previous hosing down of the undesirables. To the sodden mattresses and other debris, a new element was now added—a grotesque heap of twisted, bloody bodies. Some were still blindfolded and one had a pail over his head. None of them cried out despite the blood spurting from their open wounds. Water entered their gaping mouths and bubbled out.

A bunch of guys gathered around the body of the Camel at the entrance to 1-D to watch as young Bobby, stoned out of his mind, talked to the corpse as though it still contained life, cursing and kicking it. In a further act of savagery he stooped down, dug his fingers into a hole in the dead man's forehead, and plucked out some brains! With a satanic laugh the boy wiped his hands on his hockey sweater and disappeared into a nearby wing like an actor leaving the stage. Afraid that the army might find the body and use it as an excuse to shoot blindly, a group of prisoners tried stuffing the Camel into a nearby garbage can, but his limbs kept sticking out over the sides, so they simply left the body near the unlocked entrance to D-block.

The cellblocks were still in darkness as I turned to January Jones a few feet away from where Barrie was talking on the phone and said, "I'm going over to 1-D to see if Smokey is still breathing."

"Well, you hang on there, ol' buddy, and I'll tag along." Both of us were shivering violently in the chilly morning air as we pulled our tattered blankets more tightly around our shoulders and slowly made our way across the dome floor through groups of emotionless zombies all waiting for god knows what. Even the warriors on the top ranges were strangely silent as they sulked and fondled their crude weapons.

Approaching the steel barrier leading into 1-D, we paused to stare at the body of the Camel stretched out on his back in a pool of blood. What struck me most was not his eyes gaping wide in horror or his lips drawn back to display bared teeth, but the awful colour of his skin, a pasty white, all the blood having seeped from his gawky frame. I decided to put an end to the morbid sight by covering the body with a soggy mattress, a broken chair, and other odds and ends, which camouflaged the evidence of the foul deed. We then entered the protection block with prickles running up and down our spines. Almost everybody else avoided the area like the plague. The morning fog was drifting in through the busted windows, and in this man-made hell we could see murky forms crawling painfully like distorted turtles through the brackish water toward the dark cavernous cells. The victims must have thought it was no longer worth feigning death. As we moved through them they stared at us with vacant eyes or begged us for cigarettes as they propped themselves up against the cellblock walls. One man whom we could not recognize because of his battered face and who had one eye dangling on his cheek was instinctively seeking the shelter of an open cell by crawling on all fours. So great was his fear that when January and I bent down to pick him up he gave out a gurgling sound and fainted dead away.

Halfway down the range we located little Smokey trying to stand up by hanging on to the wall radiator, his normally friendly face a grotesque mask of battered flesh, so bloody that he looked like something out of a nightmare. Upon seeing me he gave out a funny little laugh and through broken teeth said; "I'm still alive, Roger." With those words he started to fall forward and I had to lunge to catch him. I shouted to January to drag a dry mattress for him out of one of the empty cells. As we laid him down we draped his shivering form with our blankets and told him that no one was going to hurt him any more. Both his kneecaps were smashed, and through his torn bloody shirt we could see broken ribs. Still, the euphoria of having survived certain death caused him to keep grinning and saying things like: "I took it like a man, didn't I, Roger?" Choking back tears, I assured him that he stood tall in my eyes. Smokey then told us how the riot leaders had purposely left his cell gate unlocked from the beginning of the bingo, urging him to go into the population, telling him that they knew he wasn't a stoolie, but that if he remained on 1-D he might be branded as one. But his drum was his security blanket and he refused to leave it, although he had ventured out into the population from time to time to see what was going on. In that period of madness when all his neighbours were being roughly hauled away into the dome, young Bobby refused to leave him behind.

"That Bobby is crazy!" said Smokey with a shudder. "The others wanted to let me go, even the big Russian said to him that I wasn't a fink, but the young fella beat and kicked me all the way into the circle — he's crazy, I tell ya!"

I calmed him down as January rounded up more blankets to drape over the little man, who was now puffing greedily on a blood-stained cigarette. As the sun started to creep over the prison walls, more inmates drifted into the cluttered cellblock, some to help, others to just stare numbly. Even the militants were tending to the wounded and providing blankets and mattresses. Barrie and some of his friends showed up bristling with weapons and stated that there would be no more killings. He told us to carry the undesirables from the shelter of their cells into the open. He pointed out that none of them should be left completely alone to lick their wounds, that they might be murdered, especially where there would be no witnesses.

"Do they know up front that there's a dead person in here?" I asked Barrie.

"Hell no!" he exclaimed.

A tired January asked Barrie if the population was going to throw in the towel and give up.

"Looks that way, leastwise nobody seems to be objecting any more. It's just a matter of working out a system for releasing the screws. Now I better head back to the blower and convince my man that everything is under control in D-block." Barrie's voice was barely a whisper and his features were ravaged by the strain and responsibility of trying to keep the lid on the human volcano.

Minutes after Barrie left D-block, Jezebel timorously entered the range. As she sloshed through the bloody water she was crying softly at the terrible sight that surrounded her and asking, "Can I help you fellas?" She was wearing a poncho made out of a red blanket, and although she was cold she peeled it off and placed it over a battered individual shivering by the cellblock wall. "Hugo is passed out in G-block; said to wake him up when the riot is over," she told me.

Bertrand Robert, the middle-aged man who was serving time for burning his children, had been removed from his cell at Barrie's orders and placed on top of a soggy mattress on the range. He was in really bad shape, but less than ten minutes later he somehow managed to stagger to his feet and, weaving from side to side like a drunk, he tried to make his way back to the dubious safety of his drum.

"Holy shit, will you look at him," shouted somebody as he pointed to Robert groping blindly for the doorway. As he tried to take another tentative step forward he made a gurgling sound and fell flat on his face. He never regained consciousness, and he died later of massive head injuries.

Back inside the dome tension had again mounted to an incredible intensity as the militants on the top ranges once more opposed surrendering without getting some kind of protection against prosecution. However, most of the fire was fading from their eyes. They became less vocal and more tolerant of Barrie's efforts to stave off a bloody battle that couldn't possibly be won. The only real hum of activity centred on Barrie as he stood gripping the telephone receiver in one hand and brandishing a pair of cutting shears in the other, while all around him anxious faces pulsated with anxiety and repressed excitement. At the other end of the line was the equally rugged Ron Haggart juggling two phones at a time, one to the prisoners in the cellblock, the other to the warden's office where Arthur Jarvis had his finger on the trigger.

"How much longer do we have to make up our minds?" croaked Barrie.

"Five-thirty, Barrie. Your men have got to put down their arms and be ready to come out of the cellblock by that time." As he spoke Haggart looked across the room at Arthur Martin, whose lips were forming the word "earlier." "Even that might be too late, Barrie. You've got to be ready to release the hostages immediately and come out when ordered."

"We're not all on the same wavelength in here," groaned Barrie in agony. "Tell them not to crowd us, we need more time!" This was followed by a barrage of voices directed at the inmate spokesman, who shouted back, "Cool it!"

Minutes later Barrie called Ron Haggart asking again how much time they had before the army and the screws came storming in. Haggart really didn't know what the brass was planning, but all his instincts screamed that an attack was imminent, especially since moments earlier he had spotted an army general. Even a civilian knew that invasions were led by generals. From where he was seated he could see a tiny slit of light appearing in the sky over the prison walls. He said, "Barrie, the army always attacks at dawn."

Like wildfire the word spread throughout the cellblocks that the army was going to attack at dawn. The place came to life. The savage sound of metal on metal resumed, and as the tempo got louder and louder confusion reigned supreme, even among the militants. "All right! All right!" shouted Barrie into the blower. "You'll get your hostages, but only on the exchange that we agreed upon: one screw for every hundred of us that gets out to the yard safely."

In seconds Haggart had the green light from the ministers to agree to the terms. "Tell them we want to see our first hostage now, right now!" said the Solicitor-General.

"There's no alternative. You tell them it's the final thing," said Deputy Warden Doug Chinnery, who was manning another phone to Regional Director John Moloney, whose command he had just relayed. Chinnery was a soft-spoken gentleman, later credited by members of the Citizens' Committee as being marvellously cool. For four sleepless days and nights he maintained a sense of optimism whenever despair was at its greatest. The brass and politicians, fighting back tears and hysteria and sensing defeat among the prisoners, suddenly decided to push hard and fast for that elusive white flag.

Without a guarantee of amnesty for those who had provoked the riot, without grandiose plans for TV appearances by inmates, Barrie Mackenzie was succeeding through sheer personality in bringing the rudderless bingo to an end without massive bloodshed. He was rallying the majority of ragged, panic-stricken men around him whose own personalities and reactions ranged over the entire human spectrum. Still, Barrie was plagued with doubts and paranoid (in spite of the Citizens' Committee's promises) about what the army and guards might do when the prisoners tossed down their weapons. Suddenly he started balking, saying that he wanted a vote to be taken among the prison population.

"We can't breathe in here, things are so tight!" croaked Barrie. "Gimme another half hour so we can vote and think straight."

In a voice that echoed Barrie's emotions, Ron Haggart breathed into the antiquated phone that was crackling with static, "I can give you no guarantee of what will happen in the next half hour. I strongly suggest that in the next two minutes you get a definite decision." Haggart could hear Barrie arguing to the crowd gathered around him, which he interpreted as meaning that some semblance of order had been restored to the dome. Even the bar pounding had stopped. That meant to the Citizens' Committee that rational decisions could be made. The reporter tried desperately to interpret the undertone of what was going on, arguing Barrie out of his worst fears and passing on his requests through the communication chain to the brass. Barrie could be heard clearly through the telephone lines shouting to his crowd, "You guys have just two minutes to make up your fucking minds!"

Although the Citizens' Committee and the brass were hearing rumours of incredible savagery and degradation, Doug Chinnery never believed that anyone was dead inside or, as he said, if there were, it was only one or two. The deputy warden kept his cool throughout the ordeal and was able to make calm decisions despite the wildest rumours.

Finally Haggart was hearing something tangible, that the prisoners were ready to file out with their hands on their heads in a pro-rata exchange for the hostages. "Can you assure me this is the unanimous, or almost unanimous, decision of the population so that there will be no fights when the movement starts?"

"Can you promise a bear won't shit in the woods?" was Barrie's reply.

Haggart turned to Chinnery and said: "Mackenzie assures me a hostage comes out with each group we release to the yard. He says there will be no fights as the inmates leave, in his opinion." The deputy warden wanted to know if the prisoners were prepared to be moved to any of the area prisons. Haggart could only judge by Barrie's mood at the other end of the line that the men wanted out in general and would accept any transfer, at least for the time being.

By this time it was full daylight and most of the brass were gathered tightly behind the machine-gun entrenchment at the hospital doorway that gave access to A-block. Standing next to the wide-open steel barrier like a friendly beacon was Professor Desmond Morton, with a cigar butt clenched between his teeth. He would be the first outsider to greet the prisoners—not the screws, not the army or the warden, but a trusted civilian who was putting himself on the line for the sake of peace.

Suddenly something went haywire and all hell broke loose as the several hundred convicts gathered around the entrance to A-block panicked and stampeded toward the hospital entrance with their personal belongings gathered in their arms. Like demented fools they clambered madly over the obstacles midway down the range as the militants on the upper tiers screamed "Traitors! Traitors!" and threw debris down on their heads.

Stationed at the telephone around the corner from where Professor Morton was standing, Ron Haggart couldn't see what was taking place, but he could hear the guards shouting: "Get back, get back!" In the rush to shut the steel barrier and the wooden door, Professor Morton was knocked to the floor. The guards then poked their weapons through the gun ports and quickly fired three shotgun blasts into the ceiling of A-block. The stampeding prisoners had already been forced to seek shelter beneath the overhead catwalks to protect themselves from the shower of debris that was descending on them. Now with the shotgun explosions resounding throughout the cellblocks, most of the convicts were forced back to the centre of the dome. Here they gathered, wincing under the hard stares of the militants on the upper ranges and checking their bodies for bullet wounds.

Sick with the fear that people might be dying at that very instant, and distressed that the plans for getting the hostages and prisoners to safety had fallen apart, Haggart had to fight back tears to keep his voice level as he spoke into the telephone. "Barrie, I would advise you not to go into the corridor, it's not safe even for you!"

"Some of the guys are still pinned down out there, tell the screws to back off!" roared Barrie into Haggart's ear.

"They're holding their fire, but Barrie, don't let a man move anywhere. Tell them to stay put and they'll be safe." Catching his breath, Haggart continued: "Is everything under control now? You say some of your men are in the corridor and are going to stay there. No, no, it's not a trap. If they stay put they'll be safe."

The blower went dead for a few minutes and in the background Haggart could hear Barrie shouting: "Mike, you and the guys hang in there, don't budge and everything will be cool."

Back on the phone Barrie asked what guarantee he had that the screws wouldn't blow him away if he personally led one of the hostages to the hospital gate.

"Believe me, Barrie, they won't throw down on you in any way. We need you and they've asked that you personally walk out each hostage, including the very last one. The understanding is, if you don't end up going back, the deal's off. Now you go ahead and bring out the first hostage."

"I'll do that, but first of all you tell them to let the first batch of our guys out to the yard without hammering away at us."

The columnist heaved a deep sigh and turned silently to the deputy warden, who was feverishly whispering into his phone. Chinnery nodded his head solemnly. Moments later those who were still trapped in the corridor of A-block once again flooded toward the hospital entrance. Forced to squeeze through the partially opened barrier one at a time, they were pushed against a wall and minutely frisked at gunpoint. All the bigwigs were there looking on with tense faces, including Desmond Morton, who was there to make sure that none of the prisoners got their brains smashed in by the screws, some of whom were bubbling over with suppressed venom.

It was almost 6:00 a.m., and Barrie was ready to cut loose the first hostage, but the militants refused to give one up, saying they wanted proof that the two hundred men who had poured out to the yard through the hospital entrance had not been beaten. Haggart assured Barrie that the movement had been carried out peacefully by the army, but the radicals wanted solid proof. Professor Morton volunteered to go out and check for himself. He talked to a lot of the cons sitting down in the middle of the yard guarded by soldiers. This was not good enough for the militants, so in desperation Barrie suggested that the dome clerk, an old respected bank robber by the name of Johnny Hance, be enlisted to go out to the yard to talk to the guys and then report back. The brass agreed to this reluctantly. Johnny really didn't want to get involved in this no-win situation. Nevertheless he went along with it and was escorted out to the badlands by a crusty old keeper who had known him for many years. With his heart in his mouth, Johnny clambered over the obstacles in no-man's-land, squeezed past all the soldiers and screws in the hospital, then walked nervously out to the yard in full view of the gun towers. Happily, the dome clerk was able to report that all was well.

The first grateful guard to be released was young Kerry Bushell, whom the population voted should be the first to go. He had not been a screw long enough to have made any real enemies. Still decked out in inmate clothing, Bushell was led down the winding staircases, trembling and only half believing that he was going to be freed. The young hostage was supported by Big Wayne Ford and Barrie Mackenzie, who had to bulldoze their way through the throngs of prisoners blocking the way. At the entrance to A-block Ford left the hostage with Barrie, who took a deep breath and moved slowly toward the machine-gun nest and the waiting officials. Halfway down no-man's-land Barrie heard a noise high above him and looked up just in time to catch some of the radicals about to push down an avalanche of steel on the guard hostage. With an angry gesture and an accusing look he somehow prevented the act from being carried out, and the final few feet were navigated safely. At the hospital entrance the brass practically scooped Bushell up into waiting arms, and the iron gate slammed shut.

Forgotten in the emotional welcome, Barrie Mackenzie returned silently to his position in the dome to negotiate the release of yet another hostage, thus keeping the communication channels open.

However, the militants came up with yet another reason for not releasing a second guard, stating that they firmly believed that their fellow inmates in the yard were not really being transferred to area institutions, that they were probably being bused through the front gate, then right back in through the rear gate. The fear was that all the rioting convicts would be forced to live in the devastated fortress and be brutalized every day. The militants demanded that proof positive somehow be obtained that those gathered in the yard for a strip search did indeed reach other prisons safely. So, once again, a reluctant Johnny Hance was pressed into service, this time to count busloads of prisoners roaring out through the big front gates where throngs of people were gathered in a circus-like atmosphere. Although the old bank robber was tightly encircled by military personnel, he was nevertheless threatened by hard-line guards who said that he was "going to get his" once the insurrection was quelled.

Satisfied with Johnny Hance's report that the buses could be seen heading away from the penitentiary, the militants then gave the thumbs-up signal to release another hostage on the agreed terms. Johnny agreed to remain between the front gates for a few more hours counting and checking the busloads as they left for parts unknown. The Sunday weather had started with a 35°F chill. Nevertheless "the best show to hit town since the winter carnival" brought out hordes of gawkers who swelled the ranks of media, police, and penitentiary staff. Some had even brought their transistor radios to make sure they didn't miss the afternoon hockey game between the Montreal Canadiens and the Chicago Blackhawks, who were vying for the Stanley Cup. Vendors were busy selling cold and hot drinks, hot dogs, and popcorn. Even a bootlegger got into the act by selling booze from a picnic basket until the local fuzz collared him and threw him into the paddy wagon. Also given the bum's rush was a television cameraman who had climbed high up into a tree in front of the prison gates. It wasn't long before the local police had their hands full directing traffic jams and ducking military helicopters as the release of the hostages and the transfer of prisoners slowed down to a more cautious pace.

Watching all the activity with a look of awe on his sad old face was the dome clerk, who hadn't been out in the free world almost since the days of horse and buggy. "I oughta be out there where I can see further," complained the retired bank robber. "The lads are counting on me."

"I would have to be crazier than a shithouse flea to let you do that," fumed his escort as he pointed to a tightly knit group of young people bravely brandishing placards in support of the prisoners' grievances. "Those poster-carrying hippies out there would jump at the chance to slip you some marijuana!"

"You ain't just shitting, boss," cracked Johnny. The screws could never quite figure out whether that old con retort was insulting or not.

The men and women standing up for "prisoners' rights" were mostly university students. They received no plaudits from the prison authorities, who were itching to tear-gas them. "Bad taste," muttered a beefy-faced police sergeant staring hard at the young people in T-shirts and faded jeans, "bad taste." When an army jeep carrying a courier armed with a sub-machine gun pulled up to the front gates, the group dashed across the street holding their signs aloft for the sudden flurry of TV cameras. "Justice for the Prisoners!" read one sign. "We Support the Prisoners!" said another. One of the soldiers guarding the front entrance pointed his rifle at the demonstrators and shouted: "You're on federal property, get out!"

And so it went. Talk, laughter, and the sound of robins in the elm trees as the day got warmer and warmer. Sometimes the townspeople ignored the life-and-death drama that was unfolding inside the grey walls to bicker with one another about who was going to win the hockey game, other times they philosophized about the criminal justice system, but mostly they circulated wild rumours.

"I hear there are fourteen dead already," whispered a research lab technician to a young couple carrying sandwiches and a picnic blanket. "It has to do with a power struggle among the convicts."

"Sixteen!" chimed in another.

"Those prisoners should all be put in the army and sent to Viet Nam," argued an elderly variety store operator. "Too many nice boys are getting killed over there."

One jogger in a red gym suit seemed oblivious to the crisis and just kept jogging down King Street without so much as a look. Assistant warden Edgar Babcock, a 46-year-old crew-cut scoutmaster who claimed to have slept only four hours in the four days of rioting, still found time to collect film canisters discarded by the television crews for use as survival kits whenever his Boy Scout troop went on hikes. "They are watertight and they float, just what we need," he said.

Until the buses loaded down with prisoners started pouring out through the front gates, everybody agreed that the best spectacle had been the changing of military guards. The machine guns and automatic rifles were a special delight for the children, who greeted their ominous appearance with cries of delight and applause. A policeman standing guard near the front lawns chided the crowd, claiming that there would be few smiles if they were able to glimpse what was taking place inside. But even the police, grim and increasingly impatient, smiled when a lone soldier carrying a portable TV and a family-sized bottle of pop appeared at the front entrance. Meanwhile the smaller tots amused themselves by methodically collecting discarded pop cans and patiently building a "can tree."

Suddenly two buses loaded with about sixty prisoners manacled to each other roared through the front gates of the penitentiary led by OPP cruisers with sirens screaming. Unaccustomed to all the excitement, one of the civilian drivers swiped a concrete pillar, prompting a roar of approval from the large crowd of spectators. Shoving clenched fists through the small windows of the chartered buses, the prisoners gave victory signs and shouted,

"Power to the people!"

"They are taking us against our will!"

Following closely behind the cavalcade of vehicles was a black prison scout car piled high with tear gas and riot sticks that would soon be dripping with blood. Painted in bold letters along the sides of the Frontenac Coach Lines bus were the words "Scenic Motor Coach Tours." Watching the circus on wheels go careening madly down the narrow street was Johnny Hance, gingerly picking himself up inside the gates after leaping for his life. Brushing himself off, the old bank robber turned to his keeper and said quietly,

"You can take me home now, boss. I've seen it all."

Still flapping high in the wind at the very top of the dome was the banner proclaiming "Under New Management!"

AFTERWORD

SUNDAY MORNING stretched out for the survivors of the bingo like the memory of a horrible nightmare. The convicts sprawled about the ruins like dead men. A crude sign painted in dripping red paint on the dome wall declared "The Devil Made Me Do It!" Another black-humoured remark requested a tommy gun, a case of thermite grenades, and a pepperoni pizza to go. Satan had supped here, and now that his disciples had danced to his bloody tune they all seemed deflated. Although still outwardly tough, the militants' consciences were making them cringe. Even the Yankee had remorseful tears in his eyes as he tended to the injured in the protection block.

The last hostage to be released was keeper Ed Barrett, whose wallet containing $270 was slipped to him intact as Barrie Mackenzie escorted him into the waiting arms of his comrades. The news media would hail Barrie in front-page headlines as a hero, the individual who single-handedly prevented a bloodbath. The Solicitor-General would finally meet him at the hospital entrance with a warm handshake and a word of appreciation.

A far different sort of reception committee was waiting for Billy Knight and his five co-conspirators, most of the militants, and a large number of innocent inmates who had the bad luck to be riding on the buses that were singled out for special treatment. As the heavy vehicles loaded down with prisoners and club-wielding guards pulled in through the rear gates of the Millhaven complex, they were deliberately decoyed away from the front of the institution where the brass and media were gathered, so that the unloading could be carried out at an isolated rear dock out of sight of civilians.

Waiting on the loading platform were two long lines of riot-equipped guards, renegade screws whose thirst for revenge was making them just as crazy as the militants who had beaten the undesirables. But these club-wielding con-haters didn't discriminate. They were psyched up to crush any skull belonging to a prisoner, mine included. The evil that had gripped the militants in KP had now come around full circle to take possession of the meanest screws, goons who seemed to forget that the hostages had walked out of the riot alive because they were protected by the very men whose bones they were about to break.

With our chains clanging loudly against the concrete floor, we were forced to move quickly through the human gauntlet, totally unable to defend ourselves. Our tyrannical keepers inflicted a hail of crushing blows from both sides. Billy Knight was struck over the head so hard that his skull cracked like an egg. Unable to get back on his feet, he was kicked and cursed, then roughly dragged away to a solitary cell to await further punishment for leading the rebellion. With each blow the screws landed they'd shout that they were now in charge of the zoo and that we were going to learn the hard way who was boss. One gaunt prisoner who was felled by a nightstick clawed at his face in anguish and cried out: "Yes, yes, we have sinned! Beat us, torture us!"

Throughout all the brutality and pandemonium only one man dared to shuffle at a leisurely pace with his head held high, almost impervious to the clubs that thumped his head and shoulders. Dishevelled and sporting a huge black eye, Step-Ladder was an awesome sight as he plunged right into the enemy without bothering to raise his manacled hands to protect himself. With one baleful eye he glared at the screws, muttering right and left, "Bunch of cowfuckers!" (One month after the bingo ended, Step-Ladder, who seemed to have gained a new stature in life, was informed by the prison chaplain that his only brother had gone berserk, shot his wife and two children, then killed himself. This time Coolidge was unable to break away from the invisible webs that gripped him. He was dragged away, screaming, to the funny farm.)

In later years there would be those who would jokingly remark that the Millhaven Super Maximum Penitentiary must have been constructed over a sacred Indian burial ground. In this way they would try to explain the spine-tingling horrors that stalked the cellblocks of the multi-million-dollar nightmare where violent death became a way of life. The barbed wire complex was, and still is, the scourge of Canadian prisons, with more murders, riots, and unrest than all the other institutions put together. Millhaven was plagued with bad luck from the day it was forced to open its gates prematurely. The evil that had lurked for so long inside the walls of old KP had now been shifted to the "Haven."

The remaining inmates were dispersed to area institutions of lesser security. Those of us who were transferred to the maximum security complex were kept dead-locked inside our electronic cages licking our wounds in surly silence while the repercussions of the Kingston riot continued for months to be hotly debated in front-page headlines across the country.

Often from our cell windows we would hear the melancholy sound of the Montreal-bound train speeding past somewhere into the night. It never failed to trigger off howls from the attack dogs inside their kennels, which in turn would spook the jackrabbits grazing by the barbed-wire fence, giving the screws in the gun towers the opportunity to chase the furry little critters with their spotlights. During the day bored prisoners would also amuse themselves by snaring quarrelsome seagulls outside their cell windows. After dragging the flapping, squawking birds through their cell bars, they would paint them gaudy colours or attach long kite tails to their legs, then release them amid roars of encouragement from the faces behind the gallery of tiny windows.

With only our nagging consciences for companions, we had to struggle daily for survival in the isolation of our cells, while boisterous guards tucked safely away inside their impregnable spaceships controlled our lives with the mere press of a button. The Haven continually erupted in violence and destruction amid clouds of tear gas. At night we dared not sleep soundly for fear of being pounced upon by nocturnal goon squads who prowled the dark ranges with their bingo blacklist in an effort to even the score. My next-door neighbour was a hulking inmate called Cabana, a noisy clown whose bark was worse than his bite. He became the first murder victim inside the maximum security complex. I could hear a violent struggle but no outright cries, for to cry out even in the grip of death was against the prisoners' code of silence. His killer had terminated Cabana because he was "too lippy."

A young prisoner called Glen went crazy with grief when he learned that his brother had committed suicide in the segregation block of the Haven. In desperation he tried to climb the barbed-wire fences in broad daylight and was shot dead by a guard in a nearby gun tower. Although the bullet left a hole the size of a baseball in his chest, the screws later pouted like juveniles and demanded even more powerful weapons.

Glen and his brother were feared and hated by the hard-line guards for the roles they had played in a prisoners' solidarity movement that sought prison reform and recognition for all prisoners' human and civil rights. The violent deaths of the brothers and those of the forty or fifty men and women who die every year behind bars in Canada have become the focus of a national rallying cry. Every year on August 10, a peaceful one-day hunger strike and work stoppage is held in all the federal penitentiaries across the country to commemorate the dead. They are also paid a silent tribute in the prison chapels on what has become National Prison Justice Day.

It wasn't until four months after the riot that justice came into the picture and individuals started paying their pound of flesh, including eleven guards charged with assault in the infamous gauntlet, a landmark case that was unprecedented in penal history in that the evidence that was bringing the guards to court was based solely on the credibility of prisoners who were alleged to have been beaten. Adding to the circus-like drama was the electrifying trial of eighteen convict militants, twelve of whom were charged with the double murder of two of the undesirables, and six others with the kidnapping of the six guards taken hostage. Add eighteen flamboyant lawyers plus a small army of prison guards and policemen to the courthouse scene, and the stage was set for pandemonium to reign supreme. By the time the jury trial had stretched into its second month both sides were throwing their hands up in despair and agreeing that plea bargaining to lesser charges was the best way to end the charade.

Brian Beaucage pleaded guilty to assault and had two years added to his ongoing sentence. Dave Shepley got fifteen years on a reduced charge of manslaughter. Their ten co-accused averaged three to eight years. They would in fact be punished twice — the harshest treatment awaited each of the mutineers inside the solitary confinement cells in Millhaven at the hands of revengeful guards.

Of the original six who started the bingo, five pleaded guilty to forcible seizure and received three years apiece, including one of the defendants who ended up with a broken back.

As for Billy Knight, the man who started the riot, he was found not guilty! This was further proof of his awesome ability to manipulate people, this time through the art of disguising himself so cleverly that the guards taken hostage were unable to pick him out in the courtroom. Billy was delighted, but no one else was, least of all his fellow cons, who all turned against him and placed his life in jeopardy.

Billy Knight was to spend the next eleven years in protective custody, where he died of a heart attack, a bitter man, spewing out his political speeches to the end. Dave Shepley died of a drug overdose, perhaps trying to forget the dead that haunted him. No one was to escape the jinx of old KP, not even Barrie Mackenzie, now serving time for manslaughter, reduced to a skinny, shaggy creature washing pots and pans in the kitchen, where he speaks to no one, his mind destroyed by the memories of the bingo.

The dozen penitentiary guards appearing in court on charges of assaulting the prisoners in their custody were either all acquitted or else the case against them was quietly dropped. Nevertheless, just watching them sweat bullets before a judge was like letting a gust of fresh air blow through the antiquated penitentiary service. Even more revolutionary in scope were the sixty-five bold recommendations made by a parliamentary investigative committee probing the causes of the riot. The inquiry was serious, fair, and thorough in its struggle to drag the penal system out of the dark ages and humanize the punitive aspects of doing time. Some of the first real changes in Canadian penology came not long after the riot in the form of new directives instructing the wardens to implement policies such as upgrading the qualifications for new and old-line guards in an effort to promote professionalism. A new dress code for inmates was also instituted in which ID cards with photos replaced the old tag numbers sewn to our denim tunics. They even allowed us to grow our hair longer to encourage individuality. Both sides received substantial pay increases. Conjugal visits in family-type trailers were cautiously implemented for long-term prisoners, and more letter-writing and visiting privileges were allowed. The wardens were urged to open stronger communication lines with the prison populations via elected inmate committees who reported back to their fellow cons by way of minutes tacked to bulletin boards. Most important of all were the new avenues we had to air any grievances we might be harbouring. One was the new position of a correctional investigator appointed by the Solicitor-

General, through whom an inmate could launch an appeal on internal decisions made by the warden or prison staff. Another was the formation of a community advisory council of independent observers who would visit the penitentiary on a regular basis to hear any complaints. Thirdly, all maligned prisoners were free to write unscrutinized letters to their local Members of Parliament.

As for Kingston Penitentiary, one half was salvaged, and after a hasty reconstruction period its infamous gates once again swung open as a place of confinement, but this time it had a new role as the medical and psychiatric treatment centre for the region of Ontario. Recently KP celebrated its one hundred and fiftieth anniversary by parading antique cars down the main street and launching a coffee-table book that depicts the old bulwark in pictures and text. It just goes to show that old penitentiaries never die, they just rust away.

On May 21, 1971, a telegram from Professor Morton was shoved under my cell door. It read: "Sentence quashed — new trial ordered — congratulations!" Moments later a tremendous cheer resounded throughout the cellblock as word of my astonishing victory was carried via the grapevine to every con in the joint. A few days later I was returned to the city jail in Toronto to await a third jury trial in July on the same old charge, but this time around I had a legal genius in my corner. I also had a bellyfull of bitterness at having to be put through the legal grinder once again for a crime I had not committed.

As a result of the mistreatment of the inmates by the penitentiary staff, the Citizens' Advisory Committee felt betrayed, and with Professor Morton at the forefront they waged a relentless media campaign against the Solicitor-General to have the prisoners' civil rights restored. Thus I was particularly happy for the ailing professor that he had been able to gain such a triumphant success in the appeal courts. Not only did he receive glowing accolades from the legal community, but he was able once again to tilt the scales of justice in favour of the underdog.

The professor was just as tenacious during my ten-day trial, electrifying a packed courtroom with his legal expertise. At one point the prosecutor threw up his hands in despair and declared with a wry smile: "How can I be expected to compete against such an esteemed colleague who obviously knows the books by heart!'' When a grim-faced Sergeant Kane took the stand he was asked point-blank: ''Did you not at one point kick my client right in the balls?'' For the observers, many of them young lawyers, the trial was tremendously exciting and dramatic; but for me sitting quietly in the dock it was all horribly painful. The verdict was rendered at the ungodly hour of one o'clock in the morning — not guilty! The joy of being completely exonerated was wonderful after almost two long years of uncertainty.

Later, in the privacy of the cloakroom, everybody had tears of relief in their eyes. I sat there trembling violently with the professor's judicial robes draped over my shoulders. Breaking out a bottle of cheap Spanish brandy, Gunter told me, ''Roger, what you need is a good stiff drink.''

''Good idea!'' said a gruff voice. ''I think we can drink to that.'' Looking up I was disturbed to see Kane and Lupo standing in the open doorway. ''I was humbled in there today,'' Kane continued in a mellower voice, ''but it will never happen again. I've learned something.'' The two detectives each had a quick drink, then as they were leaving Kane turned and said to me over his shoulder: ''I'm giving you twenty-four hours to get out of Toronto. Good luck.''

For a minute there was heavy silence, then with that Irish bulldog smile on his face, the professor exclaimed, ''Roger, I think he likes you!''

EDITOR'S NOTE

ROGER'S INITIAL reaction to being exonerated of the charges against him was one of joy. But the reality was that he had spent almost two years in prison, two more years of his life wasted. Overwhelmed by the injustice and scarred by the horrifying experiences he had witnessed, he was a wounded and haunted man when he left the courtroom that night. Ordered to leave Toronto, he boarded a train east and got caught up in the Montreal underworld. He embarked on a binge of bank robberies which resulted in his arrest four months later and a sentence of twenty years. Ironically, this sentence became his ticket to freedom. He went back to prison and finished *Go-Boy!*, the writing of which enabled him to come to grips with his nightmares and personal demons and to find some peace of mind. He was paroled in 1979.

GLOSSARY

A.R.   *armed robbery*

B & E   *break and enter*
beef   *criminal charge*
bingo!   *riot*
bit   *prison term*
bitch   *indeterminate sentence*
blower   *telephone*
bootlegging   *selling unauthorized booze*
bug   *a homemade water heater*
bull   *prison guard*

can man   *safe cracker*
chain   *prisoners in transit*
cherub   *disastrous situation*
cooler   *the hole*
con artist   *smooth-talking crook*
county bucket   *local city jail*
crank up   *inject dope*
croaker   *prison doctor*

damper   *the hole*
darvons   *a depressant drug*
dead-locked   *not permitted to come out of your cell*
dead time   *unproductive*
diddler   *child molester*
digger   *the hole*
dissociation   *solitary confinement*
double sawbuck   *twenty-year sentence*
downer   *a disappointment*
drag-queen   *female impersonator*
drum   *cell*

ducket   *put on report*
duds   *clothes*
dummy   *bread*

fin   *five-year sentence*
fish   *newcomer*
four-time loser   *has been in prison four times*

good time   *time off for good behaviour*
goof   *jerk*
goofballs   *capsules of valium*
goon squad   *custodial bullies*
grapevine   *word-of-mouth transmission of rumours*
grub   *food*

hacker   *prison guard*
harness bulls   *uniformed policemen*
head-shrinker   *psychiatrist*
heat-score   *troublesome individual*
heeled   *armed*
high sign   *everything is okay*
hung jury   *jury unable to reach unanimous verdict*
hung up   *delayed*

jacked up   *charged with a crime*
jackrabbit parole   *break out of jail*
jailhouse bit   *prison sentence*
jailhouse merchant   *a prisoner who barters in contraband*
java   *coffee*
jo-jo   *bulky winter coat*
joint man   *prisoner who behaves like a guard*
joint time   *penitentiary sentence*
jug man   *bank robber*
jug-up   *meal time*

kangaroo court   *warden's court*
keep six   *be on the lookout*
kite   *a contraband letter*
knowing the ropes   *jailwise*

laying track   *lying*
lugging   *transporting contraband*
lunch bucket brigade   *civilian work force*

mechanical stool pigeon   *metal detector (walk through)*
melon   *a person's head*
molotov cocktails   *gasoline bombs*
mooch   *someone looking for a handout*
mover   *ambitious person*
mugged & printed   *photographed and fingerprinted*

nark   *drug enforcement officer*

old man   *dominant homosexual partner*
on point   *alert and ready for anything*

patch   *bribery, fix, deal*
pete   *safe*
pete-man   *safe cracker*
piece   *gun*
pipe-dream   *unrealistic goal*
piped   *hit over the head with a bar*
power tripping   *trying to be a big shot*

railroaded   *convicted by means of fabricated evidence*
rat   *informer*
reefers   *marijuana*
repeater   *someone who's been in jail more than once*
rounders   *underworld figures*

sand   *sugar*
sawbuck   *ten-year sentence*
scoff   *food*
scratch   *money*
shafted   *double-crossed*
sham   *a pretence*
shank   *homemade knife*
shiv   *homemade knife*
shockers   *electric-shock treatments*

shooter   *important person*
short-timer   *sentence near completion*
shrink   *psychiatrist*
six!   *trouble on the way*
six-man   *a lookout*
sixty-five!   *full alert*
skin-frisk   *strip-search*
skinner   *rapist*
sky pilot   *priest*
slammer   *prison*
slash job   *self-mutilation*
sleaze   *creep*
snow job   *a deliberate lie*
solid con   *respected prisoner*
speed freak   *someone hooked on amphetamines*
stash   *to hide something*
stir-crazy   *punch-drunk from doing too much time*
stock-jobbing   *bartering*
stool pigeon   *informer*
sucker punch   *unsuspecting blow*
sweet kid   *youthful homosexual partner*

TM's   *tailor-made cigarettes*
tappers   *inmate trusties*
through the mill   *having served hard time in prison*
toking   *smoking marijuana*

wolf   *an inmate who is bisexual*
wolf pack   *inmate bullies*